EMBEDDED

BOOKS BY DANNY SCHECHTER

Media Wars: News at a Time of Terror, Rowman & Littlefield, USA 2003.

Inovatio Books, Bonn, Germany 2002.

The More You Watch The Less You Know, Seven Stories Press, 1997, 1999.

News Dissector: Passions Pieces and Polemics 2000, Akashic Books (2000), Electronbooks.com (1999)

Falun Gong's Challenge to China, Akashic Books, 1999, 2000.

Hail to the Thief, How the Media "Stole" the 2000 Presidential Election (Ed. with Roland Schatz), Inovatio, 2000, Germany, Electronpress.com. U.S.A.

EMBEDDED:: WEAPONS OF MASS DECEPTION

HOW THE MEDIA FAILED TO COVER THE WAR ON IRAQ

DANNY SCHECHTER
Published in association with MEDIACHANNEL.ORG

 Prometheus Books

59 John Glenn Drive
Amherst, New York 14228-2197

Published 2003 by Prometheus Books

Inquiries should be addressed to
Prometheus Books
59 John Glenn Drive
Amherst, New York 14228–2197
VOICE: 716–691–0133, ext. 207
FAX: 716–564–2711
WWW.PROMETHEUSBOOKS.COM

07 06 05 04 03   5 4 3 2 1

Library of Congress Cataloging-in-Publication Data

Schechter, Danny.
    Embedded—weapons of mass destruction : how the media failed to cover the war in Iraq / Danny Schechter.
        p. cm.
    Contents: Winners and Losers — Producing the war — Countdown to war — Mobilizing opinion — Battlefield blues — Surrounding Baghdad — War kills journalist — So this is victory? — Remembering the fallen — What can you do about it? — International perspectives.
    ISBN 1–59102–173–1
    1. Iraq War, 2003—Mass media and the war. I. Title: Weapons of mass deception. II. Title: How the media failed to cover the war in Iraq. III. Title.

DS79.76.S34   2003
070.4'4995670443—dc22

                                                                    2003016015

Printed in the United States of America on acid-free paper

DEDICATION

To all who fought and the many who died to penetrate the "fog" of war in search of truths hidden in the sands of Iraq, the files of government agencies and the studios of media companies.

And to my colleagues at Globalvision and Mediachannel.org for giving me a platform for these dissections. And to Tony Sutton of ColdType.net for believing that others should have access to them.

And, as in all my earlier books, to my daughter Sarah Debs Schechter who knew that there was something horribly flawed in what she was seeing, hearing and reading about this "war."

Hopefully, this work will help her understand why and how.

CONTENTS

PROLOGUE TO A POST LOG

IT is safe to predict that the debate over the rationale for and effects of the 2003 war on Iraq will fester for decades to come. Why did the United States act as it did? Did Saddam Hussein's Iraq ever really represent a threat to world security? Was Baghdad seriously violating United Nations restrictions on weapons of mass destruction? Did these weapons still exist when the war began? Did Washington's pre-emptive invasion, at a cost of $917,744, 361.55, according to Pentagon accountants, free Iraq's long-suffering people?

Other questions: what was the full and final costs in lives, military and civilian, limbs, and destruction of Iraq's infrastructure, economy and cultural treasures? Did that country's people really welcome the "liberation" promised to them in some 31,800,000 leaflets dropped on their country along with an unknown amount of deadly ordnance. (Newsweek estimated that all of this paper could have been put to more practical use in the form of 120,454 rolls of toilet paper.)

The war had its official statisticians just as sporting events do. They counted everything, including the 423,988 members of U.S. military units deployed (as opposed to less than 10 percent of that number in other forces, just 42,987 "foreign" troops rustled up into what was clumsily labeled a "coalition of the willing."

What was unaccounted for, at least by the invaders and rarely shown in western media, were the civilian casualties. As a matter of policy, the United States refused to release any figures or even estimates. The United Nations was tracking the problem. At the end of May, their agencies were guestimating that the toll may surpass ten thousand, a stunningly large number, considering all of the assurances given that every effort would be made to limit damage to the society and its long suffering civilian population.

According to Ian Bruce in the Glasgow Herald: "The toll will exceed the 3500 civilians killed in the 1991 Gulf war and the 1800 to 2000 innocent Afghans known to have perished during the 2001 invasion to oust the Taliban and wipe out al Qaeda's training camps." Haidar Taie, who runs the Red Crescent's tracing department in Baghdad, said: "We just don't know for certain. But thousands are dead, thousands more injured or missing. It will take time to reach a definitive count. It was certainly a disaster for civilians caught in the fighting."

"The War For Iraqi Freedom," as the Pentagon and at least two networks branded it, went on for 720 hours. It was well documented by the Pentagon, which transmitted 3,200 hours of video and took 42,000 pictures, most of which the public did not, and may never, view.

What we did see, and read about the Iraq War is the subject of this book fashioned in the heat of the conflict. If journalism is a matter of course considered the first draft of history, this is one of the first book-length attempts to focus on the coverage and its many flaws, written before our memories fade. It focuses on the different versions of the Iraq war that were transmitted on television and in the press, the versions that shaped impressions and public opinion.

This book is about more visible WMDs than the ones discussed in the media. It is about the media itself viewed as a weapon system: Weapons of Mass Deception. Those weapons drove a media war, a war that many now believe perverted freedom of the press in the name of serving it. Many used patriotism as a promotional tool, pandering to fears and nationalist sentiment.

There was warfare within the media, too, as media companies battled each other for scoops, exclusives, branding and positioning. They fought for market share, "mindshare" and ad-spend share. Within the trenches of the industry, and sometimes within the companies themselves, journalists and program producers wrestled with their colleagues and counterparts for guests and a competitive advantage. They worked with the military discipline of soldiers, only they were paid for their overtime. (When I worked at ABC, staffers were called "the troops.")

Yet, even as they competed against their counterparts, they also collaborated with each other, often drawing on the same footage, carrying the same stories, echoing the same administration claims and following the Pentagon's lead. Often they cloned each other's looks, formulas, formatting and "enhancement" techniques. They often looked and sounded more alike than they thought. Their sameness trumped their differences.

All news organizations rehearsed their coverage, pre-produced graphics and features, and "deployed" the latest techno toys. This media war brought out some of the best in journalism and too much of the worst. It showed the news business' vast technological capacity to bring us live coverage from the battlefield, but also demonstrated its power to sanitize that coverage and spin it propagandistically. It shamelessly recycled stories, repeating key themes, updating updates, all while promoting its own coverage.

This media war promoted the war it covered. It mobilized approval among opinion-making elites in Washington, London and other world capitals. First, it constructed the political environment, contributing to the sense of inevitability about the need for war and then fostered approval for it. Critical voices quickly vanished as fighting got underway.

The media war targeted the larger public, too, and in the United States at least, built what was reported as a consensus for the war and a national acceptance of its official goals and effects. The war coverage sold the war even as it claimed to be just reporting it. Media outlets called attention to their news gathering techniques, but never to their effects. During the first Gulf War, communications scholars found that people who relied exclusively on television for their news and information tended to know the least about the issues. I am sure similar studies will produce similar findings about this war. Most Americans lacked much knowledge about the issue before the war. Only 13 percent of America's teenagers could even find Iraq on a map. So much for the educational job done by the media and the schools.

Not everyone who watched the build-up to the war or the war itself bought into its terms or was persuaded by its storyline. The war and its coverage also turned off and tuned out tens of millions who took to the streets, rejecting the pro-war media frame, in the largest global protests in history. Relying on independent media, international newspapers and feisty web sites for their information, they criticized both the policy and the press. In the aftermath of the giant February 15 2003 protests, The New York Times commented that there were then two opposing global superpowers: the military might of the United States and world public opinion. As the war erupted, the critics were "disappeared" from the media view just as Saddam disposed of his critics. He used violence; our media used inattention.

Even as those protests were often badly and in some cases barely covered, they nevertheless spoke for millions who rejected the media war aimed at their minds and spirits. One can only hope that, as the claims and "evidence" used to stoke up the war are unmasked, the media role will also be seen for what it is.

As Paul Krugman commented on The Times Op-ed page. "Over the last two years we've become accustomed to the pattern. Each time the administration comes up with another whopper, partisan supporters (a group that includes a large segment of the news media) obediently insist that black is white and up is down.

"Meanwhile, the 'liberal' media report only that some people say that black is black and up is up. And some democratic politicians offer the administration invaluable cover by making excuses and playing down the extent of their lies."

Most of us were not on the battlefield. Our understanding of what happened, our perceptions, points of view and prejudices were forged and framed by our media choices. We need to see that as a problem that demands to be addressed. Just as we consider politicians lying to us a problem, media accountability and responsibility are as important as political responsibility   ●

INTRODUCTION

BLOGGING THE WAR AWAY

Few of us escaped seeing the non-stop reports from Iraq, from journalists embedded and otherwise, reports from what have been described as the front lines of the fight for "Iraqi freedom." Throughout the American media world and beyond, there has been a hearty sense of a job well done, except of course, for regrets over those colleagues and soldiers who never made it home.

We all watched the war as if it was only a military conflict. It wasn't.

There was also a carefully planned, tightly controlled and brilliantly executed media war that was fought alongside it. For the most part, that other media war was not covered or fully explained even though it was right in front of us.

The media war was there in living color but many didn't realize it had a life of its own, influencing as well as transmitting the BIG STORY. It has to be viewed on more than one level. Not all the news was what it appeared to be. In fact, it all followed a scenario, and served a function forecast years earlier by Canadian media guru, the late Marshall McLuhan who predicted: "If there were no coverage . . . there'd be no war. Yes, the newsmen and the media men around the world are actually the fighters, not the soldiers any more." McLuhan spoke of the media environment and television as a medium that rarely calls attention to itself. He called it "pervasively invisible."

The war coverage inundated us for weeks, as if there was no other news in the world. It was blow-by-blow and wall-to-wall, with the focus on the U.S. military campaign as it rolled across the desert. We watched as "the coalition" fought its way into Baghdad, stronghold of strongman Saddam Hussein, capital of the regime whose overthrow had been demanded – and accomplished. We saw the images and heard first-person accounts from many of the journalists about their adventures, difficulties, scoops and disappointments.

War as propaganda

THE Baghdad-based reporters who worked under limitations imposed by the now defunct Iraqi Ministry of Information were not shy about telling us what they had to put up with. When that ministry and the TV station it managed were "taken out" in bombing attacks that may have flouted international laws, American newscasters cheered. Its propaganda function was crude and obvious.

There was also propaganda flowing from other regional media aimed at the "Arab Street" and that also was crude and distorted – and, from its perspective, also was effective. Many commentators accepted pro-Iraq propaganda. They expec - ted far more Iraqi resistance than materialized.

While outlets like Al-Jazeera and Abu Dhabi TV strived to offer professional reporting that in some instances out-scooped western networks, other commentary reflected longstanding cultural biases, anti-Americanism, inflammatory antisemitism, with loads of violence and no attention paid to Saddam's human rights abuses or women's rights. Kurdish journalists, who lived through the impact of Saddam's ethnic cleansing of rebellious Kurds in the north, criticized Arab satellite stations for these serious shortcomings.

Many U.S. newscasts pointed to these flaws and biases in part to project their own work as being free of similar biases. "They" – the "other" – practiced propaganda common to backward societies. We of the developed world practiced world-class bias-free journalism, or so we wanted the world to believe.

Propaganda was pervasive

THE truth is that there were pervasive pro-Western propaganda techniques built into American media presentation formats. Many may be disguised; others obvious. They were also rarely commented upon or critiqued, except by war critics. Few journalists put their reporting skills to work to report fully on their own government's propaganda campaign and its interface with their own media products.

Washington's anti-Iraqi propaganda was multidimensional and a key component of the "coalition" war plan (Deceptive words like "coalition" were themselves part of it.) Aimed at the Iraqis was a well-crafted arsenal of psychological operations or Psy-Ops carried out by an IO (Information Operations) directorate that simultaneously targeted and destroyed the county's communication system and replaced it with its own. A second front – and perhaps a more important one – was the western public. Iraqis were targeted by bombs and information warfare while western audiences

had a well executed propaganda campaign often posing as news directed their way.

Explains British-based propaganda expert Paul de Rooij, in several well-sourced assessments: "One generally doesn't think of psychological warfare as something waged against the home population; but this is perhaps the best way to appreciate the U.S. experience during the past few months. The objective of such a campaign was to stifle dissent, garner unquestioning support, and rally people around a common symbol. Americans, and to a lesser extent Europeans, have been subjected to a propaganda barrage in an effort to neutralize opposition to the war, and this fits directly into a psy-ops framework."

Suddenly all the networks had platoons of retired generals and pro-war military experts interpreting war news. U.S. TV quickly resembled Chilean TV after the coup. CNN's news chief Eason Jordan revealed that he had sought approval from the Pentagon for his network's key war advisors. One Canadian critic called the network, "the Pentagon's bitch." At war's end, critic Michael Moore demanded the "unilateral withdrawal of the Pentagon from America's TV studios."

War as a political campaign

PENTAGON media chief Tori Clarke, who worked with PR firms and political campaigns before bringing a corporate style, and politically oriented spin operation into the Pentagon, admitted that she was running her shop the way she used to run campaigns. This approach was coordinated throughout the administration with "messages of the day" and orchestrated appearances by the President and members of his cabinet. They were not just selling a message but "managing the perceptions" of those who received them. Politically, they used "stagecraft," a term that once was used to refer to covert operations. On May 16th, 2003, The New York Times detailed how the Bush Administration relies on TV entertainment techniques to sell the President and his policies. Significantly, media people are directing the effort. Elisabeth Bumiller wrote:

"Officials of past Democratic and Republican administrations marvel at how the White House does not seem to miss an opportunity to showcase Mr. Bush in dramatic and perfectly lighted settings. It is all by design: the White House has stocked its communications operation with people from network television who have expertise in lighting, camera angles, and the importance of backdrops.

"TV news people have been tapped in this aspect of the media war. First among equals is Scott Sforza, a former ABC producer who was hired by the Bush campaign in Austin, Tex., and who now works for Dan Bartlett, the White House communications director. Mr. Sforza created the White House "message of the day" backdrops and helped design the $250,000 set at the United States Central Command forward headquarters in Doha, Qatar, during the Iraq war.

"Mr. Sforza works closely with Bob DeServi, a former NBC cameraman whom the Bush White House hired after seeing his work in the 2000 campaign. Mr. DeServi, whose title is associate director of communications for production, is considered a master at lighting. 'You want it, I'll heat it up and make a picture,' he said early this week. A third crucial player is Greg Jenkins, a former Fox News television producer in Washington," Bumiller revealed.

These smartly polished sales techniques worked and typified the way the war was sold – and covered. It all underscores once again that we no longer live in a traditional democracy but, rather, a media-ocracy, a land in which media drives politics and promotes the military.

New York Times columnist Paul Krugman, who has written about how media coverage shapes public opinion, makes another point about the way TV coverage distorts reality. "The administration's anti-terror campaign makes me think of the way television studios really look. The fancy set usually sits in the middle of a shabby room, full of cardboard and duct tape. Networks take great care with what viewers see on their TV screens; they spend as little as possible on anything off camera.

"And so it has been with the campaign against terrorism. Mr. Bush strikes heroic poses on TV, but his administration neglects anything that isn't photogenic," Krugman wrote.

No wonder we had newscasts in which images trumped information. Clearly, just as the Pentagon boasted of its war plan, there was another plan alongside it–a media marketing plan that was even more carefully guarded lest it fall into the wrong hands. News management always works best when those who are its target are unaware of its dynamics.

War as a TV show

THIS war was a TV show on a new scale with as many "events" as a televised Olympics. Media outlets were willing, even enthusiastic participants in presenting the made-for-television spectacle. It would be wrong and overly deterministic to conclude that these TV news operations were taken over, duped or manipulated by the kind of crude force that prevails in some other countries between government agencies and the media. The Pentagon was not faxing instructions to the newsrooms, nor would they have to. Media companies had their own reasons for playing the role they did, as did the "yellow press" publisher William Randolph Hearst who used – and, many say, started – a war as a way to sell papers. He is reported to have said: "You furnish the pictures and I'll furnish the war" – at the beginning of the Spanish-American War.

Today the relationship between government and media is more symbiotic, even synergistic. Wars like the one in Iraq are staged to project American power to the world. The pictures advertise that power (and market weapons systems at the same time).

The news business is more than happy to oblige because war attracts viewers in large numbers. Journalists quickly become intoxicated by the ether of war and all the excitement and danger that awaits on the front line. For many reporters, war is where the action is. It is also a career builder. Covering war has always been a way for journalists to prove their bona fides, win bragging rights and, of course, move up the ladder in the corporate news world.

Some journalists are drawn to war as moths are drawn to flame and light. For them, war represents the highest form of professional calling and appeals to their sense of patriotism and pride. Many promote the mission of those they cover as their own, just as many beat reporters are often co-opted by the officials and the agencies on which they report. The seduction is subtle. Some may be bought as intelligence assets, but most would resent any suggestion that they have sold out – or sold in. Years ago, Humbert Wolfe penned a famous ditty about the way many journalists voluntarily and enthusiastically serve the interests of others, without distance or skepticism:

"You cannot hope to bribe or twist
Thank God! The British Journalist
But seeing what the man will do
Unbribed, there's no occasion to."

Networks like war. It offers riveting programming "reality". They produce it as "militainment," to borrow a term from TIME Magazine. Its life and death drama brings in viewers and holds attention. The spectacle builds ratings and revenues. It also imbues news organizations with a sense of importance and self-importance. It allows executives to demonstrate how valuable they are to the national interest. Executives at MSNBC boasted of how their war coverage brought Americans together and "emphasized the positive, not the negative."

Positive coverage also helps networks gain more access to the powerful, satisfying their advertisers in an industry where three out of every four commercials are bought by the 50 most powerful companies. In 2003, pleasing the Bush Administration also promised an economic benefit, since while the war was being waged, media companies were lobbying for regulatory changes that would benefit their bottom lines. FCC Chairman Michael Powell, son of the Secretary of State who was serving the war policy, rationalized the need for more media consolidation on grounds that only big media companies could afford to cover future wars the way this one was being covered.

The embedded journalist

THIS book focuses on the campaign that involved co-opting and orchestrating the news media. The most visible center of this strategy was the effort to embed reporters whose work was subsidized by the Pentagon, overseen by "public affairs" specialists and linked to TV news networks dominated by military experts approved by the Pentagon. When the war was over, Rem Rieder, the editor of the American Journalism Review (AJR) gushed: "It is clear that the great embedding experiment was a home run as far as the news media and the American people are concerned." Military Commander Gen. Tommy Franks agreed and pledged that embedding would be used in future conflicts.

AJR writer Sherry Ricchiardi amplified the view most favored by the mainstream media organizations that participated in the embedding experiment: "... despite initial skepticism about how well the system would work, and some dead-on criticism of overly enthusiastic reporting in the war's early stages, the net result was a far more complete mosaic of the fighting – replete with heroism, tragedy and human error – than would have been possible without it." She quotes Sandy Johnson, The Associated Press' Washington bureau chief who directed coverage of the 1991 Persian Gulf War.

"Compared with the scant access allowed then," Johnson says, "This system has worked incredibly well.

"The naysayers," she adds, "will be eating their words."

Will we?

Most embedded reporters claimed that they were not really restrained but rather assisted in their work by Pentagon press flacks. This is probably true – and the reason the system worked so well. Manipulation is always more insidious as well when the manipulated do not fully recognize how they are being used in a carefully calibrated media spin operation. Many of the "embeds" acknowledged that they came to identify with and sometimes befriend the soldiers in the units they tagged along with, usually with the caveat that it was no different from covering any beat.

Former TV reporter Michael Burton offered a different view: "The idea originated with the Pentagon, where military and political strategists pitched the idea to editors last year as a compromise. The Pentagon strategists, already planning for the Iraqi war, wanted proud, positive, and patriotic coverage over the national airwaves. If the editors agreed to all their provisions for security reviews, flagging of sensitive information, limitations on filming dead bodies, and other restrictions, then journalists would be welcome. The editors not only went along – they accepted the ground rules without a fight.

"Now, the story of war is seen through the eyes of the American battalions, but without the real violence. American children see more images of violence on nightly television than they do in this war, because of the deliberate editing at home. Instead, they see a fascination with high tech weapons, battle tactics, and military strategy reporting," Burton says.

He claims this leads to bias, although he acknowledges that many of his former colleagues demur: "Some reporters disagree, saying that eating, sleeping and living with the U.S. troops does not make them biased (in spite of the constant descriptions of "we" and "us" when reporters talk about the military units). They say they are revealing more human-interest stories in real-time. But, while embedded journalism provides more opportunity for human interest, it only does so from the American military's perspective."

Veteran New York Times war reporter Chris Hedges seems to agree with this view. He told Editor & Publisher magazine that he preferred print reporting to the TV coverage but said that both were deeply flawed. "Print is doing a better job than TV," he observes. "The broadcast media display all these retired generals and charts and graphs, it looks like a giant game of Risk [the board game]. I find it nauseating." But even the print embeds have little choice but to "look at Iraq totally through the eyes of the U.S. military," Hedges points out. "That's a very distorted and self-serving view."

The Project on Excellence in Journalism studied the early coverage and found that half the embedded journalists showed combat action but not a single story depicted people hit by weapons. There were no reporters embedded with Iraqi families. None stationed with humanitarian agencies or the anti-war groups that had brought more than 15 million people on the streets before the war in a historically unprecedented display of global public opinion. The cumulative impact of the embedded reporters' work prompted former Pentagon press chief Kenneth Bacon to tell The Wall Street Journal: "They couldn't hire actors to do as good a job as they have done for the military."

War as sport

THEY were actors in a news drama that had all the earmarks of a sporting event. In fact it seems to be designed as one. I found propaganda analyst Paul de Rooje's perspective on this aspect very insightful He writes: "Propaganda campaigns usually follow a theme ... During the 1991 Gulf War, the theme was the "video game", which was evident due to the number of demolition video clips. This theme couldn't be reused because the video-game scenes raised some uncomfortable questions about this enterprise especially among opponents of the war. It was therefore necessary to conjure a new theme, and all indications are that this campaign followed a "sports show" metaphor. The main advantage of this approach is that Americans are very comfortable with the "sport show" – it is part of their daily diet, it is intelligible to them, and it gives them a passive "entertained" role. Casting propaganda in such a known, comfortable framework makes people adjust favorably to the message...

"...When one watches a sports game, there is no need to think about the "why" of anything; it is only an issue of 'supporting our team'. You are also only supposed to root for the 'good guys' team, and hate the 'Iraqi meanies'. Dissident voices are also drowned out – you are only supposed to cheer for the home team... The 'play-by-play' military analysts incorporated the sports analogy completely–with maps/diagrams, advice to players, and making the audience think about the marvelous strategy..."

How the war was shown

MANY of the cable news networks pictured Iraq

as if it was the property of, and indistinguishable from, one mad man. Accordingly, attention was focused endlessly on where Saddam was, was he alive or dead, etc. Few references were made to U.S. dealings with his government in the l980s or the covert role the CIA played in his rise to power.

Saddam was as demonized in 2003 as Osama bin Laden had been in 2001, with news being structured as a patriotically correct morality soap opera with disinterested good guys (us) battling the forces of evil (them/him) in a political conflict constructed by the White House along "you are either with us or against us" lines. Few explained that there had been an undeclared war in effect for more than a decade with Iraq (and Islamic fundamentalists) well before the hot war of 2003 was launched. That was a war fought with systematic bombing in the name of defending no-fly zones and a campaign of U.N.- imposed sanctions that may have caused as many as a million deaths. This context, in fact, most context was missing. The coverage recalled the title of a book on our media culture published some years ago, aptly entitled "The Context of No Context."

The imbalances of coverage

THERE were many stories in this war but most followed a story line that reduced the terms of coverage to two sides, the forces of light versus the forces of darkness. This is typical of all war propaganda. In this war it was presented on one side, the "good side," by endless CENTCOM military briefings, Pentagon press conferences, Ari Fleischer White House Q&As, administration domination of the Sunday TV talk shows and occasional Presidential utterances riddled with religious references. Counter posed on the other side, the "bad side," were the crude press conferences of Iraq's hapless minister of misinformation, a cartoon figure whom no one took seriously. The two armies were spoken of as if there was some parity between their capacities. There was endless focus on the anticipated chemical or biological weapons attacks that never came, and on the weapons of mass destruction – finding WMD was a major reason for the war – that have yet to be found (at this writing).

Omitted from the picture and the reportage were views that offered any persuasive counternarrative. There were few interviews with ordinary Iraqis, or experts not affiliated with pro-administration think tanks. Or with military people, other than retired military officials who quibbled over tactics not policy. Or with peace activists, European journalists and, until late in the day, Arab journalists. We saw images from Al-Jazeera but rarely heard its analysis. This list of what was left out is endless. Footage was sanitized, "breaking news" was often inaccurate" and critical voices were omitted as Fox News played up martial music and MSNBC ran promos urging "God Bless America."

The role of Fox News, an unabashed 24-hour- a-day booster of the war, probably deserves a book of its own. Its aggressive coverage pandered to the audience, simplified the issues and attacked competing media outlets and correspondents who deviated in any way from the "script" they were promoting. Fox's apparent success in attracting viewers with its non-stop hawkish narrative led to a "Fox Effect" that caused many competitors to try to emulate its approach. MSNBC was accused of trying to "outfox Fox." Its coverage polarized the media war and bullied war critics.

War as staged spectacle

ONE of the most dramatic stories of the war was a dramatic rescue of U.S. POW Jessica Lynch from an Iraqi hospital. It was covered for days as triumph for the U.S. military. A month after it occurred, The BBC took a second look. Its reporters found that the truth of what happened contradicted what seemed at the time like a Made for TV Movie (and yet may inspire one!).

Reported Ellis Henican in Newsday: "Her rescue will go down as one of the most stunning pieces of news management yet conceived." And John Kampfner, a British journalist who has taken a hard second look at the case for the BBC and the Guardian newspaper, concurs. His documentary, "Saving Private Jessica: Fact or Fiction?" aired in Britain on March 18."

Robert Scheer of the Los Angeles Times added: "Sadly, almost nothing fed to reporters about either Lynch's original capture by Iraqi forces or her 'rescue' by U.S. forces turns out to be true. Consider the April 3 Washington Post story on her capture headlined 'She Was Fighting to the Death,' which reported, based on unnamed military sources, that Lynch 'continued firing at the Iraqis even after she sustained multiple gunshot wounds,' adding that she was also stabbed when Iraqi forces closed in.

"It has since emerged that Lynch was neither shot nor stabbed, but rather suffered accident injuries when her vehicle overturned," Scheer wrote. "A medical checkup by U.S. doctors confirmed the account of the Iraqi doctors, who said they had carefully tended her injuries, a broken arm and thigh and a dislocated ankle, in contrast to U.S. media reports that doctors had ignored Lynch," he concluded. (Later, the claims in the piece would be challenged as distorted by Geoffrey Sherwood on Asia Times: "Kampfner's analysis was flawed on several levels. If CENTCOM went to great lengths to manipulate the war reporting, as Kampfner alleges, then it failed miserably." This debate is likely to continue.)

The war's other "most dramatic moment" was the toppling of the statue of Saddam Hussein. Many media critics like Ted Rall debunked this story thoroughly. "The stirring image of Saddam's statue being toppled on April 9th turns out to be fake, the product of a cheesy media op staged by the U.S. military for the benefit of cameramen staying across the street at Baghdad's Palestine Hotel. This shouldn't be a big surprise. Two of the most stirring photographs of World War II – the flag raising at Iwo Jima and General MacArthur's stroll through the Filipino surf – were just as phony."

Competing narratives

OUTSIDE the United States, there were competing narratives in the coverage of the war. Americans saw a different war than the one presented in the media in Europe and the Arab world. These differences raised "vexing questions" for media scholar Jacqueline E. Sharkey "about the responsibilities of the press in wartime, journalistic values such as objectivity, and the relationships among the press, the public and the government . . . During the war in Iraq, television news operations in Arab countries provided viewers throughout the world with an alternative view of the conflict, " she wrote in the AJR.

"Arabs and Muslims are getting a dramatically different narrative from their American counterparts," says Fawaz Gerges, who holds a chair in

INTRODUCTION

Middle Eastern studies and international affairs at Sarah Lawrence College and is an ABC news consultant on the Middle East. The U.S. networks have focused "on the technologically advanced nature of the American military armada," he says. "The Arab and Muslim press tend to focus on the destruction and suffering visited on Iraq by this military armada."

The U.S. government has at times sought to silence Arab media outlets. In other instances, U.S. media outlets like Fox News denounced their news coverage, in one case, as "culturally Arab." The U.S. military bombed Baghdad's Arab media center during the war, claiming two lives. In mid May 2003, The Wall Street Journal reported from Mosul: "The U.S. Army issued orders for troops to seize this city's only television station, leading an officer here to raise questions about the Army's dedication to free speech in postwar Iraq, people familiar with the situation said. The officer refused the order and was relieved of duty. The directive came from the 101st Airborne Division's commander, Maj. Gen. David Petraeus, who has ultimate authority in Mosul and the rest of northwest Iraq, the people familiar with the matter said. He said it was aimed at blocking the station from continuing to broadcast the Arabic news channel al-Jazeera."

Media Writer Norman Solomon noted in a syndicated report carried on Al-Jazeera's website: "Widely watched in the Arab world, Al-Jazeera's coverage of the war on Iraq has been in sharp contrast to the coverage on American television. As Time Magazine observed: "On US TV it means press conferences with soldiers who have hand and foot injuries and interviews with POWs' families, but little blood. On Arab and Muslim TV it means dead bodies and mourning."

Coverage in Europe also differed from that offered by U.S. media outlets. Writing from Spain, professor Herman Gyr noted, "It is often hard to believe they are covering the same events and the gap between American and global perceptions of this war will certainly have significant repercussions for some time to come."

"In the end, I think, the difference between the two views of the war (that of America & Israel versus that of the rest of the world) boils done to a single question: Were there alternatives? Americans were told by their media that there were no alternatives and that the only option was for Americans to get in there and get the job done (=war) and let the rest of the world be damned. The rest of the world was told by their media that there were numerous other options (diplomatic, economic, etc.) that would have involved less death and destruction In short, there were two very different wars to watch: one almost entirely military in nature (the American version) and another portrayed in unrelentingly human terms (the global version)," Gyr concluded?

What many Americans don't know is that some U.S. outlets offered competing narratives as well. CNN mounted two expensive news gathering operations. CNN America offered coverage for the "homeland" that was often a thinly disguised form of boosterism, while CNN International served the rest of the world, with a more nuanced picture.

Independent journalist Michael Massing who spent part of the war encamped at the CENTCOM media center in Doha, Qatar, explained this seeming conflict in The New York Review of Books:

"The difference was not accidental. Six months before the war began, I was told, executives at CNN headquarters in Atlanta met regularly to plan separate broadcasts for America and the world. Those executives knew that (Paula) Zahn's girl-next-door manner and Aaron Brown's spacey monologues would not go down well with the British, French, or Germans, much less the Egyptians or Turks, and so the network, at huge expense, fielded two parallel but separate teams to cover the war. And while there was plenty of overlap, especially in the reports from the field, and in the use of such knowledgeable journalists as Christiane Amanpour, the international edition was refreshingly free of the self-congratulatory talk of its domestic one. In one telling moment, Becky Anderson, listening to one of Walter Rodgers's excited reports about U.S. advances in the field, admonished him: "Let's not give the impression that there's been no resistance." Rodgers conceded that she was right.

"CNN International bore more resemblance to the BBC than to its own domestic edition, a difference that showed just how market-driven were the tone and content of the broadcasts. For the most part, U.S. news organizations gave Americans the war they thought Americans wanted to see.'"

Obviously I could not see all the coverage or compare and contrast it in any systematic way. What is clear and important to recognize is that there are different ways stories can be covered. Media diversity matters.

The outside view of a media insider

THIS book brings together an outsider's coverage of the war focused on covering the coverage.

I was 'self-embedded' in my small office in New York's Times Square, the media capital of the world, as editor of the not for profit Mediachannel.org, a global media monitoring website with more than 1000 affiliates worldwide. I focused on covering the coverage on a global basis every day, and disseminating my findings, ruminations and dissections (I am known as "the news dissector") in a daily weblog. Many of these weblogs run 3,000 to 4000 words a day, and often appear seven days a week, which speaks to my obsession, fixation and passion on this subject. Call it what you will.

In addition, I write regularly on media issues for the Globalvision News Network (www.gvnews. net) that has 350 media partners in 100 countries. I was able to access this unique international news source as well.

I also bring to this work nearly 30 years of experience inside the U.S. media system. There is a mission to my "madness," as well as a method. From years of covering conflicts on the radio in Boston and on TV at CNN, ABC News and Globalvision, the company I co-founded, I have come see how often inadequate is the "first draft of history," as daily journalism is called. How it excludes more than it includes. How it narrows issues while framing them. How it tends to mirror and reflect the worldview of decision-makers while pandering to the patriotism of the audience. And, most interesting, now that we have the web for daily comparative access to stories in different countries on the same subject, how ideology and cultural outlook shape what we report and choose not to report.

That made it possible for me to monitor and review, with the help of readers and other editors in our shop, coverage from around the world. Clearly some of it brought biases as strong as our own, but also offered information, context and background missing in U.S. media accounts. Most of our news outlets, for example, covered a war IN Iraq; others spoke of the war ON Iraq.In the U.S., there was often no line between jingoism and journalism.

This is the essence of the analysis I offered, day after day, cobbled together from articles from the world press, independent sources, international agencies and my own observations of the U.S. cable coverage, network shows, BBC and CBC News. I relied on the coverage from around the world to offer far more diverse accounts of the facts on the ground as well as their interpretation.

I began each morning at 6:00 a.m., watching TV at home with a remote in my hand and a notebook by my side. Daily, I scanned CNN, BBC, MSNBC, Fox and whatever else was on. I read The New York Times, the New York Post and other dailies and weeklies, as well as news magazines and opinion journals. I clipped away in a frenzy.

I was in the office at 7:00 a.m. and was soon hop-scotching between web sites and email over flowing with stories I missed. I would cut and paste, collate and collage and then start writing. I worked fast, and sometimes sloppily. I squeezed in as much as I could and thought relevant and a useful corrective to the main media frame. Fortunately, I had few distractions. No phones. No one bugging me. I posted at 9:00 a.m. with an editor to oversee the copy and correct my many typos. Within an hour, we tried to send the weblog out to the many Mediachannel readers who subscribed.

After work, I'd be radar-locked back on the tube, watching the late news, the talk shows and even comedy programs. I found that the Comedy Channel's Jon Stewart was often more on target than the news networks. I preferred Canada's newscasts to our own. Sometimes CSPAN featured talks or hearings worth paying attention to. When I couldn't take it anymore, I tuned out and dropped off to sleep and then did it again the next day. Sometimes I had trouble sleeping as the stupidity of the coverage recycled in my brain.

I guess I am one of those "feelers" who empathize with war's victims more than the soldiers whose deadly work was often sanitized. On the tube I kept hearing about the "degrading" of Iraq's military while witnessing the degrading of journalism itself.

Watching the media war took a personal toll on me. I was often bleary-eyed, wandering to work in empty streets, as the city woke up to new terror alerts and fear that the war had consequences that we were not ready for. What kept me going was the constant supply of items, extracts from news stories and comments from readers. As well as a lot of encouragement of a type that most journalists rarely get. Journalists tend to resent our readers and rarely interact with them, but they help me enormously.

Fortunately, the weblog gave me the space and the freedom to have a rather extended say. Could it have been shorter? Probably. Would it have been as comprehensive? No. Clearly the haste of the effort did not permit as much reflection as I would have liked. I am sure my work is flawed with unintended errors, some of my making, and some in the reports I quoted. Covering war is often as chaotic as war itself.

You will encounter duplication. The reason is simple. While I was blogging daily for Media Channel, I also produced weekly reports on war coverage for the Globalvision News Network and occasional articles for Alternet, Znet and other outlets. So there is some repetition even though I tried to avoid overdoing it. I decided against rewriting everything for this book because I believe there is value in putting all of this material written at the time together in one place. I believe even those who saw the original reports will welcome a chance to reread this body of work, especially, now, before our memories fade or when we prefer to forget all the pseudo news that bombarded us. It is important to remember our minds were invaded along with Iraq. We were targeted, too. Taken together, it is my hope that the book may be a useful in encouraging more critical reporting when Washington starts to prepare for the next war, and the one after that.

I deluge. You decide.

Not alone

IT may all sound crazy, and admittedly idiosyncratic, but at least I know am not alone. Increasingly I hear comments like "disgusting" applied to the way the war news was being presented. At one point, I led the blog with comments by the head of the BBC, Greg Dyke, as reported in the Guardian:

"BBC director general Greg Dyke has delivered a stinging rebuke to the U.S. media over its "unquestioning" coverage of the war in Iraq and warned the government against allowing the U.K. media to become 'Americanized.'"

What bothers me about his remarks is the all-too-common view that "unquestioning coverage" is what all of American journalism has become. It has not. I hope we are demonstrating that this one-note war journalism charade (parade?)

doesn't speak for all Americans.

I have collected excerpts from weblogs and longer pieces for this book. My hope is that it will encourage others to scrutinize the coverage and take responsibility for their media choices and for trying to improve our press. I hope it will contribute to the construction of a counter narrative that challenges all the half-truths we saw.

America's media is too important to be left in the hands of the few who own it, and the marketers who run it. Media responsibility has to become an issue, not just a complaint. Condemning governments for exaggerated claims about WMDs and an invented war rationale is not enough. Our media has to be held accountable for serving as their megaphone.

The future of our democracy depends on it.

Questions to ponder

IN this regard I, like so many others, am left with deeper questions than the ones I began with. There are no easy answers.

Some years ago, an old friend, social historian Stuart Ewen posed a few such questions in "PR: A Social History of Spin," on the power of public relations, showing how scientific and well advanced the engineering of consent has become. He asks:

"Can there be a democracy when the public is a fractionalized audience? When the public has no collective presence?

"Can there be a public when public agendas are routinely predetermined by "unseen engineers?

"Can there be a democracy when the tools of communication are neither democratically distributed nor democratically controlled?

"Can there be a democracy when the content of media is determined almost universally, by commercial considerations?

"Can there be a democracy in a society in which emotional appeals overwhelm reason, where the image is routinely employed to overwhelm thought?"

Finding answers to these questions has been given a new urgency by the war in Iraq and the coverage of that war. Let us ask these questions anew – and join the struggle for answers that will revive our democratic culture and foster a more responsible media.

Gratitude

THIS book could not have emerged without the support of Globalvision and the MediaChannel. org. It was designed and produced initially with the committed help of Tony Sutton, an international newspaper consultant based in Toronto, Canada, who runs ColdType.net in his spare moments. He stepped in when other publishers lacked the capacity or the guts to get this work out quickly. It could not have been completed without the active help and editorial support of a friend who prefers anonymity and who worked tirelessly with me to shape this book over a spring weekend. I am thrilled that Steven L. Mitchell of Prometheus Books recognized its importance and decided to rush it into print.

I appreciate Victoria Graham's professional eye and hand as an editor. The book could not have happened without weblog editor Jeanette Friedman, and later Bill Curry; without support from Rory O'Connor, Tim Karr, and Michael Summerfield of the Globalvision News Network. I am grateful for the technical help of Doug George and Anna Pizarro's administrative and editorial assistance.

And I sincerely thank the readers who send in items, comments, donations and so many kind words. Happily, my daughter Sarah Debs Schechter was among them.

You can give me feedback on the analysis and contents of this book by writing dissector@mediachannel.org. Please visit my daily online weblog http://www.mediachannel.org/weblog and help us keep Mediachannel.org alive.

Just one last point: this book begins at the end of the war with the post-war reporting and works its way backwards. Knowing how the story is evolving helps us put all the lies and deceptions that led up to it, and which were repeated throughout, into a new framework.

As you will see, a war brought to us with constant "Breaking News" was not above faking news. A war whose rationale had to do with disarmament and finding weapons of mass destruction was fought in large part with Weapons of Mass Deception.

That's how I saw it. Now, it is your turn.   ●

Danny Schechter
News Dissector
New York, May 23, 2003
Parts of this introduction were written
for the Nieman Report, the journal of
the Nieman Foundation for Journalism
at Harvard University.

CHAPTER ONE

WINNERS AND LOSERS

TRAINING MEDIA FOR WAR

By KATHLEEN T. RHEM

WASHINGTON, NOVEMBER 22, 2002 – The scene atop Cardiac Hill at Marine Corps Base Quantico, Va., was somewhat surreal today. A group of about 30 media representatives were poised at the summit waiting to photograph and interview trainees on a road march.

But as the trainees hiked into view, it was quickly apparent this was no ordinary military unit. Nearly 60 reporters in a ragtag mix of military protective equipment and civilian outdoor apparel tromped up the hill with a dozen or so Marines and soldiers offering directions along the way.

The media on the march were completing the final leg of the seven-day Joint Military Contingency Training for Media course. They had spent the past week with the Navy and Marine Corps gaining a familiarity for military operations. The last steps of the way was this five-mile road march, carrying 25-pound packs, complete with "ambushes" and a "gas attack."

The media waiting for them atop the hill had been invited to get a taste of the training and interview their counterparts. Most spoke freely of the situation's irony.

All irony was forgotten, however, when the Marines launched the first simulated attack. The trainees dove for cover, seeking the best possible hiding the woods had to offer. They got even more serious when smoke began wafting around them in a simulated poison gas attack.

Some got their protective masks on like seasoned military pros; other struggled and lamented that they'd be dead in a real attack. But all seemed to realize the seriousness of what they were learning.

"The most useful training by far was the nuclear, biological and chemical training," ABC News's Jim Scuitto said. He has covered military operations in Afghanistan and is currently based in the tiny Persian Gulf nation of Qatar.

The media trainees assumed they were preparing to cover a war with Iraq, even though military officials are quick to remind all that no decision has been made regarding using military force in Iraq.

"The one thing that will be different about this war will be that (chemical) threat," Scuitto said. He said the briefings on different types of chemical and biological agents and their symptoms were particularly useful.

The "confidence chamber," in which participants were exposed to tear gas to demonstrate how military protective masks work, brought the seriousness of the potential threat to focus for a lot of people.

"Even when you do it right, you're likely to get a taste of (the gas). It gets into your skin, and a little bit is going to get down your throat invariably," Scuitto said. "That just shows how dangerous the environment can be, because even when you're prepared, and even when you're forewarned, it's not necessarily completely safe. That's a sobering thought, but that's also useful because it's the kind of thing you have to be prepared for."

Reporters lauded other training as well. "We landed in a hot (landing zone), figured out where

31

we were supposed to be in relation to where the troops were going to be, how to get on and off helicopters, what to do for a gas attack, how quick you have to react," said Fox News Channel's Pentagon correspondent Bret Baier.

Baier has also covered military missions in Afghanistan and said in the next war he'd like to embed with a unit. "I think this next war is going to be a lot different media-wise. I trust (the military) that they're trying to get a lot more people in more forward areas," he said. "I think that if that happens and you're able to file stories with the military, then that's the most compelling story out there and maybe the safest place to be."

That's exactly what the military wants reporters to think. Military officials would rather have media members embed with units and remain under their protection than running around the battlefield on their own. It's safer for the media and safer for the military.

"We believe in this. There has been a lot of discussion about how best to prepare journalists for embedding in a more conventional conflict should the president order us into whatever is next, perhaps Iraq," said Marine Brig. Gen. Andrew Davis, director of Marine Corps Public Affairs.

"We want to have journalists with us who are knowledgeable enough to write smartly about the military, get the ranks right, understand the tactics and the equipment and also have enough self-protection and field skills so that they wouldn't endanger themselves or endanger the mission or endanger the Marines," he said.

Pentagon spokeswoman Torie Clarke traveled to Quantico to participate in the march this morning. She said she thinks the military and media members who participated each recognized how hard the others work.

"One of the things I'm hearing from both the media and the military is they have a new and greater appreciation for how hard each other's jobs are," she said.

ABC's Scuitto agreed. "I already had a lot of respect for what these (military) guys do," he said. "But you gain more respect when you see the type of training these guys go through."

Embedding media members with military units isn't without controversy. On the evening before the big march, some media members expressed their discomfort with being seen wearing camouflage military equipment. Many used white tape to write "press" or "TV" boldly on their gear.

Media members want to clearly define their role as noncombatants on the battlefield.

"Particularly in certain parts of this world it's already perceived that the American media is on the military's side," Scuitto said. "I don't believe it true, but that's the perception."

Davis said the military recognizes the potential problems and agrees wholeheartedly. "We have been scrupulous about keeping the distinction between noncombatants and combatants," he said.　●

Source: The Defense Department's American Forces Press Service

NEW YORK, MAY 23, 2003

PENTAGON PUTS JOURNALISTS TO USE IN SELLING THE WAR

They have to decide whether to embed or stay out of bed

Embed me, please. Ari, beam me up. I have sent the following request to Ari Fleischer, the soon to be departing White House minister of media pacification, the man who Howard Fineman of Newsweek compared with some party line promoting mouthpiece of the old Kremlin.

"Before you leave us, Ari, would you consider a request for embedment in the office of Karl Rove, the White House's Machiavelli of the moment?

"I crave an up-close and personal insider view of his movements and machinations. You gave us unprecedented access to the war in Iraq.

"How about the war at home? And in this case, unlike Iraq, I will pay my own expenses.

"Signed,

"Your News Dissector

"Danny Schechter"

No, I am not holding my breath for a positive response, but as I read and write about the embed experience, I decided I would like to try it for myself. As a former assistant to the Mayor of Detroit, I know that the inside-the-entourage view can be more revealing than the view from the outside where one hangs around waiting for handouts and pithy sound bites.

I have been as skeptical as every other journalist has been about the impact of the embedding. I know the Pentagon rated it a big success and plans to do it again.

Former TV reporter and author Michael Burton explains, "This is the first American war where journalists are 'embedded' with the troops. The idea originated with the Pentagon, where military and political strategists pitched the idea to editors last year as a compromise. The Pentagon strategists, already planning for the Iraqi war, wanted proud, positive, and patriotic coverage over the national airwaves. If the editors agreed to all their provisions for security reviews, flagging of sensitive information, limitations on filming dead bodies, and other restrictions, then journalists would be welcome. The editors not only went along — they accepted the ground rules without a fight.

"The majority of editors and publishers are pleased with the program, because it allows reporters to be much closer to the action than in the 1991 Gulf War."

Also pleased were some media analysts and military leaders. Rem Rieder, the editor the American Journalism Review (AJR), gushed, "It is clear that the great embedding experiment was a home run as far as the news media and the American people are concerned." The disgraced former National Security Advisor and Fox News embed in Iraq, Oliver North, was beside himself with praise for the access it gave him. U.S. Military Commander Gen. Tommy Franks agreed and pledged that embedding would be used in future military operations.

Now that the war is over, some of the "embeds" are more candid about their experiences than they were when they were on the battlefield. Talk Radio News reporter Gareth Schweitzer, who was with the 3rd Infantry, told Mother Jones that he valued his experience but had misgivings.

He told Michelle Chihara: "Physically, there was a lot of stuff they simply couldn't not show you. You were riding with them. It was there. There was no way to anesthetize the process. At the same time, on a couple of occasions when I was taken by a colonel to a site he wanted to show me, it was just a PR rap. The army definitely had a message they wanted to get out. At one point, a colonel came back to the unit just to take me and another journalist on a guided tour. He wanted to show us places where Iraqis had been fighting and where they had been sleeping, – a weapons dump. I wanted a chance to look at the stuff myself, without the guided tour. But it just wasn't always possible.

Mother Jones: But how hard was it to be objective about the decisions being made by the troops who were protecting you, possibly saving your life?

Schweitzer: "You know, anybody who tried to claim that their reporting, as an embed, was unbiased was not telling the truth. Then you're looking for the wrong thing from the process. At least for myself, I was not trying to be embedded for mere facts. We were getting our information from our own eyes, and from American battle commanders."

The perceptions fueled by this type of reporting had political consequences, he said.

"What's struck me is that for a lot of the conservatives who supported this war, validation seems to be in the victory. We prosecute it successfully, we win and the fact that we win validates us being there in the first place. That makes no rational sense at all. The purpose of our entrance was not to defeat another army but to accomplish a lot of more difficult tasks, none of which have been accomplished, save getting rid of some of the Ba'ath Party of Saddam Hussein."

Schweitzer also noted that there had been many mistakes, including information fed to reporters that in the hot house of live television was relayed to the public without verification. Like what?

Schweitzer: "On a variety of occasions, reporters said that they had stumbled across chemical weapons sites, and it was displayed prominently on TV, on some of the news channels, and it was also broadcast by a number of people. And on each and every occasion it turned out not to be true. There were also reports of 'heavy fighting' up north by the town of Karbala. There was almost no fighting there."

The Project on Excellence in Journalism found that half the stories from embedded journalists showed combat action but not a single story depicted people hit by weapons.

Media Tenor, the international media monitoring organization, studied newscasts in six countries. It asked: "To which degree were journalists in the U.S. and abroad serving the interests of their governments, intentionally or not? Was the media merely part of a larger war strategy?"

Media Tenor continues: "Many facts about this and other facets of the war will surface only over the course of the next decades, but our research does indicate that news media in different countries, if they did not lend outright support to their governments, cloaked in voices of patriotism and criticism, certainly did not oppose them.

"Not surprisingly, we generally found overwhelming agreement with issues related to the war on U.S. news broadcasts."

So what is the bottom line? According to Burton, the former TV reporter: "The war with Iraq may indeed signal the decline of independent journalism in times of war and the loss of the adversarial role journalism once played with the U.S. government. With 24-hour coverage, Americans are seeing more wartime video than ever before, but less of the big picture than any other war. So far, the White House strategy to sell the war through the U.S. media has succeeded."

All of this gives me second thoughts about my own imaginary request. I guess I don't want that embed slot in Washington after all.

Watching this White House is hard enough. Living there could be soul-sucking.   ●

IRONY AND REALITY IN REPORTING THE POST-WAR WAR

NEW YORK, MAY 16, 2003 – We are watching a TV scene in Baghdad: A group of Iraqis is marching, marching in anger, with signs in English for a CNN camera that is recording their demands. They want a government, they want to get paid, they want the lights on, they want the garbage collected. Their rage is palpable.

The camera cuts to an American military officer, smiling at them, motioning to them to calm down. He offers no response to their specific complaints.

Cut to the sound bite that was used, for the benefit of the folks back home: "Isn't it wonderful that these people finally have freedom of speech and can express themselves?"

You can't make this up, but news networks are not very good at dealing with irony. Their focus on routinized news reality cannot cope with the surrealism that now characterizes post-war reporting. As optimism pours out of Washington, pessimism stalks the streets of Baghdad. Arab News commented on the irony of the irony, even as most American outlets do not:

"It is an irony that a nation so often accused of imperialism should prove so incompetent when it comes to playing the colonial administrator; the French and British are still so much better at these things, even decades after their empires have gone."

The liberation of Iraq was barely a week old before most of the U.S. news army staged its own withdrawal. There was a murder to cover in California, tornadoes terrorizing the Midwest, a so-called "road map" in the Middle East, a New York Times reporter blew it badly in Midtown, and, as feared and predicted, there was an ugly surprise from the Osama bin Laden brigade.

In America this week, the first of two sequels to the movie "The Matrix" opened in theaters. One of the lines in the original film had inspired the Slovenian philosopher, Slavoj Zizek, to entitle his book "Welcome to the Desert of the Real." But many analysts of the film, according to Adam Gopnik in The New Yorker, view it as inspiring the sense that "reality itself has become a simulation."

Gopnik cites Jean Baudrillard's book, "The Gulf War Did Not Take Place," as a sign of the difficulty many face in determining if the great victory we saw in the media did indeed take place. In the spirit of a once popular commercial, many of us who are now in recovery from war news addiction syndrome (WNAS) are asking, "Was it real or was it Memorex?" How real was the widely pictured desert of real war? Do we yet know why it ended with a whimper, not a bang?

The current issue of The Atlantic carries an excerpt from "Martyrs Day," a ten-year-old piece by former editor Michael Kelly, who died covering this Gulf War. He saw it as necessary to finish the unfinished business of the first one. Back then, after Gulf War I, he wrote:

"I think even then there were the beginnings of a sense that we had come out of this thing with a great deal less than we should have – that we had in a sense muffed it. This sense that we had somehow managed to snatch a quasi-defeat out of victory soon grew much stronger and became much more defined." This same sentiment is being whispered today.

Even if the TV war has ended, the real war is not over in Iraq, or for that matter, in Afghanistan. The deadly terrorist strike in Saudi Arabia demonstrates that Al Qaeda has lived to fight another day. We have not heard the last from them, even if many in the media forgot the warnings from critics that the war will not make us safer, that more terrorism is likely, that actions bring reactions.

Will these developments lead to a new wave of retrospection in an American media system that was nearly indistinguishable from the Pentagon operation throughout the conflict? Will hard questions and tough investigations finally puncture the spirit of triumphalism that President Bush is counting on to tough it out for five more years?

Don't count on it.

In Washington, it is back to business. According to the Financial Times, Rupert Murdoch, who served the administration well throughout the war, awaits his reward in the form of a lifting of FCC restrictions on the number of TV stations he will be able to own. That is expected to come down June 2, once Colin Powell's son, Michael, the FCC Chairman of a regulatory commission who never saw a regulation he liked, is able to deliver. Powell Jr. has said that more media consolidation is needed to insure that there are news organizations big enough to cover future wars. That circle is about to be squared.

Meanwhile, dissenters look on in anger but without the clout to stop the give-away of the public airwaves, or this anschluss and expansion by the big players. The dissenters are still asking for counts of casualties in the war, and assessing how badly the media system turned them into a casualty by marginalization.

The data confirming that we were ill served by the media is now in from Fairness and Accuracy in Reporting. It studied U.S. war coverage and found "the guest lists of major nightly newscasts were dominated by government and military officials, disproportionately favored pro-war voices, and marginalized dissenters.

Starting the day after the invasion of Iraq began, the three-week study covered the most intense weeks of the war (March 20 to April 9). It examined 1,617 on-camera sources in stories about Iraq on six major evening newscasts: ABC World News Tonight, CBS Evening News, NBC Nightly News, CNN's Wolf Blitzer Reports, Fox News Channel's Special Report with Brit Hume and PBS' NewsHour with Jim Lehrer.

Among their findings: "Official voices dominate: 63 percent of all sources were current or former government employees. U.S. officials alone accounted for more than half, 52 percent, of all sources."

The New York Times columnist Paul Krugman contrasted U.S. and British coverage, charging that U.S. outlets "behaved like state-run media." Geneva Overholser, a former ombudsperson at the Washington Post, now with the Poynter Institute, agrees. "The comments I've been hearing about U.S. media becoming ever more like state-run media seem to me to evoke something deeper than partisanship or ideology.

"What I sense is a narrowing of the discussion, a ruttedness – call it an echo chamber of conventionalism. Sure, we have the appearance of controversy, what with our shouting heads and sneering pundits. But real debate – substantive representation of viewpoints not currently in vogue, of people not currently in power, of issues not currently appearing in our narrowly focused eye – is almost absent."

It seems clear that this pattern of coverage is unlikely to improve unless and until the media system itself is reformed. For that to happen, more Americans need to see media as an issue, not a complaint.   ●

NOW THAT THE WAR IS OVER, MEDIA SHAME SURFACES

NEW YORK, MAY 08, 2003 – "Disgusting" is a strong word to apply to the Iraq war coverage, but that's the epithet author Russell Smith invokes in the new issue of The New York Review of Books in a column about "new newspeak" that indicts "patriotic lapses in objectivity."

Even as NBC rushes out a new book lionizing its war coverage, a small undercurrent of criticism from within the news industry threatens to turn into a flood of denunciation as the shock and awe wears off, and journalists realize how badly they have been had.

This tends to follow a rule first enunciated by the German philosopher Arthur Schopenhauer who wrote: "All truth passes through three stages. First it is ridiculed. Second it is violently opposed. Third it is accepted as self-evident."

Stage One: Ridicule. In the aftermath of President Bush's flight to an aircraft carrier for a heavily-staged photo-op, questions, comments, sneers and jeers are slowly rising up from a press corps that heretofore has been compliant, complicit and in the words of James Wolcott in Vanity Fair, easily bullied.

Stage Two: Violent Opposition. We have witnessed a mild dissent on coverage, from the lips of MSNBC's Ashleigh Banfield who questioned the media's accuracy during a lecture at Kansas State University, for which she was savaged as a traitor by media bores on the right. Michael Savage, her right-wing MSNBC talk show colleague, denounced her as a "slut." Rush Limbaugh told her to go to work for Al-Jazeera.

Stage Three: Accepted as Self-Evident. We're getting there. As politicians question the Victory at Sea setting for Bush's photo-op, Eric Zorn of the Chicago Tribune questioned the lack of hard reporting about the man's own efforts to dodge active service during the Vietnam war, the event and its significance:

"There was no relentless examination (of Bush's military record) on cable news outlets, no interviewing the commanders who swear Bush didn't show up where he was supposed to, no sit-downs with the veterans who have offered still unclaimed cash rewards to anyone who can prove that Bush did anything at all in the Guard during his last months before discharge.

"So much for the cynical distortion that has become conventional wisdom in many circles. So much for the myth of the 'liberal media.'"

There is a deeper cultural dimension to this problem, this patriotic lapse in objectivity, claims Wolcott: "If the press has given Bush and his Cabinet a horsey ride it isn't because they are paid submissives. They are not prostitutes. They are pushovers."

He also argues that the political damage done is incalculable: "The American press sniffs at the cult of personality that once plastered the walls and billboards of Iraq with portraits of Saddam Hussein while remaining oblivious to the cult of personality that has cowed most of them. The

press in this country has never identified less with the underdog and more with the top pedigrees. The arrogance of the Bush Administration is mirrored in the arrogance of the elite media."

For more insights on elite media, jump past the Versace ad at the end of Wolcott's scathing piece and you arrive in Dominick Dunne's high-tone gossip country. Vanity Fair's man about town admits to getting upset with himself for breaking away from the war coverage to put on a tux in order to slip out to the next party.

He tells us about all the celebs who turned St. Patrick's Cathedral into citadel of luminaries for the funeral of NBC's Embed-in-Chief David Bloom. In his last e-mail, read at this grand event, Bloom seemed to have a premonition of his own demise.

Enthuses Dunne: "The all white flowers were perfect. The music triumphal. A head of state couldn't have gotten a better send off. I never saw so many priests on one altar."

While the greater glory of God was invoked in New York, up at Yale a senior editor of Newsweek was spilling his guts. The New Haven Register reports: "A senior editor at Newsweek, Michael Hirsh, told a Yale audience that he was fairly appalled, by television's coverage of the Iraq war.

"This has not been the media's finest hour," said Hirsh, who won the Overseas Press Club Award in 2001. He said war broadcasts from Great Britain and Canada were so different from American broadcasts that one might have thought the reporters were covering two different wars. He called American TV "self-absorbed" and "jingoistic" and said, "The natural skepticism of the media was lost after 9/11."

We are only now beginning to hear first-hand

what really transpired in the briefing rooms and embed posts, even if the scale of civilian casualties is still unknown.

Michael Massing reports in The New York Review of Books about those CENTCOM sessions that spun the story of the day complete with military video and lots of map pointing. He charges that many of the colleagues he was imprisoned with in that bunker in the Doha desert knew nothing about the region, the culture or the context. They were functioning as stenographers, not critical journalists, he said.

Russell Smith says he was more peeved by CNN, "The voice of CENTCOM" as he called it, than Fox News, which one satirist describes as "the Official News Channel of the Homeland. ('Ein Volk. Ein Reich. Ein Fuhrer. Ein News Channel.')"

"CNN was more irritating than the gleefully patriotic Fox News channel because CNN has a pretense of objectivity," Smith writes. "It pretends to be run by journalists. And yet it dutifully uses all the language chosen by people in charge of 'media relations' at the Pentagon."

Clearly there is much we still don't know about what happened on the ground in Iraq and the details of why the media covered it the way it did. Unfortunately, too, the growing chorus of criticism is still too little, too late.

Mark the words of a media monitoring news dissector: Observations like these and even sharper criticisms to come will move soon from the margins to the mainstream on their way to becoming the conventional wisdom, "self-evident" truth, as per the very late Dr. Schopenhauer.

In the end, with hindsight and reflection, all of journalism will look back in shame. ●

THE LINK BETWEEN WAR, THE FCC AND OUR RIGHT TO KNOW

NEW YORK, MAY 01, 2003 – By now, all of us realize that there is a high-powered media campaign aimed at promoting the war on Iraq and shaping the views of the American people, relying on a media-savvy political strategy to sell the administration's priorities and policies.

There is an intimate link between the media, the war and the Bush Administration that even many activists are unaware of. Few administrations in history have been as adept at using polling, focus groups, "perception managers," spinners, and I.O. or "information operations" specialists to sell slogans in order to further a "patriotically correct" climate. Orchestrating media coverage is one of their most well-honed skills, aided and abetted by professional PR firms, corporate consultants and media outlets.

Our Republican Guard relies on Murdoch-owned media assets like the Fox News Channel, supportive newspapers, aggressive talk radio hosts, conservative columnists and an arsenal of on-air pundits adroitly polarizing opinion and devaluing independent journalism.

They benefit from a media environment shaped by a wave of media consolidation that has led to a dramatic drop in the number of companies controlling our media from 50 to between five and seven – in just 10 years. Then there is the merger of news biz and show biz. Entertainment-oriented reality shows help depoliticize viewers while sensation-driven cable news limits analytical journalism and in-depth, issue-oriented coverage. Is it any wonder that most Americans admit to being uninformed about many of the key issues we confront? Is it surprising that many blindly follow feel-good slogans or appeals to national unity and conformity? This media problem is at the heart of all the issues that we face. And it is getting worse, not better.

If we want to save our democracy, we have to press the media to do its constitutionally protected job as a watchdog of the people in power. We must insist that all views be given access, and that concerns of critics of this administration be heard and debated.

We live in a climate in which even journalists are being intimidated for stepping out of line. In Iraq, the hotel assigned to journalists was fired on by soldiers, who killed two media workers. In the U.S., Pulitzer Prize winner Seymour Hersh was baited as a "media terrorist" by Pentagon advisor Richard Perle. Hundreds of journalists were "embedded" in order to sanitize war coverage. Independent journalists were harassed or ignored. Antiwar commercials have been suppressed and censored, while conservative talking-heads outnumber all others by 700 percent.

Last week MSNBC's Ashleigh Banfield spoke at a college about the coverage of the Iraq war. She was honest and critical. "There were horrors that were completely left out of this war. So was this journalism? Or was this coverage?" she asked. "As a journalist, I have been ostracized just from going on television and saying, 'Here's what the leaders of Hizbollah, a radical Moslem group, are telling me about what is needed to bring peace to Israel,'" she said. "And, 'Here's what the Lebanese are saying.' Like it or lump it, don't shoot the messenger, but that's what they do."

The "they" undoubtedly were her bosses at the General Electric and Microsoft-owned channel, the same men who fired top-rated talk show host Phil Donahue and then used the war to try and outfox Fox's jingoism with promos proclaiming, "God Bless America."

They quickly sought to silence Banfield. "NBC News President Neal Shapiro has taken correspondent Ashleigh Banfield to the woodshed for a speech in which she criticized the networks for portraying the Iraqi war as 'glorious and wonderful,'" reported the Hollywood Reporter. An official NBC spokesperson later told the press, "She and we both agreed that she didn't intend to demean the work of her colleagues, and she will choose her words more carefully in the future."

It was the kind of patronizing statement you would expect in the old Pravda or Baghdad's old ministry of misinformation. In Saddam's Iraq, she would have been done for. Let's see what happens at NBC. Already, Rush Limbaugh is calling on her to move to Al-Jazeera. Michael Savage, the new right-wing host on MSNBC who replaced Donahue, has branded her, his own colleague, a "slut" on the air!

Even mainsteam media monitor Howard Kurtz of the Washington Post is now looking back on the war coverage in anguish. "Despite the investment of tens of millions of dollars and deployment of hundreds of journalists, the collective picture they produced was often blurry," he wrote in his column. He raises a number of questions: "Were readers and viewers well-served or deluged with confusing information? And what does all of this portend for coverage of future wars?"

There are other questions that need asking.

What is the connection between the war, the pro-Bush coverage we have been seeing and the upcoming June 2 FCC decision that is expected to relax broadcast regulations? Is it unthinkable to suggest that big media companies stand to make windfall profits once Colin Powell's son, FCC chief Michael Powell, engineers new rules that permit more media mergers and concentration? Would these big media companies want to appease and please an administration that frequently bullies its opponents?

According to experts cited by the Los Angeles Times, if the media moguls get what they want, only a dozen or so companies will own most U.S. stations, giving them even more control over the marketplace of ideas than they already have.

Jeff Chester of the Center for Digital Democracy explains, "The ownership rules on the FCC chopping block have been developed over the last 50 years. They have been an important safeguard ensuring the public's basic First Amendment rights. The rationale for these policies is that they help provide for a diverse media marketplace of ideas, essential for a democracy. They have not been perfect. But the rules have helped constrain the power of the corporate media giants."

The FCC is, in effect, holding out the possibility of freeing the networks from restrictions on owning more stations. At a time when the industry is hurting financially, big bucks are once again being dangled in front of media moguls. No wonder none will challenge the government on the current war effort. Would you be surprised that the Conservative News Service gave its award for best Iraq war coverage of the war to Dan Rather (and not Fox because of Geraldo's antics)? This is the same CBS that was once admired for the reporting of Edward R. Murrow and Walter Cronkite.

Powell makes the connection between the war and his agenda. He says that bigger media companies are needed more than ever because only they can cover the war the way the Iraq war was covered. Need he say any more?

At first glance, the relationship between media concentration and what we see on TV seems tenuous. But is it? The cutbacks in coverage of world news that left so many Americans uninformed and unprepared for what happened on 9/11 took place in the greatest wave of media consolidation in history. It has already had an effect.
– *AlterNet, May 7, 2003*   ●

WHITE HOUSE PRESS PARTY BECOMES A BUSH RALLY

NEW YORK, APRIL 29, 2003 – It was an uncomfortable scene: a roomful of some of the most powerful journalists in America applauding the President as he boasted of his success in Iraq. It didn't happen in the White House but it might have, since the positive reception was offered up by White House correspondents at their association's annual dinner in Washington.

It was April 26, the 70th anniversary of the bombing of Guernica in Spain. But the symbolism was no more appreciated there than it had been at the United Nations some months earlier. At that time a tapestry copy of Picasso's famous painting of that wartime atrocity displayed outside the Security Council chambers was draped at Washington's request when Secretary of State Powell came to make the case for a war on Iraq.

As is the custom at these annual dinners, the President was on hand, traditionally as the target for a comic assault. Not this year. There was no humor, no satire, no criticism, no real barbs allowed. The New York Times called it the most subdued such event ever. Just one big happy family, with Press Secretary Ari Fleisher on one side of the dais, and his nemesis, the dean of the White House reporters and war critic Helen Thomas, on the other. She was not invited to speak.

This was the year for an aging Ray Charles to play old standards, and for President Bush to ask for God's blessings for the souls of two American reporters who died covering his war. Once again, he was playing preacher, not president. He cited approvingly the late NBC reporter David Bloom's last email speaking of his love of wife, children and Jesus. The President was giving not a speech as much as a benediction.

The press is there year after year, it is said, as a sign of respect for the office of the President. Reporters like to see themselves as having an adversarial relationship with the officialdom they cover, but except for a few stalwarts like Helen Thomas and perhaps Dana Milbank of the Washington Post, they seem more like adulators than journalists.

In this year of triumph, Bush spoke of the great successes of the war, and praised embedded reporters. He spoke of toppling the tyrant and used other applause lines that worked so well in his many speeches at military bases.

To my surprise, this audience of professional skeptics gave him a big hand, as if victory in Iraq had been assured.

Yes, the smoke is clearing, the looting is subsiding and the President is declaring an end to the military phase of the invasion. But was there "Victory in Iraq"? And if, so for whom?

As American newscasters gloated when each former regime member was snagged, described by his place in the Pentagon's deck of cards – "We got the ace of spades, heh-heh" – it seemed as though the rout was complete.

Saddam is out of commission. But, is he alive or dead? Tariq Aziz says he is still alive. But it doesn't seem to matter as much as it once did.

Our Republican Guard has defeated theirs.

Iraq is in ruins. The infrastructure is busted up pretty good, along with the country's stability, economy and former sense of enforced unity under Saddam. Now the country is fractured into political factions, many demanding that the U.S. get out.

Is this Iraqi freedom?

If the Afghanistan experience is any guide, reconstruction and order will be a long time coming. On April 26, the day that The New York Times reported the Pentagon was sending a "team of exiles to help run Iraq," The Times's Carlotta Gall reported from Kabul, "In a very real sense, the war here has not ended." She is one of the few U.S. journalists still in the Afghan capital.

According to media monitor Andrew Tyndall, the Afghanistan story, in network parlance, has all but "gone away." He reports, "The war in Afghanistan received 306 minutes of coverage on the newscasts in November 2001, but that dropped to 28 minutes by February 2002, and last month it was one minute."

The Bush Administration had also deemed that Afghan war a victory, and much of the press concurred, even though Osama bin Laden and Mullah Omar were never found. Terrorists remain in Afghanistan, and they may be regrouping and getting stronger.

As one who covered the victory parades after the first Gulf War, I remember the yellow ribbons flying and the crowds chanting, "We Are Number One!" That conflict, too, was proclaimed a victory until it was clear that it wasn't. Yes, Kuwait was returned to some of the richest people in the world who own it. But Saddam survived, hanging on for the next 12 years.

Soon the initial media-supported image of Desert Storm was revised. The sense of victory was short-lived. In the aftermath, the media complained about having been had, as atrocities were revealed and it turned out that the smart bombs used were not so smart. The President who won the war would soon lose his bid for reelection.

Fast forward to Iraq, 2003.

Who won? And who lost?

A high-tech U.S. military equipped with the best weaponry in the world overwhelmed a second-rate, no-tech defense force. It was no contest. If it was a prize fight, the ref would have called it in the first round. It was just as those who planned it knew it would be – a bloody and one-sided massacre. The coalition of the willing quickly became a coalition of the killing. All the fears of the anticipated use of bio-chemical weapons that aroused the public and made the war SEEM so risky never came to pass.

"I never thought Saddam would use those weapons," ABC's Ted Koppel confided after the war was over. He revealed that the general he was embedded said he didn't believe the weapons would be used either.

The war's biggest and most spectacular operations, the shock and awe and the decapitation strikes, all were pricey failures. The "collateral damage" that we were told would be minimal was enormous.

Warnings about the dangers of looting cultural treasures were ignored. U.S. soldiers stood by and watched, sometimes plunging in to pick up a souvenir or two. A employee of Fox News was busted and later fired for stealing two paintings, one of which he said he wanted to give to the head of his super-patriotic channel. They fired him for his gesture.

"We" won, but what have we won?

There is oil of course – nothing to snipe at, at least not in the way that those who suggested that oil was the rationale for war were sniped at.

The successful battle plan so great at quickly liberating territory was half-assed when it came to liberating people. The precision bombing somehow knocked out the lights and the water supply. No one knows how many Iraqis died. "We don't do body counts" was the military commanders' standard response to questions about estimates of how many died. There were sure enough casualties to overwhelm Iraq's understocked hospitals.

For U.S. viewers, this reality of war-as-hell was mostly out of sight and out of mind.

It was sanitized from view, admitted Ashleigh Banfield, the MSNBC correspondent who had been groomed as her network's answer to CNN's Christiane Amanpour. Banfield told a college crowd at Kansas State – but not her TV audience:

"We didn't see what happened when Marines fired M-16s. We didn't see what happened after mortars landed, only the puff of smoke. There were horrors that were completely left out of this war. So was this journalism? Or was this coverage?"

43

ABC's Koppel would agree when interviewed by Marvin Kalb, the veteran NBC warhorse who retired to a cushy job at Harvard. Koppel admitted that most Americans, both on the battlefield and off, never saw the true face of war. "Watching war on TV from a distance," he said. "is pulse pounding entertainment. That's damn good entertainment. We need to show people the consequences of war. People die in war."

We know about some of those who died, mostly Americans. There was endless airtime given over to POWs who were glorified as heroes even though most were victims. But the Iraqis were faceless. We rarely heard their names. No reporters were embedded in their world. Their fighters, the "soldiers of Saddam," the "enemy," were always presented as fanatical and worse.

The idea that people fight to defend their country is true everywhere, whatever the regime. The Russians died in the millions resisting the Nazi invasion of their country, even as many disliked the dictator who ruled them. When those communists were fighting as allies by our side, they were praised, not baited, in the press.

In the end, America's TV viewers who were given so much televised access to the war lost out when it came to understanding the conflict and realizing its impact. There was little empathy in the coverage, and hence little understanding when so many Iraqis greeted their liberation with demands that the liberators leave. "No To Saddam and No To America" is their slogan.

Ironically, one of the unspoken "winners" in this conflict was America's nemesis, Osama Bin Laden. As Jason Burke recently explained in The Guardian, "the primary objective of the terrorist actions that Bin Laden sponsored has not been to hurt the economies or the society of the West through physical damage. Instead they have been designed to rally the world's 1.2 billion Muslims to Bin Laden's banner. By radicalizing the Middle East, the war in Iraq has played straight into Bin Laden's hands."

A big loser was the credibility of American journalism. The losses were not only those journalists who died but also the many who lived and will have to live with the role they played as publicists for policies leading to a preemptive war, a war that outraged and alienated the world.

Alexander Cockburn of The Nation who is not known for understatement, may have been understating when he characterized the impact of the coverage as signaling the "Decline and Fall of American Journalism."

It was not only writers on the left who were challenging the coverage. Even Howard Kurtz, of the Washington Post, whom I debated on CNN while the bombs fell, and who was defending the coverage then, now that the war is over, is raising the larger questions.

On April 28, Kurtz began to sound like me, admitting, "Despite the investment of tens of millions of dollars and deployment of hundreds of journalists, the collective picture they produced was often blurry."

"The fog of war makes for foggy news," said S. Robert Lichter of the Center for Media and Public Affairs. "War is too messy to package into sound bites and two-minute stories."

Now that the shooting is over, these questions hang in the air: What did the media accomplish during the most intensively and instantaneously covered war in history? Did the presence of all those journalists capture the harsh realities of war or simply breed a new generation of Scud studs? Were readers and viewers well-served or deluged with confusing information? And what does all of this portend for coverage of future wars?

Please realize: I am not against the press, nor dismissive of the enterprise, hard work and tenacity shown. Many of our reporters were brave, most hard working and a few even brilliant in the stories they filed. I can't fault the technique or the way in which they worked to give us an insider's seat at a war. The technology was amazing and some of the imagery unforgettable.

At the same time, one must ask, what was the cumulative impact of this news army, what are the stories that went uncovered in a heavily managed system? Bear in mind that propaganda works best when you are unaware of it. Censorship is most effective when it is subtly achieved. Without "shooting the messenger" we can and must evaluate the message, its social meaning and political effect.

There has been a gradual erosion of the adversarial stance of many on high-status beats, reporters who appear to be seduced by the aura of power and the prestige of those whom they have been assigned to cover.

The White House correspondents' dinner is a case in oint. Journalists there were "em-tuxedoed," socializing with war makers. It is one thing to be polite. It is another to be co-opted.

President Bush knew he had a friendly crowd to wow and woo. He spoke eloquently of journalists he knew who died, especially the conservative Michael Kelly, without touching on any of the issues that worry advocates of free expression. He was preaching to those who should be watchdogs, who should be scrutinizing his poli-

cies, not complicit in his project.

There was no dissent shown from any of these correspondents and stenographers of power, nary a negative word. Instead, they cheered. They cheered. At one point, the outgoing president of the White House Correspondents Association commented that some reporters had even suggested that anti-war musicians like the Dixie Chicks or Harry Belafonte be invited to entertain. He scoffed at that proposal. "Imagine!" he sneered. "You can't make this stuff up." He was right on that point. You can't make this stuff up. ●

WAR AS NEWS BECOMES WAR AS HISTORY

NEW YORK, APRIL 23, 2003 – The non-stop news cycle turns instant events into history with a new rapidity. Soon we will be flooded with books, videocassettes and documentaries about Operation Iraqi Freedom through a media recycling operation already in high gear.

New media products offer one way of amortizing the investment in so much news coverage. But it is also a way of reinforcing the U.S. TV view that good has triumphed over evil, that the war was welcomed and worth it. Soon, the News Business will start handing out awards for best coverage by an embedded journalist under fire and, later, memorial plaques for those who died. Our heroism and valor cannot be forgotten.

What is needed more is real introspection and a critical reassessment. Were some media outlets acting more like publicists and promoters of the war than journalists with a duty to remain neutral, balanced and fair?

Were the warriors given an expensively produced free ride?

The Pentagon seems pleased as Punch at the positive spin it received despite the carping of the thin-skinned Secretary of Defense Donald Rumsfeld who has never read a critical comment he could agree with. "Gee," "Gosh" and "No" were his three favorite words when confronted with critical queries.

CSPAN spent a day with Pentagon media chief Tori Clark who did a good job of avoiding self-congratulation, even as it seemed that was the way she felt. Her predecessor Kenneth Baker had praised her in the pages of The Wall Street Journal, gushing, "You couldn't hire actors to do as good a job as the press has done" from the Pentagon's point of view.

There are many issues that remain unresolved, unexplored, uninvestigated, unreported and under-played. And some involve the role of the "embedded" journalists who had a rare front-row seat to the war, but ended up giving us only a partial view. The controversy over the embedding is only one aspect of a deeper debate that is emerging over what did and didn't really happen in the war. Every narrative tends to produce counter narratives, especially when new documents and other sources emerge. Revisionism is now part of the craft most historians pursue. Just as the first Gulf War was originally proclaimed a big win until it wasn't, so this war has also given rise to troubling unanswered questions, perhaps as numerous as the unexploded ordnance littering the streets of Iraq's cities.

Among the concerns to be pursued:

1. How was the Weapons of Mass Destruction issue constructed and why did it succeed despite solid evidence to the contrary? Ditto for the link between 9/11 and Iraq.

2. Was the circumvention of the U.N. planned in advance? What political forces were involved in the pre-emptive war strategy?

3. How did the looting begin in Baghdad? Was it unexpected? Was some of the looting an inside job by criminals with keys to the vaults? Were U.S. troops encouraging it?

4. Was the toppling of the Saddam statue a staged event? Why were no other statues, many of them larger, not toppled earlier by Iraqis?

5. Did Baghdad fall or was it handed over? Was there a deal with Saddam, members of his regime, or the Russians?

6. Why were journalists fired on? Accident or part of the war plan?

7. How did U.S. companies like Bechtel lobby for a profitable role in the reconstruction? Were targets selected with lucrative reconstruction in mind?

8. What was the extent of civilian casualties? What was the extent of damage to the country?

9. What behind-the-scenes role did Israel play?

10. What was the relationship between the uncritical coverage we saw and the lobbying underway at the same time by media companies seeking FCC rule changes that will benefit their bottom lines?

Wars transcend media coverage: Some outlets become winners, others losers. In America, the Fox News Channel with its patriotic posturing, martial music and pro-war boosterism has used the conflict to build a right-wing base and polarize the media environment. Fox won the cable news ratings war, even as most critics complained that it degraded journalism in the process. The so-called "Fox effect" has moved its competitors, like CNN and MSNBC, to the right.

In global terms, Al-Jazeera has emerged with new respect and a bigger audience. As Michael Wolff noted in New York Magazine: "The network is being transformed the way Gulf War I transformed CNN – but then CNN's audience has never exceeded more than a few million, whereas Al-Jazeera already speaks to a good 35 million people every day.

"By the time this whole thing is over," I said to three (Middle East) correspondents, "you'll be far and away the dominant media organization in the region – one of the largest in the world! You could end up being Time Warner Al-Jazeera."

The Al-Jazeera man responded: "No, Al-Jazeera Time Warner." Clearly, they understand brand positioning.

The real war may have ended but the media war grinds on and heats up. While most of the world had its eye on Baghdad, Rupert Murdoch had his on the Direct TV satellite that he wants to add to his arsenal of media weaponry.

In Washington, the FCC, under the leadership of Colin Powell's son Michael, announced plans to lift media rules that limit concentration of media in the hands of a few companies, this on June 2. Michael Powell has already cited the war coverage as the reason America needs media Goliaths.

This story bas been badly covered in the American press, but not in England where The Guardian's Annie Lawson reported, "U.S. broadcasters' war stance under scrutiny." Unfortunately, only non-profit groups not the government are calling for such scrutiny. The Center for Digital Democracy, which promotes diversity in digital media, says it believes news organizations in the U.S. have a "serious conflict of interest" when it comes to reporting the policies of the Bush Administration.

"It is likely that decisions about how to cover the war on Iraq – especially on television – may be tempered by a concern not to alienate the White House," said Jeffrey Chester, the Digital Democracy Center's executive director, in a recent article. "These media giants stand to make untold billions if the FCC safeguards are eliminated or weakened."

This issue has yet to surface in the American media. Does anyone wonder why? ●

CHAPTER TWO

PRODUCING THE WAR

IRAQI 'MONSTER' SEEKS TO WIN OUR HEARTS AND MINDS

Saddam takes to the airwaves with Dan Rather in prime time

Tonight's the night that the Iraq War truly goes prime time in America with the airing of Dan Rather's heavily hyped exclusive interview with Saddam Hussein. Already the right wing press is up in arms because cameramen from Iraqi Television actually shot the standoff between one of the world's most controversial anchors and its most contentious dictator.

The frequency this time is CBS, but there is already static on the horizon, with the Murdoch media insinuating that Rather was used. (News junkies remember how CNN's Peter Arnett was demonized as a traitor for even reporting from Baghdad during Gulf War I). In contrast, Rather is pleased with himself, telling the Washington Post how he scored a scoop TV bookers call the "big get."

"You work hard, work your sources, make your contacts, not get discouraged, just keep coming," Howard Kurtz reveals. When Rather got to Baghdad, he says, "I went to my hotel room and started preparing lists of questions and tried to memorize an outline of the questions. I had 31 or 32 questions. I put them in three different orders. I practiced them. I sat in front of the mirror and pretended he was on the other side and tried out the questions."

News outlets are not looking in that mirror, but musing instead about the interview's likely impact. Britain's Independent speculates: "Assuming CBS gets the tape in time, the choice segments will be aired tonight opposite what was previously seen as the scoop of the season, the interview with Robert Blake, Hollywood B-lister and accused wife-killer, by ABC's indefatigable Barbara Walters.

"A true connoisseur of American television might wonder what the difference is, in terms of luring the punters, between a film star accused of one murder and a foreign ruler who is known to have murdered millions. Was it not Stalin who said that "one death is a tragedy, a million deaths are a statistic"? But in this land of the 15-minute sensation, President Saddam is the exception.

"The contents of Rather's interview are deadly serious, which presumably is why Iraqi television, which taped it, has not made available extracts for CBS to air as promised, either on its Monday evening news or on its Tuesday breakfast show, and why no transcript had been provided by the Iraqis at the time of writing.

The Independent concludes: "Rather's inter-

51

view may do wonders for CBS' ratings but not for the all-but-vanished prospect of a peaceful solution to the crisis."

The New York Times places the interview in the context of a more mundane media war: "This is the last night of the all-important sweeps period, when networks broadcast their most-hyped programming, and TV news is increasingly hijacked to report on the results of manufactured "reality," as if the bachelorette's choice of suitors or the latest expulsion from the island were events of global consequence. The appearance of Mr. Hussein in the midst of it makes for a truly eclectic, if not peculiar, mix.

"The nation may be cruising toward one of those moments of cultural humiliation when the world compares the number of people who watch the Hussein interview with the 40 million who last week watched Joe Millionaire pick wholesome Zora over Sarah, the presumed gold-digger. CBS may be hoping only to match the 27 million viewers who watched ABC's Michael Jackson documentary earlier in the month — and even then it's unlikely that Fox will be rushing in to air unseen scraps of the Baghdad interview. But it's hard to imagine how Mr. Hussein, who claimed 100 percent of the vote in last October's referendum in Iraq, would react to news that he lost the ratings battle to Barbara Walters's visit with the jailed ex-star of "Baretta."

This reference to Walters calls to mind a juicy "exclusive" one-on-one she snagged years ago with Fidel Castro, then Washington's most hated evil-doer. That interview, shot by ABC News, was carefully edited to leave out most of Commandante Castro's more political points. The full text was later released by the Cubans to be published side by side in an alternative paper showing how politicized U.S. TV editing can be. Sanitizing media is not just the province of dictators.

One of the more fascinating propositions in the interview is said to be Hussein's offer of a televised debate between him and George Bush. The White House immediately shot this down, revealing that the President may be authorizing a covert assassination team to take its own shot at the man who has said he would rather die than leave his country. Such a debate is already grist for the comedy mill, with all the makings of one of those World Wrestling Federation "smackdowns," and could probably make millions as a Pay TV event. That is, if MTV doesn't scoop its competition with a special edition of "Celebrity Death Match."

The winner of this latest episode in the media war remains to be seen and it will be shortly. Whatever Saddam says is still a first in giving the Iraqis real "face time." For the moment, they achieved parity in a media war which has until now, had a 'rather' one-sided spin.

(At the war's end, the conservative Media Research Center in Washington gave Dan Rather an award for the best war coverage. Howard Kurtz of the Washington Post reported that Rather's boss was dismissive of media critics. "CBS News President Andrew Heyward dismisses criticism that media outlets were too jingoistic, in their coverage. American journalists are rooting for America to win," he said. "You're not going to find a lot of Americans rooting for Iraq. That doesn't mean they're not objective and fair in their reporting.")　●

WAR CALLS AND THE NEWS BIZ RUSHES TO ENLIST

NEW YORK FEBRUARY 25, 2003 — War calls, and many a journalist is answering. Throughout the world, media organizations are planning their sojourns to Baghdad. All want to be in place for the "big one." They are lining up at Iraqi missions asking for visas. Others are trying to get the U.S. military to give them a front row seat.

In the old days, there was a sharp debate about whether to get 'in bed" with the people you are covering. Today it is the military that is pursuing a policy of "embedding" journalists with U.S. units. Back in the Gulf War, reporters had to demand access. Today, it is the military doing the demanding.

Why? "What is driving this is a fear that Iraq will win the propaganda war if reporters are not on the ground with troops," writes Dave Moniz, of USA Today. As a result, explains News World: "The Pentagon has pledged that reporters will gain more access to troops on the ground during a war with Iraq. But the promise has met with a mixed response from journalists. Most welcomed the move, but some questioned whether the fine words would be translated into action, while others questioned the Bush administration's motives. The U.S. press corps heavily criticized the Pentagon for keeping journalists away from the action during the recent war in Afghanistan."

At a recent media panel in New York, Judith Miller of The New York Times says that the press will "not allow" the Pentagon to exclude them. She and other journalists are also taking training in self-protection. If she goes, she says she will learn how to use a suit to defend against chemical warfare. Chris Cramer, president of CNN International, revealed that 500 CNN journalists have already taken war safety training. Globalvision recently lost an intern to the adventure promised in taking pictures of the soldiers in training in the deserts of Qatar.

Access to the war is one concern – shilling for it is another. Far too many journalists take an uncritical, even fawning attitude towards men in uniform. Says Cokie Roberts on NPR: "I am, I will just confess to you, a total sucker for the guys who stand up with all the ribbons on and stuff and if they say it's true, I'm ready to believe it."

Independent radio producer and author David Barsamian amplifies this point: "When the U.S. marches to war, the media march with it. And within the media the generals generally are heavily armed with microphones. The din of collateral language is rising to cacophonous levels. The mobilization and ubiquity of present and past brass on the airwaves is an essential component of manufacturing consent for war."

He assessed U.S. media coverage earlier this month. On PBS' NewsHour on Thursday, January 2 with Ray Suarez as host, the lead story was Iraq. The guests were Patrick Lang, U.S. Army and John Warden, U.S. Air Force. Geoffrey Kemp, a war hawk and ex-Reagan NSC staffer joined them. The discussion totally focused on strategies and tactics.

"How many troops would be needed to do the job? What would the bombing campaign look like? And the inevitable, when will the war begin? It's kind of like placing bets on a bowl game. Suarez, formally of NPR's 'Talk of the Nation,' played the classic role of the unctuous and compliant questioner.

"There were no uncomfortable inquiries about the U.N. weapons inspection process, casualty figures, international law, the U.N. Charter or the notorious U.S. practice of double standards on Security Council resolutions. Instead, the pundits pontificated on troop deployments, carrier battle groups and heavy infantry forces such as the 3rd Mechanized Division," Barsamian said.

This type of pro-Pentagon punditry also informs the reporting in major U.S. newspapers, says Mathew Engel, a Guardian reporter based in Washington who notes that military leaks are often not accurate. "Most of these stories, which look like impressive scoops at first glimpse, actually come from officials using the press to perform on-message spin. Whatever the category, the papers lap this up, even when it is obvious nonsense, a practice that reached its apogee last year when palpably absurd plans for the invasion of Iraq emerged, allegedly from inside the Pentagon, on to The New York Times' front page."

"It's a very cynical game," says Eric Umansky, who reviews the papers for Slate.com. "The reporters know these stories are nonsense and they know they are being used. But it's an exclusive. It's an exclusive built on air, but CNN says 'according to The New York Times', so the paper's happy, and it stays out there for a whole news cycle. So what if it's popcorn?"

"In the face of this," Umansky continues, "only one White House reporter, Dana Milbank of the Post, regularly employs skepticism and irreverence in his coverage of the Bush Administration – he is said to dodge the threats because he is regarded as an especially engaging character. It

is more mysterious that only the tiniest handful of liberal commentators ever manage to irritate anyone in the government: there is Paul Krugman in The New York Times, Molly Ivins down in Texas and, after that, you have to scratch your head."

Scratching your head won't necessarily fill it with the information you need to stay informed. That's why news like that offered on Globalvision News network or critiques like the ones offered on Mediachannel.org are trying to fill the growing gap between news and truth   ●

THE MEDIA WAR AND THE ANTI-WAR MOVEMENT

NEW YORK, FEBRUARY 18, 2003 – In the run up to the massive February 15th protest in New York, a group of media activists proposed to the organizers of the anti-war rally that the headquarters of media organizations also be targeted, since it was likely that not all who wanted to join could do so. They suggested that all that opposition energy be channeled against the companies that, more often than not, are misinforming the American people about the issues.

The small group, calling itself "The Information Liberation Front," an offshoot of the Indy Media movement, argued that the movement's goal should not only be to get a few seconds of episodic airtime for an event – but also to pressure media outlets to offer more balanced coverage all the time.

Their argument is that media is not a side issue, but a central one. Most activists acknowledge the problem, but do little about it. They seem to want to be in the media more than they seem to be concerned with transforming it. One organizer, who like many militants uses a nom de guerre, "War Cry," makes this complaint: "Going to empty government buildings like the U.N. and City Hall is a waste of time – sort of a hollow symbolic gesture. But going to the MEDIA and DEMANDING a national platform is NOT symbolic. It might be worthwhile both in terms of opposing the war effectively by getting the public support we need, and asserting our basic rights of freedom of speech and assembly. (Rapidly eroding rights I might add)."

Protest organizers, understandably caught up in testy negotiations with police, city officials and members of their own coalitions jockeying for platform time, were unwilling to entertain a more multi-dimensional approach. They were bent on orchestrating the one big photo op – showing sizable and significant protest.

Undeterred, the Information Liberation Front tried to mount a side protest anyway. CNN was the target. The police proved less receptive than the mainstream-oriented movement. An intra-First Amendment conflict resulted, with cops defending CNN's "freedom" of the press over protesters' freedom of speech.

Here's what they say happened: "A few dozen people showed up with signs at CNN HQ in NYC. However the cops managed to cut off a contingent headed to CNN and detained them (based on what we don't know) until people had dispersed from CNN to join the larger marches. Also, the ILF had received a last minute email from UFPJ saying that CNN was going to cover the rally and that we should not antagonize them. They said our protest was only organized in a week and a half time, and that's not enough

time to do adequate outreach and build or express the kind of pressure it takes to make corporate giants acknowledge our demands."

Within this conflict are the seeds of a larger challenge. Should protest movements adapt a passive hands-off attitude towards media institutions in hopes of getting coverage?

The ILF people think this strategy aimed at getting on some show here or there is fated to fail. Cries War Cry: "After witnessing F15 and subsequent corporate media coverage (TV and print), it's clear that most of it was superficial and not in depth about the issues we were out there for. When they didn't ignore us, they either distorted our numbers and/or downplayed our intelligence (almost never saw an interview or meaningful soundbite from a protester), however, this is not surprising."

A protest against CNN does not a strategy against media myopia make. Clearly media plays a central role in defining issues and the political environment. This point was made in The New York Times, which ought to know, by Paul Krugman who explained that the massive European rejection of U.S. policy occurred in part because of a supportive media there, while our media downplays and undercuts opposition.

Krugman approvingly cited The Nation columnist Eric Alterman's new book, "What Liberal Media?" to argue, yes, it is the media, stupid, writing, "At least compared with their foreign counterparts, the liberal, U.S. media are strikingly conservative and in this case hawkish. . . For months both major U.S. cable news networks have acted as if the decision to invade Iraq has already been made, and have in effect seen it as their job to prepare the American public for the coming war."

This is an issue that protest movements ignore at their peril. While a Nation editor may pop up on a talk show, usually "balanced" by a bullying neo-con and conservative anchor, most of the news and analysis that shapes the activist agenda is not reaching the mass audience. Is this not a political challenge?

Putting anti-war ads on TV is important but insufficient. We need to sharpen our own understanding of the way media works and doesn't. How can we believe that government will be responsive to pressure, protest and lobbying but that the media isn't? The far right targeted the so-called liberal media and took it over. Pressure works. It's time to press the press to make media coverage an issue, not just a complaint to cry about. •

MARCH 10: HOW TO KEEP THE MEDIA ON MESSAGE

IMAGINE the scenario. It is Saturday night at the State Department and more is stirring than a few mice. The Sunday New York Times has arrived. In it, that newspaper's first editorial against the war. "If it comes down to a question of yes or no to invasion without broad international support, our answer is no. Even though Hans Blix, the chief weapons inspector, said that Saddam Hussein was not in complete compliance with United Nations orders to disarm, the report of the inspectors on Friday was generally devastating to the American position."

You can just hear one of their media spinners exclaim: "We are losing New York!" As they rambled through the Op-ed page, it got worse. Jimmy Carter, our other Born-Again President, says the war will not be just. Tom Friedman seems to be sliding into the anti-war camp since no one in power seems to be listening to his complaints that "We" will need international support to rebuild Iraq, so let's not piss off the whole world. And the coup de grace: Maureen Dowd calls Bush "The Xanax" President, commenting on his s-l-o-w performance last week at that White House press conference that seemed to suggest he was on drugs. She came right out and said it while others spoke of his sedate manner. "Sedated" was her conclusion.

Orchestrating a story

WHAT to do? Since the propaganda war is as important as the real war in the wings, they would have to find something to keep their agenda as the main frame of the debate. They needed to find something to give Secretary of State Powell a "smoking gun" to reveal/expose, and to take the offensive during the Sunday TV talk shows – on which he seems to have become a permanent fixture. And sure enough, there it was on page 169 of a 176 U.N. inspector's technical report. Iraq *may* have rockets suitable for delivering chemical or biological weapons.

Gotcha

On Sunday, on Fox, the homeland network, Powell cited the existence of drone aircraft that could unleash black rain on our boys. He hinted at what was to come: "That's the kind of thing we're going to be making some news about in the course of the week," he said. "And there are other things that have been found that I think more can be made of." Underscore the thought: "MORE CAN BE MADE OF."

The big leak

FAST forward, to Fox News this morning. The message of the day: Blast Blix for covering this up. It is on all the networks, too. And The New York Times. Take that, Howell Raines. The administration leaked the story to The Times to undercut the editorial direction of the paper. And where did The Times play it? Why, page one, of course. It is today's BIG story:

"U.S. Says Iraq Retools Rockets for Illicit Uses"
By John Cushman with Steven R Weisman

"Weapons inspectors recently discovered rockets configured to disperse chemical or biological agents, U.S. officials say . . . "

Check the source.

Note the reference to the U.S. recently discovering the issue. That was not played up on the TV channels that reported Washington's claims as fact. Actually The Times story traces this "new" disclosure back to 1996. But, never mind. The fact is that this story, played up by all the TV channels, is another item of which "more can be made." It is an allegation from officialdom, not some revelation that Times reporters investigated on their own. No inspectors are quoted in the story. Not one Washington official is cited. And all sources are unnamed.

More telling, there is no reference in the article to the report last week that DISCOUNTED, challenged and debunked earlier U.S. claims about aluminum tubes, magnets and uranium from Africa. That latter issue was, it was revealed, based on phony documents.

So here you have it, the newspaper of record,

out to prove its impartiality, prominently reporting a claim by only one side in the world debate – on the pro-war side – with no skepticism or context that would help readers evaluate its credibility.

Remembering the Pentagon Papers

THIS is how the propaganda war is fought. One bombshell after another that later proves bogus. If you wanted some background on all of this, all you had to do was to watch the excellent TV movie on Daniel Ellsberg and the Pentagon Papers that aired on, of all places, FX, one of Mr. Murdoch's channels. (Did you know he was called "Red Rupert" back in his college days when he kept a bust of Lenin next to his bed? Honest!) Anyway, the film explained how the Pentagon Papers, a secret history of the Vietnam War, showed how the public was being told one thing about the war, while the President was being told the truth. And this took place during FOUR administrations – Republican and Democratic.

Ellsberg was pictured as a hawk who became a dove when he discovered the truth and felt he had a duty to inform the public. It was powerful television and timely. Its finale reminded us of the Supreme Court decision that affirmed the press could publish documents like these. That was The New York Times's finest hour. I wish the editors of The Times had read their paper's own positive review and watched it before they gave over their front page again to the claims of an administration lacking in all credibility in matters involving "evidence."

Unofficial leaker in trouble

MEANWHILE, in England, another Pentagon Papers case may be brewing. You will recall that Observer article a week back that exposed U.S. spying on members of the Security Council. (U.S. buying of Security Council members is far more open.)

At the time, few U.S. newspapers picked it up and White House spokesman Ari Fleischer declined to comment on it. It was DOA , as far as most U.S. news outlets were concerned. The Washington Times challenged its authenticity, as did Matt Drudge. Well now, Ed Vulliamy, one of the reporters who broke the story, tells us:

"This is to inform you that there has just been an arrest at the British Government's Communications Headquarters (GCHQ – equivalent of the NSA) in connection with the leak of the memo. If charges are made, they will be serious – Britain is far more severe in these matters than the U.S. (So far!).

"They could result in a major trial and a long prison sentence for the alleged mole. It is also a criminal offence to receive such information in Britain (some of you may recall the 'ABC' trial of the 1970s), and this may also become an issue of press freedom. The authors of the piece will defy any attempt by the government to discuss our sources.

"It is important that maximum international – as well as domestic British – pressure be brought to bear on the Blair government over this impending case, the prosecution of which will inevitably have a political agenda, and to protect this prospective defendant all we can. Pleading motive will be impossible because there is no defense of justification in Britain."

That U.N. vote

MEANWHILE, all the media is buzzing with reports that Washington wants the Security Council to vote tomorrow on the new resolution that would sanction war after St. Patrick's Day. The Times speaks of "urgent diplomacy" and says it has so far failed. What is "urgent diplomacy"? It seems that translates into money changing hands, with promises of new U.S. Aid projects to come. The U.S. may succeed in turning the votes of many nations who want to be on the side of a winner.

"It is a good time to be a Ghanaian," said Joe Klein on ABC yesterday morning, apparently not knowing the difference between Ghana and Guinea unless I heard him wrong. CNN reported that French President Jacques Chirac and German Chancellor Gerhard Schroeder might fly over to cast their countries votes personally. Will Bush? Times agit-propster Maureen Dowd's "Xanax Cowboy" might show up, too. CNN also said that we will we see which cards fall where, a direct steal of President Bush's language which compared the Security Council's deliberations to a card game. Interesting how a presidential metaphor quickly finds its way into 'objective' news language.

As for the President's presence at the U.N., he may like the showdown aspects of it, and see it as a new chance to grandstand. We will see. The Daily Mirror in Britain tells us about another recent invite that the Commander-in-Chief turned down:

"George Bush pulled out of a speech to the European Parliament when MEPs wouldn't guarantee a standing ovation.

"Senior White House officials said the President would only go to Strasbourg to talk about Iraq if he had a stage-managed welcome.

"A source close to negotiations said last night: "President Bush agreed to a speech but insisted he get a standing ovation like at the State of the Union address.

"His people also insisted there were no protests, or heckling" since reception of U.S. war plans is worsening fast – this won't help."

Where are the humanitarian aid supplies?

TO its credit, CNN did feature a report from Kuwait by Richard Blystone, who spoke of the humanitarian disaster that is predicted to follow the war. He interviewed a U.S. official who waffled on whether humanitarian supplies have been shipped in the high-priority way the bombers have been shipped. He gave the distinct impression they had not. The Mail and Guardian of South Africa also takes up this question, noting, "With a war against Iraq perhaps days away, the world's richest governments have given the United Nations barely a quarter of the funds its agencies have asked for to deal with the expected humanitarian catastrophe."

Can the U.N. still do anything to stop the war?

WHY, I wonder is a U.S declared war not considered a violation of the U.N. charter? Writer Jeremy Brecher has done some research and believes there is one possibility left: "If the U.S. attacks Iraq without support of the U.N. Security Council, will the world be powerless to stop it? The answer is no. Under a procedure called "Uniting for Peace," the U.N. General Assembly can demand an immediate cease-fire and withdrawal. The global peace movement should consider demanding such an action. Resolution 377 provides that, if there is a threat to peace, breach of the peace, or act of aggression and the permanent members of the Security Council do not agree on action, the General Assembly can meet immediately and recommend collective measures to U.N. members to maintain or restore international peace and security." ●

MARCH 11: KEEPING THE CARDS BELOW THE TABLE

THE White House blinked, at least for the minute. All last week, we were hearing how the U.N. Security Council had to vote on the new resolution giving Saddam until the day of the leprechauns to get out of Dodge. Show your cards, said the President with a sedated but unmovable resolve at what passed for a press conference. In the media echo chamber at TIME, an old friend, Joe Klein, all but cheered him on:

"George W. Bush abandoned his studied air of mild sedation only once during his prime-time press conference last week. His eyes lighted up when he was asked if he would call for another U.N. vote on Iraq. A poker metaphor escaped from his Inner Cowboy. 'It's time for people to show their cards,' he said, as if he actually enjoyed the prospect of a confrontation with France, Russia and the others. The tactic was unexpected; the belligerence, revealing."

You heard Colin Powell say that today is the day, the moment of truth, during the showdown at Turtle Bay. Win or lose, the President had called the bets – until, sometime yesterday, when the mother of all votes was surprisingly POSTPONED, not because of rain, but because Russia has joined France in vowing to veto. The administration took a small step backwards. Why? What happened?

Daddy to Junior: Don't Diss the U.N.

FIRST, it appears as if Daddy Bush has weighed in with a strong recommendation that the administration do all it can to rally the U.N. (Even as the polls and the press keep lambasting the institution.) "More Americans now faulting U.N. on Iraq, Poll Finds," reports The New York Times on its front page. There is no suggestion in the article that all the U.N. bashing on TV might have anything to do with this shift in public opinion. For that matter, next to that article was another: "US SAYS UN COULD REPEAT ERRORS OF 90s." The U.N. has become the latest target for Bush supporters to beat up on, with analysts like George Will and his crowd labeling the international organization a bad idea and calling for its demise.

These nattering nabobs of anti-U.N. negativity, to borrow a Spiro Agnew-ism, are of course distressed whenever the U.S. cannot bully or bribe its way into a hegemonic role. The lack of media attention for the U.N. contributes to misconceptions, which led the ultra-paranoid right to fear "black helicopters" from the U.N. invading America. A report by Media Tenor, published in my book, "Media Wars" showed that the major media largely ignore U.N. activities, except when it is politically advantageous not to.

Militainment: What's next?

IT may be that war is not quite ready to roll yet. I am hearing from informed sources close to someone high up in the network news hierarchy, who is privy to informed sources, (how's that for pretty typical sourcing?) that our military mavens are expressing fears that their "E-BOMB" – designed to knock out all communications – is not up to par. But beyond that, in this age of Millitainment, the set is not ready yet. The set, you ask? Yes, the set is being built, as the New York Post reported today:

"March 11, 2003 – CAMP AS SAYLIYAH, Qatar – The Pentagon has enlisted Hollywood to present its daily briefings to the world.

"Fresh from the latest Michael Douglas film, one of Tinsel town's top art directors has been hired to create a $200,000 set for Gen. Tommy Franks and other U.S. commanders to give daily updates.

"George Allison, 43, who has designed White House backdrops for President Bush and worked with the illusionist David Blaine, has been flown into the U.S. Central Command base in Qatar as part of a reputed $1 million conversion of a storage hangar into a high-tech hub for the international media. Allison's credits include the set for "Good Morning America," as well as Hollywood productions for MGM and Disney, such as the Kirk and Michael Douglas film, "It Runs in the Family," due to be released next month.

"His work in Qatar reflects the Pentagon's realization that it needs to look good on prime-time television. Gone are the easel and chart, solitary television and VCR machine with which Gen. Norman Schwarzkopf showed fuzzy images of smart-bomb raids during the 1991 Gulf War."

The media is the illusion

I LOVE the reference to illusionists, don't you? That is because the idea of a real press corps is itself becoming an illusion. Columnist James O. Goldsborough writes about the media ABDICAT- ING its role in the pages of The San Diego Union- Tribune, once one of the most conservative newspapers in America. Why is the public buy ing the war? His answer:

"I think the media deserve most of the blame. Bush officials have explained in detail their rea- sons for war, and the media have not sufficiently challenged those reasons. They are endorsing Bush's war by default. The public is confused because its gut feeling is that the government/ media reasoning doesn't add up.

"Television is Bush's ally in war because it is a visual medium. It shows pretty pictures of ships sailing, flags waving, troops landing. Television loves Bush photo-ops and shrugs off anti-war protests. C-SPAN and PBS alone present fair pic- tures because they don't depend on advertising.

"Unlike television, newspapers are not a pic- ture show. Unlike television, newspapers have editorial and opinion pages whose job it is to analyze, endorse or refute official policy. These pages have ties to their communities, not to some multinational news machine in New Jersey. Reporters report what Bush and Donald Rums- feld say or do, but the job of opinion pages is crit- ical analysis. Short of that, we are useless."

In a nation bitterly divided, this editorial enthusiasm for Bush's war amounts to profes- sional crime. The media, led by cable television (which wasn't there) has forgotten the lessons of Vietnam. Soon we will be remembering the words of Tacitus, referring to the Romans: "They make a desert and call it peace."

Missing in action

THAT is the first time I have seen a leading jour- nalist call his colleagues criminal. Peter Bart of Variety offers his own spin, using a military metaphor. He asks, "Are journalists missing in action? Where is that magic mix of interpretive journalism that lends both vitality and credibility to a free press?

"Ask working journalists about all this and they'll explain their woes in reporting on the presidency. TV newsmen tell you the numbers crunchers have eviscerated their staffs. Some also hint there's been a subtle shift to the right as a result of the ascension of Fox News. Maga- zine writers complain about corporate con- straints at a time when ad revenues are plung- ing. The right is very well organized, they say, and not inhibited about complaining.

"Probably there's a germ of truth in all these explanations. The bottom line, however, is that journalists already seem to be missing in action. And the war hasn't even started yet.

Blair blows it

"WITH journalists out there hyping the build up or in there cozying up to the powerful," he con- tinues, "politicians continue to try to use the press. Our own correspondent Garry Nash sends this report along from London. Sometimes even the best plans backfire:

"On prime time TV, and still smarting from one of his Cabinet, Clare Short, naming him reckless over his new Iraqi war, Prime Minister Blair faced thirty Iraqi and British women, including Gulf War veterans and two who had lost sons in 9/11, and tried to convert even one of them to his view. He failed dismally. After nearly an hour of frustration from his audience, the end arrived and clapping began. Mr. Blair's noble brow began to rise but lowered immediately. It was a slow handclap from about ten of the women, while the rest remained stonily silent.

"A reprise clip played on the 22.00 ITV main network news immediately after, was suddenly cut short – and apologized for by the news anchor. WHY? Well, some editor had made a mistake. Over cut clips of the women's faces one phrase was repeated ad nauseam. It was Mr. Blair's own voice – and his repetitive phrase during the entire confrontation, "I am working flat out for a second resolution . . . I am working flat out for a second resolution . . . "

Axis of Evil Film Fest

SEARCHING for other perspectives, some students at Duke University are studying films made by the other side. The New York Post calls this "the cinematic cream of the Axis of Evil."

"Reel Evil," a film festival that runs into next month, is featuring movies from Iraq, Iran and North Korea, as well as from a trio of countries designated by the State Department as "rogue states" – Cuba, Libya and Syria.

"Organizers said they wanted to provide insight into a world sharply different from America's.

"We know how Bush sees 'the Axis of Evil,'" said Professor Negar Mottahedeh, the series' co-curator. "How does someone from the Axis see everyday life? The screening drew a lot of media attention and both positive and negative e-mails

– but no protests, he said.

"But the next screening, of the 1985 North Korean film "Pulgasari," could be the biggest draw. It was produced by Dictator Kim Jong II, who kidnapped a South Korean director to film the tale of a metal-eating monster who helps an army of farmers overcome a tyrannical king.

Funny, just last night, I was talking with some Italian filmmakers about why a science fiction film might be the best way to capture the craziness in U.S. culture. They smiled and agreed. Maybe North Korea's "Dear Leader" is available to direct it.

Is PBS sanitizing a new series on war and peace?

GETTING hard-hitting programming on the air in the U.S. is getting harder by the moment. I have been chatting with Chris Koch, a veteran journalist and filmmaker. He found himself abruptly fired as the executive producer of a TV documentary series on weapons of mass destruction produced by Ted Turner's company for WETA, the PBS station in Washington, D.C. He says WETA has taken over the film and is sanitizing it and softening its content.

Chris was understandably perplexed and torn up about this one more sign of how PBS is not immune to the tendency to 'KISS,' keep it simple and stupid. By the way, his background is impressive. He was executive producer of NPR's nightly news program, "All Things Considered," and won many awards, including a Peabody, the Overseas Press Club's Edward R. Murrow Award, a Cable Ace and five national Emmys. He sent me a copy of a letter he has sent to Ted Turner – who is unlikely to intervene. It points to the problems facing journalists who want to get edgier stories on the air.

"A statement prepared by WETA-TV and Safe World Productions praised me for the work I had done to date, then said: As the production progressed, particularly in light of changing world events, we felt we needed to install a new team to bring the project to completion. Frank Sesno and Chris Guarino are respected news producers and journalists.

"Less than an hour after I was fired, Marlene Adler, Walter Cronkite's personal assistant, called me. Mr. Cronkite wanted to speak to me. I explained that I'd been fired. Adler was shocked. Mr. Cronkite wanted to tell you himself how much he liked the scripts. He didn't even feel the need to have his own editorial review. It has been my experience that the person delivering the words on camera is usually the most critical because it is their [sic] reputation and face that is out there," Koch said.

Amy Goodman charms the WashPost

MEANWHILE, in the center of U.S. power, the Washington Post, accused of boosting the war while ignoring critics, has discovered Amy Goodman and the Democracy Now! show on Pacifica and other stations. Michael Powell writes:

"Its politics can veer toward communion for the progressive choir. But in this age of corporate media conglomeration, when National Public Radio sounds as safe as a glass of warm milk, Democracy Now! retains a jagged and intriguing edge.

"Goodman is the show's center, a slight 45-year-old in a pullover vest, jeans and sneakers. Her unruly brown hair is streaked with gray. She can break out a playful smile, and punctuate an interview by opening a hatch in her office floor and sliding down a fire pole to the floor below.

"More often, though, her intensity burns through. Her eye sockets look a bit hollowed out. It's hard to leave phone messages for her because her voice mail keeps filling up.

"She doesn't say 'no' very well," says Michael Ratner, a friend and an attorney and president of the Center for Constitutional Rights.

"Sleep? Her friend, Elizabeth Benjamin, head of the Legal Aid Society's Health Law Unit, chuckles. "I wish she got more of it. Amy has so much passion to right the wrongs of the world."

Perle calls Hersh a terrorist

WHAT happens to reporters who don't buy the administration position line hook and sinker? They get called terrorists. This shocking email from Kathy Sampson of Cambridge, Mass., deserves to be printed in full.

"I am writing to you to inform you of an event that is deeply disturbing and frightening. Yesterday on Late Edition on CNN, Wolf Blitzer asked Richard Perle what he thought of an article written by Seymour Hersh in the 17 March issue of The New Yorker magazine. According to Mr. Blitzer, Mr. Hersh explores the question of whether Mr. Perle may have a conflict of interest due to his role with the administration and his investments in Homeland Security-related companies. Mr. Perle then stated that Mr. Hersh is the closest thing American journalism has to a terrorist.

"Mr. Blitzer seemed quite surprised at this response and asked, "Why do you say that? A terrorist?

"Mr. Perle: Because he's widely irresponsible."

"Mr. Blitzer asked, "But I don't understand. Why do you accuse him of being a terrorist?

"Perle: Because he sets out to do damage and he will do it by whatever innuendo, whatever distortion he can – look, he hasn't written a serious piece since Maylie (sic)". (DS: This may be reference to the My Lai Massacre in Vietnam that Hersh reported. He had to use a small news service to distribute it because most newspapers refused to print it.   ●

THE MEDIA WAR MIRRORS THE COMING WAR

THE juxtaposition of stories on the front page of The New York Times captures a fault line in American politics. On one side of the page, there is a report on Jimmy Carter's Nobel Peace prize address with his call to avert war. Two columns to the right, there's the report that the Bush Administration will "respond with all of our options to any use of weapons of mass destruction aimed at soldiers in the U.S.-organized coalition." That sentiment, downplayed for elite readers, was translated for the masses by Rupert Murdoch's New York Post as "We'll Nuke You."

The conflict within the American media is mirroring the larger conflict in the world as opinion polarizes and positions harden. Anti-war organizers have placed three full-page ads in The New York Times to promote support for a multi-lateral diplomatic solution, not pre-emptive strikes. Over a hundred Hollywood celebrities have signed on to one such call. The groups placing the ads say that paying for pricey ads is the only way to get heard in a media system filled with

programs structured around "showdowns" and "countdowns" with Iraq. Many say the media is preparing the public for war. Conservatives challenge that, saying that President Bush is already doing what they want, even if the tone of the administration's rhetoric seems extreme.

That may be because the U.N. Security Council seems to be stage managed by the U.S. State Department. Secretary General Annan, for one, has just mildly criticized a U.S. decision to control the distribution to council members of Iraq's weapons declaration document and only share it with fellow big powers. At the same time, one of the potentially juiciest disclosures in the document dealing with which nations supplied Iraq with weapons making material is not being released – ostensibly because the weapons inspectors may need the data.

Earlier reports naming names seems to have disappeared down the media memory hole. For example, last September's report in Glasgow's Sunday Herald by Neil Mackay and Felicity Arbuthnot asked, "How did Iraq get its weapons?" Their answer " We sold them." Their conclusion:

"The U.S. and Britain sold Saddam Hussein the technology and materials Iraq needed to develop nuclear, chemical and biological weapons of mass destruction.

"Reports by the U.S. Senate's committee on banking, housing and urban affairs – which oversees American exports policy – reveal that the U.S., under the successive administrations of Ronald Reagan and George Bush Sr., sold materials including anthrax, VX nerve gas, West Nile fever germs and botulism to Iraq right up until March 1992, as well as germs similar to tuberculosis and pneumonia. Other bacteria sold included brucella melitensis, which damages major organs, and clostridium perfringens, which causes gas gangrene."

Also missing in many news accounts worldwide is any analysis about the motives for the war. Mainstream journalists and more radical critics seem to agree that there is more at play than meets the eye. Rolling Stone magazine gathered a group of top journalists and policy makers to kick this question around. Among the participants was veteran journalist, Youssef Ibrahim of The New York Times.

He says: "In my 30 years covering the Middle East for The Wall Street Journal and the N.Y. Times, I have not seen a bigger group of imbeciles than the current administration in the White House . . .Our war on terrorism has been a miserable failure. . .The moment we distract ourselves with Iraq, al Qaeda will see its golden moment has arrived."

Like many critics, he opines that oil and energy strategies are what is behind the ratcheting up of war talk. Already Iraq's Tariq Aziz is contending that "region change, not regime change" is what is motivating U.S. strategists. Says the well-informed Ibrahim: "I firmly believe our oil interests are driving this war. . .Their attitude [people in the Administration] is: This is our big chance to make Iraq into a pumping station for America."

On the other hand, a radical critic, who you would expect to have a similar economic-centered analysis, has a more political one. Author and anti-war icon Noam Chomsky told the BBC earlier today, that the current war fever is an extension of the policy established during the Reagan Administration (whose members now hold key posts in the second Bush Administration). He believes they push international conflicts to distract the American public from the negative things happening inside the United States.

Whatever the motive – and there could be many – most of the U.S. media may be the last place to turn to learn about them. ●

MARCH 12: PARTYING WITH MSNBC.COM

FIRST there were the chads of Florida. And now there is the Chad of CNN, the early morning happy-talk weather-wonder, telling us about heat rising in the deserts awaiting devastation, with a forecast for Baghdad and Basra and the rest of the neighborhood. He warned New Yorkers like me that it would reach the 50s today, before snows hit tomorrow. This is how it's been – sharp ups-and-downs, expected U.N. votes demanded with great sanctimony and righteousness allowed to slip slide away.

This ying-yanging weather mirrors the volatility of the times. Just look at Tony Blair, already reeling from the defection of most of his country from policies that inspire websites like Poodleocity.com. He finds himself under attack from motor-mouth Donald Rumsfeld who dissed the idea of British troops on the front line. The British Parliament will be asking its PM some questions about that any minute now, as Rummy mounts a rhetorical retreat.

Bomb away

MEANWHILE, Bush has had to back down for a few days, even as his military shows off the new "mother of all bombs," the 2,500-pound MOAB that is being called operation "Desert Stun." This is the closest thing the Pentagon has to a non-nuclear nuclear bomb. It even leaves its own mushroom cloud for effect, and threatens mass destruction with the power to flatten everything in its path for one mile around its epicenter. Including people. The New York Post sings its praises this morning. It is being used as a weapon of intimidation before it sees action.

Meanwhile in Iraq, the BBC's John Simpson was asked about Iraqi soldiers expected to surrender to get out of the way of the onslaught of what's to come. Simpson who covered Gulf War I reminded his viewers that many Iraq soldiers were mowed down by U.S. troops as they tried to give up. He called it a "tragedy." He expressed the hope that it won't happen again. File this away for future reference.

As for the U.N., The New York Times reports: "The White House also said President Bush would force a vote by the end of the week on an American-backed resolution." Over on Fox, we had the assurance this morning that the U.S. had every right to do whatever it will in Iraq, and that the law was with us. Da Judge, who started as a guest on the News Channel, may soon be traded to Comedy Central, as he mocks international law and cites as the rationale for attack, the standard of self-defense. And never mind, he adds, a nation doesn't have to be attacked to defend itself. It can act before such an attack occurs. Never mind that there has been not even a threat of such an attack or any serious evidence linking Saddam to the attacks of 9/11.

Finally, but perhaps\ too late, Kofi Annan is speaking up in defense of the U.N. and its charter – which has all but been ignored. (The argu-ment is that the Gulf War resolution of 1991 is still in effect and permits U.S. unilateral action. Huh?). Annan is saying if the Security Council fails to come to an agreement, "and action is taken without the authority of the Security Council, the legitimacy and support for any such action would be seriously impaired."

As I pondered all the talk of the Council and the hostility being directed towards France for threatening a veto, (You know, French fries to be replaced by "freedom fries," even as the fries were always of Belgian origin, never French, but no matter) I flashed back to an earlier moment from the annals of that august body in light of all the denunciations of threatened vetoes that flout the majority's supposed desires. The year was 1988, and the Security Council was debating sanctions against South Africa. Ten members voted yea, a few abstained but two vetoed. At a time when the people of South Africa were being terrorized by the thugs upholding apartheid, The U.S. and Great Britain cast vetoes. The U.S. delegate said sanctions would hurt the people they were intended to help. Ah, what we forget in these United States of Amnesia. Have you seen this referenced anywhere on TV?

Under assault

FORGET facts. America is under ideological assault from within, from the Fog machine and the whole echo chamber that resonates with the same arguments around the clock, 24 hours a day, just shoveling it out, with know-it-all pretty-boy anchors and sarcastic mini-skirted blondes and military experts and selective polls. I am less upset about Fox, which has repackaged Murdo-chitis while hiding behind a claim of "real journalism." The problem is that absent a real alternative; the rest of the media essentially adoptsed its Fox's worldview, even if it does cool down some of rhetoric and arrogance.

At the center of it all are a group of smart media strategists led by Roger Ailes, loyal servant of Republican politics, and aided and abetted by the neo-con intellectuals led by William Kristol, editor of The Weekly Standard, Rupert's loss leader into influence and power in Washington. Some of the left websites spend time denouncing them, but most of these critics are not trying to come up with competitors or support alternatives. They see them as fools not fanatics who must be taken seriously. Example:

"Who are these idiots? From talk radio and right-wing chatter to national policy – anti-U.N., unilateral, finger in your eye foreign policy – aggressive military – and see what we have – the country weaker not stronger, poorer not richer, more despised, more fractured, GREAT WORK GUYS! We have found the Homebase, the nest of vipers of the Brilliant Fools who have made a new record – never have so few done so much damage to so many so quickly – Fox News Channel analyst William Kristol is the center of the ring of evil."

Evil is no faceless stranger

THINKING about evil, may I share this verse from the "Book of Counted Sorrows? I like it better than the rhetoric of denigration.

"Evil is no faceless stranger
Living in a distant neighborhood.
Evil has a wholesome, hometown face,
with merry eyes and an open smile.
Evil walks among us, wearing a mask
which looks like all our faces."

MARCH 13: MESSIAHS AND MORE MEDIA MISHIGAS

TONY BLAIR was defiant yesterday in Parliament. I watched some of his Question Time in Parliament on CSPAN last night. It seemed that his supporters were lined up in advance to pitch softballs that he could hit out of the proverbial park. His new proposal, with its cheeky "benchmarks" was rejected by Iraq, which called it a pretext for war, by the U.S., which said nothing, and by France, which called it a non-starter. So we are back to square one, except for one development.

It seems that the U.S. full court press has ground down resistance from more members of the Security Council who have been bribed and bullied for weeks. Some have apparently capitulated, but not enough to give the U.S. the nine out of the 15 votes it demands. My hunch is that several presidents in other countries have agreed to give the U.S. anything it wants as long as they don't have to take another phone call from President Bush. When newscasters say he is "working the phones," I can't help wondering what it would be like to be on the other side of one of those Saddam-is-evil rants. How much could you take?

The final daze

AS for the religious not so subtle subtext in all of this back and forth, Tarif Abboushi offers a view on Counterpunch.org that takes seriously all the religious mumbo jumbo that seems to be driving the jihad and its mirror image.

"For Christian fundamentalists, the notion of Iraq possessing weapons of mass destruction is not in and of itself an anathema; it's the timing that is bad. Armageddon can't happen without forces of evil, presumably bearing nuclear arms, to fight the forces of good. But scripture dictates that the Jewish temple must first be rebuilt, and since that hasn't happened, it cannot be Saddam Hussein, the incarnation-of-evil-du-jour, that bears those arms. What better argument to disarm him? After the temple is built, then we will find evil and arm it.

"For American empire-builders, the religious fanatics can proselytize till the messiah comes or returns; what matters today is less Deuteronomy than hegemony. American hegemony, as in control of the Middle East's oil and natural gas resources, and hence the world's economy. How better to get there than by turning Iraq, with proven oil reserves second only to Saudi Arabia's, into the overseas address of the XVIII Airborne Corps? Fort Braggdad has an irresistible ring to it."

Legitimate fears?

THERE may be another wrinkle in why Britain is so gung-ho for a new resolution – which others see as not needed or irrelevant. TomDispatch.com, noticed a revealing paragraph buried deep in the bowels of the Washington Post:

"The Washington Post today in the penultimate paragraph – oh, those final paragraphs of news stories in the imperial press – of a piece entitled "Bush Lobbies for Deal on Iraq," offered this:

"British officials also expressed fresh concern that failure to obtain a resolution authorizing war against Iraq would expose them to potential prosecution by a newly established International Criminal Court with jurisdiction over war crimes. Britain is a signatory to the treaty establishing the tribunal, but the United States is not. Blair was advised by his attorney general last October that military action to force 'regime change' in Baghdad would violate international law"

The death of TV news (again)

NOW let's move into the media landscape. I begin today with some comments from Av Westin, a man who was a mentor to me and a boss I frequently quarreled with at ABC News. He ran 20/20 until the late Roone Arledge became convinced he was gunning for his job. I wrote about what it was like to work for him in my book, "The More You Watch the Less You Know." When I knew him, he was a defender of network power. Today, he like many, has become a critic. The Pioneer Press picked up a talk he gave to students in Minneapolis. Av says:

"I think we're on the death spiral of TV news. Everywhere you look, the bottom line has trumped [quality journalism]. The profit expectations of conglomerate news are such that if you're running a local newsroom, the only way you're going to meet your objectives is by going down-market and cutting staff. You look around, and you see men and women today running newsrooms who got all their training in the past 10 years. They don't know any other environment. And as for great journalism, I seriously doubt either Mel Karamazin [president and COO of CBS' parent company, Viacom] or Sumner

Redstone [chairman, CEO, Viacom] have any idea who Ed Murrow was."

Av was also specific when asked about the performance of the White House press corps: "Since 9/11, the press corps has allowed the administration to wrap itself in the flag. The press, it seems to me, has been watching the public opinion polls almost as much as the administration, which explains why it has taken quite a while for it to resume the kind of normal adversarial relationship, much less the kind that was rampant during the Clinton years and the Nixon years."

Beat the press?

AV'S comments were mild compared to Matt Taibbi's analysis in New York Press. He writes about the performance of the press at the eighth press conference that Bush has held since taking office. (Clinton had 30 by the same time in his presidency.)

"After watching George W. Bush's press conference last Thursday night, I'm more convinced than ever: The entire White House press corps should be herded into a cargo plane, flown to an altitude of 30,000 feet, and pushed out, kicking and screaming, over the North Atlantic.

"Any remaining staff at the Washington bureaus should be rounded up for summary justice. The Russians used to use bakery trucks, big gray panel trucks marked "Bread" on the sides; victims would be rounded up in the middle of the night and taken for one last ride through the darkened streets.

"The war would almost be worth it just to see Wolf Blitzer pounding away at the inside of a Pepperidge Farm truck, tearfully confessing and vowing to 'take it all back.'

"The Bush press conference to me was like a mini-Alamo for American journalism, a final announcement that the press no longer performs anything akin to a real function. Particularly revolting was the spectacle of the cream of the national press corps submitting politely to the indignity of obviously pre-approved questions, with Bush not even bothering to conceal that the affair was scripted."

Perle is pissed

RICHARD PERLE says he will sue Seymour Hersh and The New Yorker for the story this week reporting that Perle has business interests that conflict with his policy role. Perle also, it has been revealed, is a director of Hollinger International Inc., an investor in The New York Sun, which uncritically backs Ariel Sharon, and baited anti-war marchers as traitors. As you would expect, the paper also supports Perle's polices. It broke the story of the lawsuit quoting Perle thusly:

"I intend to launch legal action in the United Kingdom. I'm talking to Queen's Counsel right now, Mr. Perle, who chairs the Pentagon's Defense Policy Board, a non-paying position, told The New York Sun last night. He said he is suing in Britain because it is easier to win such cases there, where the burden on plaintiffs is much less."

Last weekend Perle went over the top denouncing Sy Hersh as a terrorist during an interview on CNN, as we have reported. Hersh, up at Harvard to get a prize for his work, criticized the Bush Administration, according to the Harvard Crimson: "It's scary," he said. "I wish I could say something optimistic. I think this guy will do what he wants to do." He said of the attorney general: "(John) Ashcroft seems to be confusing his personal definition of God with the Constitution. He's the least knowledgeable and most dangerous attorney general we've had." As for his colleagues, he added: "I have never seen my peers as frightened as they are now."

On the brink

IF you watch American television, it feels like New Year's Eve with clocks counting down the minutes before the big ball drops in Times Square. Only this time, the big ball is likely to be a big bomb and the target is Baghdad, but the anticipation, even excitement is the same. That is especially so at the news networks that are planning to share footage from Baghdad and, who may push their top shows onto cable outlets to clear time for wall to wall coverage.

With threat levels escalated in the U.S., journalists are feeling them in the field. The propaganda war has already moved into high gear. The Bush Administration strategy for managing news and spinning perception is well in place with more than 500 reporters embedded in military units, with coverage restrictions to guide them. Their emphasis will be story telling, focusing on our soldiers. Human interest, not political interests, is their focus.

Andrew Tyndall studied network news in the week leading up to the President's Declaration of War. What did he find? "ABC's Peter Jennings, who anchored from the Gulf region on three days, told us that his network has almost 30 reporters, up close and personal with U.S. troops: "These young men know there is tremendous pressure on them to do well – and in a

hurry. America expects them to win, even easily," Jennings said. The big story there was sandstorm season, the oldest enemy in the desert, blinding, disorienting, even painful, according to CBS, Lee Cowam, enough to peel off paint, grinding its way into machinery and weapons. The winds carry a mixture of chemicals, microbes and nutrients across oceans at a height of 10,000ft, ABC's Ned Potter explained: "If you see a very colorful sunset, thank the dust from a distant desert," Tyndall said of the networks, coverage of the heat and dust.

There will be no dust in the Pentagon's new million-dollar state of the art high-tech media center, built to Hollywood specifications in Qatar so that Supreme Commander Tommy Franks can be all that he can be. Trustworthy former military officers are in place inside the networks to offer the kind of analysis the Pentagon would approve of.

Elizabeth Jensen of the Los Angeles Times says these TV generals are shaping news coverage: "When a tip comes in, some of the ex-military men will get on the phone – in private, out of the open-desk chaos of a standard newsroom – to chase it down, calling sources, oftentimes old buddies, whom even the most-plugged in correspondents can't reach. Gen. Barry McCaffrey likes his NBC job because it lets him maintain influence on policy, being able to speak to these issues."

Reporters have been warned to leave the Iraqi capital, guaranteeing there will be fewer eyes on the shock and awe to come. The BBC's veteran war reporter Katie Aidie says she has been told that journalists operating on their own, the so-called unilaterals, are being warned the invading army will target them.

And what about Arab news outlets with their own sources? They will be targeted, says media war expert, Harper's Magazine publisher John MacArthur. He told Editor and Publisher he thinks Al-Jazeera, whose office was "accidentally" bombed in Kabul, Afghanistan, may face similar treatment in Iraq. MacArthur predicts Al-Jazeera will be "knocked out in the first 48 hours, like what happened in Kabul." He told Barbara Bedway: "The Pentagon is expecting a kind of Panama-style war, over in three days. Nobody has time to see or ask any questions. I think if embedded reporters see anything important – or bloody – the Pentagon will interfere. Same result, different tactic: the truth gets distorted."

But that's not all. Network news managers have effectively accepted the administration's rationale for war. Its pundits and experts tend to function as cheerleaders with few dissenting voices given voice.

A study by FAIR, the media watchdog group, found that anti-war views were conspicuous by their absence: "Looking at two weeks of coverage (1/30/03 to 2/12/03), FAIR examined the 393 on-camera sources who appeared in nightly news stories about Iraq on ABC World News Tonight, CBS Evening News, NBC Nightly News and PBS's NewsHour with Jim Lehrer.

"The study began one week before and ended one week after Secretary of State Colin Powell's Feb. 5 presentation at the U.N., a time that saw particularly intense debate about the idea of a war against Iraq on the national and international level.

"More than two-thirds (267 out of 393) of the guests featured were from the United States. Of the U.S. guests, a striking 75 percent (199) were either current or former government or military officials. Only one of the official U.S. sources – Sen. Edward Kennedy (D.Mass.) – expressed skepticism or opposition to the war.

Even this was couched in vague terms: "Once we get in there, how are we going to get out, what's the loss for American troops going to be, how long we're going to be stationed there, what's the cost going to be," said Kennedy on NBC Nightly News on Feb. 5.

Similarly, when both U.S. and non-U.S. guests were included, 76 percent (297 of 393) were either current or retired officials. Such a predominance of official sources virtually assures that independent and grassroots perspectives will be underrepresented.

The reporting will be closely managed. Robert Fisk of The Independent points to "a new CNN system of script approval," the iniquitous instruction to reporters that they have to send all their copy to anonymous officials in Atlanta to ensure it is suitably sanitized – suggests that the Pentagon and the Department of State have nothing to worry about. Nor do the Israelis.

"CNN, of course, is not alone in this paranoid form of reporting. Other U.S. networks operate equally anti-journalistic systems. And it's not the fault of the reporters. CNN's teams may use clichés and don military costumes – you will see them do this in the next war – but they try to get something of the truth out. Next time, though, they're going to have even less chance."

That was Fisk before the countdown to combat was approved. Now he advises us to move a War of Words watch up to an elevated level. More recently, Fisk issues a language alert now moving to an elevated level. His clichés to counter:

"Inevitable revenge" – for the executions of

Saddam's Baath party officials which no one actually said was inevitable.

"Stubborn" or "suicidal' – to be used when Iraqi forces fight rather than retreat.

"Allegedly" – for all carnage caused by Western forces.

"At last, the damning evidence" –– used when reporters enter old torture chambers.

"Officials here are not giving us much access" – a clear sign that reporters in Baghdad are confined to their hotels.

"Life goes on" – for any pictures of Iraq's poor making tea.

"What went wrong?' – to accompany pictures illustrating the growing anarchy in Iraq as if it were not predicted." So says Fisk.

The War is with us. The reporting will fan its flames as surely as the fires of the oil wells. ●

WORDS FROM THE WISE

"[A] NEW and subtler instrument must weld thousands and thousands and even millions of human brings into one amalgamated mass of hate, will and hope. A new will must burn out the canker of dissent and temper the steel of bellicose enthusiasm. The name of this new hammer and anvil of social solidarity is propaganda. Talk must take the place of drill; print must supply the dance. War dances live in literature, and at the fringes of the modern earth; war propaganda breathes and fumes in the capitals and provinces of the world. – **HAROLD LASSWELL, Propaganda Techniques in the World War, 1927.**

"PERSONALLY, I was shocked while in the United States by how unquestioning the broadcast news media was during this war." – **GREG DYKE, BBC Director General, 2003.**

"HE'S a warmonger. He promoted it." – **TED TURNER on Rupert Murdoch.**

"THERE were horrors that were completely left out of this war. So was this journalism? Or was this coverage…As a journalist, I have been ostracized just from going on television and saying, 'Here's what the leaders of Hizbollah, a radical Moslem group, are telling me about what is needed to bring peace to Israel.' And, 'Here's what the Lebanese are saying.' Like it or lump it, don't shoot the messenger, but that's what they do." – **ASHLEIGH BANFIELD, MSNBC.**

"Watching war on TV from a distance, is pulse pounding entertainment That's damn good entertainment. We need to show people the consequences of war. People die in war." – **TED KOPPEL, ABC Nightline.**

"THERE is something deeply corrupt consuming this craft of mine. It is not a recent phenomenon; look back on the "coverage" of the First World War by journalists who were subsequently knighted for their services to the concealment of the truth of that great slaughter. What makes the difference today is the technology that produces an avalanche of repetitive information, which in the United States has been the source of arguably the most vociferous brainwashing in that country's history. A war that was hardly a war, that was so one-sided it ought to be dispatched with shame in the military annals, was reported like a Formula One race…" – **JOHN PILGER, columnist and TV producer, U.K.**

"AFTER September 11, the country wants more optimism and benefit of the doubt, it's about being positive instead of negative." – **ERIC SORENSON, MSNBC.**

"YOU couldn't hire actors to do as good a job as the press has 'done' from the Pentagon's point of view." – **Former Pentagon Media spokesperson KENNETH BACON, in The Wall Street Journal.**

CHAPTER THREE

COUNTDOWN TO WAR

WASHINGTON DEMANDS U.N. INSPECTORS LEAVE IRAQ

High Noon as Bush team insists it will find WMDs

BACK in pre-history, in the 1970s, a headline writer at New York's Daily News captured the spirit of the then-President's unwillingness to help New York through a financial crisis with the headline: "FORD TO CITY: DROP DEAD." Today we should be seeing another one in a similar vein: "BUSH TO U.N.: DROP DEAD."

It is ultimatum time on the Potomac, as the much planned for and feared "Moment of Truth" arrives on the day that diplomacy died. (Some truth would be welcome, especially in this moment of mounting propaganda.) Dick Cheney rattled his spurs on Meet the Press Sunday, as he commented on charges that our president is a cowboy. Sayeth the veep: "I think that is not necessarily a bad idea." So saddle up, gang, as America gallops to war, and media camp followers tag along.

Inspectors: Get out!

THIS morning the U.S. ordered U.N. inspectors out of Iraq. The pretense of consultation and even respect for any nations questioning U.S. policy has ended. The U.N. meets today to respond to this resolution, which boils down to might defines right. What can they do? It reminds me of Stalin's dismissal of an appeal from the Pope when he asked how many divisions the Vatican had. Chairman Mao's ghost must be looking on approvingly — he always said political power grows out of the barrel of a gun.

After a weekend of escalating rhetoric, the public opinion polls, which always reflect what Americans see and hear on the boob tube, show 64 percent in favor of war and growing hostility towards France and any other chicken shit nation that dares question the Messiah from Midland. Bush's two main speechwriters, Karen Hughes and Michael Gerson, accompanied him on Air Force One and were reported to be drafting a speech to the nation that could come as soon as tonight.

Ultimatum

AT the Socialist Scholars conference yesterday, where I first heard about the mandate from the Azores, from the U.S. and the leaders of three former colonial powers, a French delegate described it as a dual ultimatum. Yesterday, none of the U.S. media outlets I watched described it that way. (Today the New York Post does. When CNN rebroadcast the press conference in the afternoon, they called it a "replay" as if was just a game which many columnists believe it was.)

Washington talks about "disarmament," a code word for its real intentions. The closest France's President Chirac can get to talking with the U.S. is through 60 Minutes. And what's worse, the U.S. government seems to welcome its isolation, wrapping it in the rhetoric of righteousness and unflinching resolve. The Wall Street Journal carries documents that show Washington is planning to bypass the U.N. on reconstruction plans, giving the work to U.S. corporations. There's gold in them thar deserts.

Protests downplayed

I STOPPED by one of the vigils last night, one more protest in a week that saw more demonstrations around the world, with more than 700,000 marching in Spain alone. You would think that the emergence of this global movement would be big news. And yes, there was TV coverage in the form of collages of images. But to the top-down worldview of The New York Times, they are a treated as a nuisance. The lead story on Sunday devoted one line in the 13th paragraph on the jump page, page 14, to the demonstrations: "Around the world, including in Washington, protesters assembled to demonstrate against the impending war." A story about the demos appeared on page 15 under a large photo of Iraqis marching with a photo of Saddam Hussein. The headline refers to the marchers as "throngs."

The Times, predictably, was more worried about the warnings that Al Qaeda is using the war on Iraq to step up its recruiting. One of the more bizarre media moments occurred during a Los Angeles Times- sponsored debate aired live on CSPAN Saturday night. Just as columnist Robert Scheer was speaking, CSPAN reported they were having technical difficulties. The screen went black, and within seconds we were being treated to a prerecorded urgent warfare exercise from Fort Polk hosted by a soldier. A rebroadcast of the ANSWER anti-war rally promised for midnight was never shown, at least not in the East. Huh ???????

The threat to journalists

WHAT happens now? U.S. dependents and personnel are being withdrawn throughout the region, including Israel. There's a heightened police presence in the streets of our cities. National Guardsmen carry M16s in the subways. And there are new difficulties for members of the press who are being counseled to get out of Baghdad.

A Gulf region website is reporting that independent reporting may be impossible. "Should war in the Gulf commence, the Pentagon proposes to take radical new steps in media relations – 'unauthorized' journalists will be shot at. Speaking on The Sunday Show on Ireland's RTE1 last Sunday, veteran BBC war reporter Kate Adie said a senior Pentagon official had warned her that uplinks, i.e. TV broadcasts or satellite phones, that are detected by U.S. aircraft are likely to be fired on.

Bush Sr.'s Iraq war featured tight control of the media, but the current administration intends to go further. According to BBC superstar Adie (who, overseas readers should be aware, is effectively a saint in the U.K.), the Pentagon is vetting journalists who propose to cover the war, and is taking control of their equipment. This presumably will ease the logistics of managing the hacks quite considerably, because if the U.S. has control of all the gear, then any gear it doesn't know about that starts broadcasting is presumably a target.

Adie's remarks were delivered as part of a discussion of war reporting and media freedom, along with author Phillip Knightley, New York Times war correspondent Chris Hedges and former Irish Times editor Connor Brady. The whole discussion is well worth listening to, and we particularly liked Hedges' put-down of CNN: "CNN survives from war to war; as soon as the war starts, they become part of the problem."

Protesting the media

NOW back to the media. Clearly, a bad situation is likely to get worse as an "embedded press corps" brings us Pentagon-sanitized news of the conflict to come. To date, the anti-war movement has tried with occasional success to get into the press, but not to confront it, not to challenge its bias towards war as the only real option. Can anything be done about this?

A group of activists in Los Angeles is launching a drive to call the media bosses. I was sent an email outline of the effort. They charge: "Support for a war and for police state actions by tens of millions of Americans can be directly traced to the misinformation, lack of information and wildly unbalanced commentary they get from General Electric (NBC), News Corp (Fox), Disney (ABC), AOL-Time Warner(CNN) and Viacom (CBS).

"If democracy is to have any true meaning, it must be based on a well-informed public. These companies must be compelled to provide real journalism and commentary balance. Their roles as propaganda arms of the Administration must end. We encourage you to join the mass phone-in to the TV News bosses. Ask for investigative reporting, not drum-beating; for balanced coverage and commentary, not cover-ups of government misinformation and of potential civilian deaths and injuries. Call every time you see something on the tube you know is propaganda and not news." •

MARCH 18: LIBERATION BY DEVASTATION

IT was a speech that the Liberation Theologian-in-chief has been practicing for nearly two years – and perhaps longer. George Bush delivered his declaration of war with eyes unblinking, locked like radar on the teleprompter, a mono-track mind conjuring up images of the lock box, a long forgotten Al Gore-ism. That is it, U.N.! Au revoir, Paree! Saddam, you are out of here and take your boys with you. Evil dictators, be warned, the first Air Cav, with CNN in tow, is coming to get ya! In the aftermath of THE SPEECH we all knew was coming, reaction was so muted that the networks for the most part didn't bother to go after it. The only criticism I saw as I scanned the dials came from Senator Joe Lieberman, a hawk who lamented the failure of diplomacy. I had to wait for the morning to hear Tom Daschle say, "I am saddened, saddened that this President failed so miserably at diplomacy that we're now forced to war." Now, I don't know about the forced part, but the failure is there for all to see. (Daschle himself was no profile in courage; he said he would vote for war all over again if he had to.)

The problem is that for many of the ideologues who think for this President – who pushed for this war before they were in power and continued to press now that they are in – this was not a failure, but a success. Their cabal has prevailed, steering the United States on to what amounts to a Superpower dominates all, preemptive power rules, imperial relationship to the world. In New York, a town where reality is spelled realty, I can believe that there are brokers ready to start converting the U.N. Secretariat Building into East River condos.

Dissecting the speech

ON MSNBC ("NBC ON CABLE") this morning, after a jam forced the network to rerack the tape, one analyst spoke of the President's speech as grounded in fact. Not one network subjected the speech's claims and assertions to any analysis, much less criticism or refutation.

Assertion No. 1: "The only way to reduce harm and duration of war is apply full force." The only way? Surely someone might point out that the majority of the Security Council and the General Assembly, if polled, would disagree. Were there no journalists who could assess this claim and at least point to the specific alternatives that have been proposed?

Assertion No. 2: "In a free Iraq, there will be no more wars of aggression against your neighbors." Couldn't have anyone pointed out that the U.S. government supported and encouraged Sad-

dam's war on Iran, and told him that they would not object to his "solving" his longstanding dispute with Kuwait. (The films by Frontline airing on PBS carried the scene in which the foremer U.S. Ambassador to Iraq signaled no objection to Saddam. It also showed that the U.S. government aided his rise to power.)

Assertion No. 3: "War criminals will be punished." No reference to the U.S. refusal to support the International Criminal Court.

Assertion No. 4: "The United States of America has the sovereign authority to use force."

Says who? Couldn't the networks have asked some law professors about this and noted that Kofi Annan clearly challenged this notion?

Generals in residence

ON and on, it went, assertions that went unexamined, while anchors endlessly recapped and went to their reporters in the field to see how the soldiers felt or what the military analysts in the field thought. Like NBC's General in residence Barry McCaffrey, the ex-Drug Czar who Seymour Hersh exposed as a war criminal in a documentation of his unit's massacre of Iraqis during Gulf War I. Speaking of General M, Elizabeth Jenson reports in the Los Angeles Times that these military men are helping to shape the arc of coverage: "When a tip comes in, some of the ex-military men will get on the phone – in private, out of the open-desk chaos of a standard newsroom – to chase it down, calling sources, oftentimes old buddies, whom even the most-plugged in correspondents can't reach. Gen. Barry McCaffrey likes his NBC job because it lets him maintain influence on policy, being able to speak to these issues," Jensen wrote.

PBS to the Rescue

SURELY there were journalists who could have been found to question all of these assertions and assumptions? Bill Moyers found one in Walter IsaacsFon, the ex CNN chief who in his middle-of-the-road fashion said he believed another outcome was possible. That was on PBS after HOURS of reprises of Frontline documentaries (more on them in a moment) and some fine reporting by Roberta Baskin. PBS was clearly better in its reporting than the nets. Earlier the NewsHour had an excellent report by Elizabeth Farnsworth from northern Iraq who interviewed human rights lawyers detailing abuses by Turkey. Ankara appears likely to shift positions to let the U.S. military roll through its borders while it contains Kurdish demands for self-determination.

Krugman in print, not on the air

THIS morning, Paul Krugman was his usual incisive self on the op-ed page of The Times, but it was not his voice we heard on Charlie Rose but that of another Times reporter who seemed agnostic on the war and its likely aftermath. Krugman did not get the same platform, but his words bear repeating: "What frightens me is the aftermath and I'm not just talking about the problems of postwar occupation. I'm worried about what will happen beyond Iraq in the world at large, and here at home.

"The members of the Bush team don't seem bothered by the enormous ill- will they have generated in the rest of the world. They seem to believe that other countries will change their minds once they see cheering Iraqis welcome our troops, or that our bombs will shock and awe the whole world (not just the Iraqis) or that what the world thinks doesn't matter. They're wrong on all counts."

The PR firm behind the war

WELCOMING the onslaught is former leftist-turned-conservative Richard Perle and Paul Wolfowitz protégé, the Iraqi dissident Keyan Makiya, who was interviewed by Bill Moyers. Makiya was pictured as an idealist with suggestions that hopes for democracy are likely to be dashed. (He cited a report in the Los Angeles Times last week of a State Department document that made clear that democracy is not a likely outcome.) A PR firm, Benador Associates, which places pro-administration speakers on TV shows, represents Makiya. They say they are "proud to present a highly qualified cadre of inspiring, knowledgeable speakers who are available to address your group or broadcast audience. Each of our experts is nationally and internationally recognized on issues of the Middle East and national security, among others."

Their list of clients reads like an A to Z of the right. Here are a few of their big guns:
James Woolsey
Richard Perle
A..M. Rosenthal
Charles Krauthammer
Michael A.. Ledeen
Dennis Prager
Frank Gaffney Jr.
Amir Taheri
Keyan Makiya
Richard Pipes
So the next time you see a member of this

"crew of the cantankerous" on the air, as you do almost nightly, think of the PR pluggers at Benador "working the phones" to spin media coverage. Makiya, incidentally, was at the American Enterprise Institute where President Bush made his most recent policy speech reinforcing his commitment to regime change over disarmament.

Baiting Chomsky

ON Moyers' NOW program, Makiya typically dismissed critics like Noam Chomsky and Edward Said (who, of course, were not interviewed anywhere on the air last night). Writing in The Guardian last May, Nik Cohen explained that: "He dates the schism between supporters of universal human rights and those on the Left and Right who regard any Western intervention as imperialism to the moment when the opponents of Saddam were denounced. Israel was built on the destruction of 400 Palestinian villages, Makiya says; Saddam destroyed at least 3,000 Kurdish villages. Makiya, like every other Iraqi democrat you meet in London, has lost patience with those who will oppose the former but not the latter and is desperate for America to support a democratic revolution."

Richard Perle, another Benador bookee, looked tired and worn on CNBC last night. Earlier on Frontline, he was well made up with the kind of Hollywood lighting that many marvel over. That was on video. Live, his eyes have blackened, his hair has thinned and his pomposity seemed more strained. Watching all the Frontline shows last night certainly offered the context, history and background missing on the news shows and networks.

It was a march down memory lane to cast light on the origins of the crisis, but was I wrong to feel that it was drenched with middle of the road experts, mostly policy wonks, and in effect rationalized the administration's course. It was strong in showing how Wolfowitz's doctrine of pre-emptive bullying went from a minority view to become policy, but otherwise, I came way feeling that it was showing the logic for war as the consequence of U.N. failures and Iraqi belligerence. It took some shots at the right but treated its arguments with reverence. Moyers was certainly better and Charlie Rose, was, well, very Charlie Rose-ish. Maybe Kissinger was busy last night.

Missing in the media

FAIR reports: "Despite daily reports about the showdown with Iraq, Americans hear very little from mainstream media about the most basic fact of war: People will be killed and civilian infrastructure will be destroyed, with devastating consequences for public health long after the fighting stops. Since the beginning of the year, according to a search of the Nexis database (1/1/03-3/12/03), none of the three major television networks' nightly national newscasts – ABC World News Tonight, CBS Evening News or NBC Nightly News – has examined in detail what long-term impact war will have on humanitarian conditions in Iraq. They've also downplayed the immediate civilian deaths that will be caused by a U.S. attack."

Pharmaceutical calmatives

DEBORAH STERLING, a journalist writes: "What

can we do here? 1) Rumsfeld has already told Congress that the U.S. will use 'pharmaceutical calmatives,' (i.e. gas) on Iraqi civilians (www.moscowtimes.ru/stories/2003/02/21/120.html), yet I am not aware of any mainstream media picking up on this story. This gas will be deployed using both an unmanned 'loitering vehicle' – which hovers in the air and sprays – and by mortar shell loaded with chemicals. But the use of any chemical weapon against people in wartime – no matter how supposedly non-lethal it might be – is expressly forbidden by a number of international treaties, all signed by the United States.

"Not only that, the very production of such combat weapons is prohibited – which is supposedly why Bush/Rumsfeld quietly shifted funding authority for 'calmative' research from Pentagon coffers to Ashcroft's Justice Department – to give 'domestic' cover to the military program. At the same time that we risk killing countless Iraqi civilians with OUR chemical weapons, the White House keeps saying, and our mainstream press is reinforcing, the notion that Saddam will gas his own people and blame it on us. We are being set up MASSIVELY, I think, to hear: 'SEE? Just like we said. Will that madman stop at NOTHING?' Will these embedded journalists be able to report what really happens – which side is lobbing artillery shells to gas civilians?"

Sterling continues: "I am, incidentally, a professional journalist, and it's very hard to be sidelined and sitting on my hands. I am very frightened that with the notable exception of Newsweek (whose investigative digging appeared in sidebars), the only place I can go for the truth is the internet. It doesn't help much to know that there'll be some interesting books written about the takeover role of the internet – not when it (make that We, The People) rushed in to fill the vacuum left by a mainstream Fourth Estate with a lamentable yellow streak down its back."

CSPAN interrupts

BRENT BUICE writes: "Hi, Danny, my wife and I were watching the debate on CSPAN Saturday night, and we were very disturbed to see Robert Scheer's comments cut off by a frankly 'fake' looking technical difficulty.

"It was a snow effect, the audio gradually dimming – and when the pleasantly throated announcer said that C-SPAN was experiencing 'technical difficulties,' we were immediately switched to a 'press conference' with a young crewcut explaining the chills and thrills of urban combat in the 21st century. His presentation had plenty of splash and the very best multi-media gimmicks a pentagon budget can buy, but it looked like there were 3 folks in the audience (besides the C-SPAN crew).

"We watched this surreal switcharoo for 10 minutes and never found out if Mr. Scheer's comments were re-broadcast or just lost in a digital blizzard. Did anyone else notice this, and are we the only ones who found it suspicious? . . . This administration and its media lapdogs make me fear that my suspicions are not entirely unfounded? That CSPAN debate was repeated last night. I didn't see if it aired in full this time." Overall CSPAN deserves to be commended for the diversity of its coverage which included anti-war protest and foreign news coverage.

It turns out that Nature intervened on this one – I later heard that there had been a storm that knocked the program off the air. ●

EMBED WITH THE MILITARY

By DAVID MILLER (FREE PRESS, UK)

EMBEDDED journalists are the greatest PR coup of this war. Dreamt up by the Pentagon and Donald Rumsfeld the 'embeds', as they are now routinely described, are almost completely controlled by the military. Embeds agree to give up most of their autonomy in exchange for access to the fighting on military terms.

They also gain the advantage the use of facilities such as transport and accommodation. Reporters who are not embedded are pointedly and denied such facilities. Most importantly, embeds are afforded protection from physical harm by the military. So far in this war, the main danger for journalists has come from western military. So the protection on offer is more of a threat than a reassurance for independent reporters.

Each embedded reporter has to sign a contract with the military and is governed by a 50-point plan issued by the Pentagon detailing what they can and cannot report. The list of what they can report is significantly shorter than the list of what they cannot.

According to reports, there are 903 embedded reporters including 136 with UK forces. There are none embedded with the small contingents of other nations such as the Australian military.

Only 20 percent of reporters embedded with the US are from outside the US and 128 of the embed with UK forces are from the UK.

Even countries with military involvement such as Australia have very little access to the embedding system with only two reporters embedded with US forces.

French journalists in particular have complained about being excluded.

The Anglo American dominance of the reporters is no accident, but a key part of the strategy.

The PR genius of the embed system is that it does allow unprecedented access to the fighting and, also, unprecedented identification by the reporters with the military.

British minister of Defence Geoff Hoon has claimed: "I think the coverage is more graphic, more real, than any other coverage we have ever seen of a conflict in our history. For the first time it is possible with technology for journalists to report in real time on events in the battlefield."

It is certainly true to say that it is new to see footage of war so up-close, but, it is a key part of the propaganda war to claim that this makes it "real."

In fact, the aim of the embedding system is to control what is reported by encouraging journalists to identify with their units. To eat and drink together, to risk danger and to share the same values.

Ted Koppel of US network ABC, told The Washington Post that his feelings towards the soldiers were "very, very warm".

This identification with the soldiers works to ensure self censorship is generally effective.

Phillip Rochot, a respected reporter for France 2, currently working independently in Iraq, said, "Embedded journalists do a fair amount of voluntary self-censorship, controlling what they say. In any case their views are closely aligned with the Anglo-American position. They are soldiers of information, marching with the troops and the political direction of their country. They won't say anything wrong, they feel duty-bound to defend the anglo-american cause in this war."

Christina Lamb of the London Times agrees that embedded journalists are: "Giving a more positive side, because they're with the troops and they're not out in the streets or out in the countryside seeing what's actually happening there."

Hoon has himself acknowledged the effect of this reporting in appearing to reduce opposition to the war in the first days: "The imagery they broadcast is at least partially responsible for the public's change of mood."

But toward the end of the first week of the war, U.S. and U.K. officials started to mutter about too much access and claimed that it was the pressure of 24-hour coverage that was circulating misinformation. Both U.S. and U.K. military sources blamed embedded reporters and the pressure of 24-hour news cycles for circulating misinformation. This is a straightforward propaganda manoeuvre designed to distract attention from the fact that the false stories have all been authorised by military command structures and also to warn journalists not to get out of line. The proof that this is propaganda is that they are not proposing to change the embed system which has served them very well.

Some embedded reporters fell over themselves to explain that they only reported what the military allow them to.

Late at night with very few people watching, Richard Gaisford, an embedded BBC reporter, said, "If we ran everything that we heard in the camp, then certainly there would be a lot of misinformation going around. We have to check each story we have with them. And if they're not sure at the immediate level above us – that's the Captain who's our media liaison officer – he will check with the Colonel who is obviously above him and then they will check with Brigade headquarters as well."

This open acknowledgement of the system of control is rare and was provoked by official criticism.

It illustrates the tight censorship imposed by the military, but not acknowledged in U.S. or U.K. reporting. News bulletins in the U.K. are full of warnings about Iraqi 'monitoring' and 'restrictions' on movement in reports from Baghdad. The closest that they get to this on the U.K./U.S. side is to note that journalists cannot report on where they are and other security details. In fact the embed controls are, if anything, stricter than the system imposed by the Iraqi regime.

Gaisford's comment is also interesting for the acknowledgement it makes that reporters are actually fully integrated into military commands structures.

This complements the identification revealed by phrases such as "we" and 'our" in reports of military action. Reference to the "level above" as the press officer does, indicate a fundamental subordination to military propaganda needs. But this is hardly surprising since the contract that reporters sign explicitly requires reporters to 'follow the direction and orders of the Government" and prohibits them from suing for injury or death even where this "is caused or contributed to" by the military.

Unprecedented access is the carrot, but the stick is always on hand. Two embedded journalists who have allegedly strayed over the line have been expelled and during the second weekend of the war "many embedded reporters found their satellite phones blocked for unexplained reasons".

In addition, some embeds are, according to Christian Lowe of US military magazine Army Times, being "hounded by military public affairs officers who follow their every move and look over their shoulders as they interview aviators, sailors, and maintainers for their stories."

Each military division in the gulf has 40 to 60 embedded journalists, and between five and six public affairs officers "behind the scenes".

They report up to the Coalition Press Information Center (CPIC) in Kuwait and the $1 million press centre at CentCom in Doha. From there the message is co-ordinated by the Office of Global Communications in the White-house in consort with Alastair Campbell, Tony Blair's top spin doctor in Downing Street.

The fanciful notion that the misinformation of the first weeks of the campaign were been due to journalists having conversations with "a squaddie who's shining his boots", as a British MoD official spun it, is itself a key part of the propaganda war.

All of the myriad misinformation coming out of Iraq in the first two weeks has been fed out by the U.S./U.K. global media operation. As one reporter in Doha noted, "At General Tommy Franks's headquarters, it is easy to work out whether the day's news is good or bad. When there are positive developments, press officers prowl the corridors of the press centre dispensing upbeat reports from pre-prepared scripts, declaring Iraqi towns have been liberated and that humanitarian aid is about to be delivered.

"Yet if American and British troops have suffered any sort of battlefield reverse, the spin doctors retreat into their officers at press centre and await instructions from London and Washington."

If the embeds have been an opportunity, the Pentagon and British military have seen independent journalists as a threat. There have been a stream of reports of hostility, threats and violence against independent reporters. UNESCO, The International Federation of Journalists, Reporters Sans Frontieres and the British National Union of Journalists have all condemned these threats.

Some have been subtle and others less so. On the ground and away from the cameras the threats are pointed and can include violence, as several journalists have already found out.

The subtle threats include those made by British Ministers such as Defence Secretary Geoff Hoon, "One of the reasons for having journalists [embedded] is to prevent precisely the kind of tragedy that occurred to an ITN crew very recently when a well known, hard working, courageous journalist was killed, essentially because he was not part of a military organisation. Because he was trying to get a story. And in those circumstances we can't look after all those journalists on this kind of fast moving battlefield. So having journalists have the protection, in fact, of our armed forces is both good for journalism, [and] it's also very good for people watching."

Here, Hoon takes on all the charm and authority of a Mafia boss explaining the benefits of a protection racket. The message is clear: stay embedded and report what you are told or face the consequences. ●

David Miller is a member of the Stirling Media Research Institute, Scotland. Contact him at David.miller@stir.ac.uk.

CHAPTER FOUR

MOBILIZING OPINION

RIGHT WING LIBERATION THEOLOGY DRIVES SPEECH

Liberation by devastation is Bush's ultimatum to Iraq

BEGIN writing with nearly twelve hours left on President's Bush's arbitrary deadline to war. A higher force may be speaking even if no one is listening. The desert storms in Kuwait are gumming up the helicopters and cutting visibility to near zero. As Saddam expresses hopes that Baghdad will resist the Americans as Stalingrad did the Nazis, one must be reminded that it was the weather, oft named "General Winter," which slowed Hitler's blitzkrieg. Today, sandstorms represent the first threat facing the coalition of the willing. For a cautionary note, read today's Wall Street Journal on the obstacles that colonial armies faced in subjugating Arab nations. In physical form, they signal the fog of war is swirling. In electronic form, you can see that every hour on TV.

Journalism of death

IN the "official media," led by the New York Post, Saddam poses in uniform under a headline that screams "DEAD MAN." Under the photo, the wags of war add this never-subtle thought: "Butcher tells US come and get me." It works as agit prop, not journalism and reminds me of a headline in Boston back on the day U.S. bombers brought a Christmas present to the citizens of Hanoi. That one had another point of view: "ENEMY BOMBS HANOI." (I thought of that after visiting shows by Vietnamese artists in New York, a completely normal affair that would have been unthinkable back then, when their country was demonized.)

The fatal mistake

WAR is the news these days. Our TV screens are filled with images from the front and bluster from Ari Fleischer in the White House. He said yesterday that Saddam Hussein made his "final mistake" by rejecting the Bush ultimatum ordering him to leave Iraq. Meanwhile, The New York Times's Judith Miller reports: "The plan is to rapidly find, secure and ultimately destroy the caches of chemical, biological and other unconventional weapons."

I have heard many suspicions raised about the possibility that U.S. troops might plant such weapons and then dramatically "discover them" in the manner of so many drug busts in America. Let's hope that the military has outsiders with them to verify what they claim to find.

One of the inspectors who was charged with finding such weapons is now speaking out. Aftenposten in Norway reports a story I have yet to see on American TV:

"A U.S.-based Norwegian weapons inspector accuses the USA and Secretary of State Colin Powell with providing the United Nations Security Council with incorrect and misleading information about Iraq's possession of weapons of mass destruction (WMD), newspaper Dagbladet reports.

"Joern Siljeholm, Ph.D. in environmental chemistry, risk analysis and toxicology, said that the USA's basis for going to war is thin indeed, and called it a slap in the face to the United Nations weapons inspectors.

"Siljeholm told Dagbladet that Colin Powell's report to the Security Council on how Iraq camouflaged their WMD program was full of holes. Much of what he said was wrong. It did not match up at all with our information. The entire speech was misleading, Siljeholm said.

"We received much incomplete and poor intelligence information from the Americans, and our cooperation developed accordingly. Much of what has been claimed about WMDs has proven to be sheer nonsense. From what I have seen they are going to war on very little, Siljeholm told Dagbladet. I strongly doubt that the American will find anything at all. In any case I doubt that they will find WMDs that constitute a military threat, Siljeholm said."

Peace programming: the wrong demo

REPORTING on alternatives to war is verboten. Case in point: Yesterday I was told about Jon Alpert's new project filming conversations between Iraqi high school students and their American counterparts in Iraq. He had total access, no minders and no censorship. I am told the final film is moving and timely. Reportedly he funded it himself. A top indy TV company tried to place it, sending it from network to network, channel to channel.

There were, as of yesterday, NO, repeat NO, BUYERS. Jon has won more Emmy Awards than anyone I know, except perhaps Bill Moyers. He is a gutsy reporter who alone got into Baghdad in the aftermath of Gulf War I. At the time, he was working for NBC. His own network did not air his report and canned him for an unauthorized act of enterprise journalism.

Now it is happening again. I am told from someone in the know that one three-initialed news network "passed" because the subjects of the film were "not in our demo." They said they would prefer to save the money for their war coverage. (The Nets say today they expect to lose $200 million in revenue to bring us their versions of the war. Watch for stepped up post-war lobbying so they can win new concessions from the FCC that will allow them to recoup.)

Peter Arnett is back

THE networks have decided to share their footage from Baghdad. Peter Arnett, no stranger to wars – he seems to live for their oxygen – is staying put. And NBC has him this time. As we must recall, he was fired from CNN for reporting on a story revealing that the U.S. used biological warfare in Vietnam. The network canned several producers who sued, charging censorship and insisted the controversial Operation Tailwind report was true.

CNN later quietly settled with them. They were paid off with silence bought in the process. Arnett originally was brought back from forced retirement and into action by Camera Planet, a gutsy independent company aligned with Broadcast News Networks. He did reports for National Geographic and MSNBC. Now NBC seems to have bought his services. He couldn't be happier. He is back on the air. So much for independent journalists competing with the big guys in an age of media concentration.

The newspapers are not much better

THE newspapers are not much better, argues TomDispatch.com: "Except for the WSJ, the papers all quoted some version of Bush's 'Tomorrow is a moment of truth for the world' line somewhere in the lead paragraphs of their lead stories on the "summit meeting" in the Azores. Only the Times described the three leaders' joint statements (the Portuguese Prime Minister being clearly a no-account tag-along) quite appropriately as an 'ultimatum to the United Nations,' preceding tonight's final, final ultimatum to Saddam. (Bush, in the joint news conference, resorted to his normal 'musts,' which is invariably the way he, in his imperial guise, addresses the world – 'and now they [the nations of the Security Council] must demonstrate that commitment to peace and security in the only effective way'), The Financial Times offered the strongest description of how he gave the 'Tomorrow the world' quote – 'said a belligerent Mr. Bush' – though the NY Times in a variant line, described 'his voice rising and his jaw clenched as he punched the air with his fist.'"

"In its lead editorial, 'Moment of Truth,' the St. Louis Post Dispatch called the less than two hour meeting, 'one of the more bizarre summits in history' and had this pungent description of its nature: 'Mr. Bush left a capital where tens of thousands of demonstrators marched against the war on Saturday. Mr. Blair traveled from London where thousands more protested an unpopular war. And Spain's Jose Maria Aznar left a nation where an estimated 800,000 people demonstrated in Madrid and Barcelona. No wonder the leaders decided to get together on an island.'"

What we will see (and see not)

ROBERT FISK of the Independent is making some guesses of how the coverage of the war will go: "American and British forces use thousands of depleted uranium (DU) shells – widely regarded by 1991 veterans as the cause of Gulf War syndrome as well as thousands of child cancers in present day Iraq – to batter their way across the Kuwaiti-Iraqi frontier. Within hours, they will enter the city of Basra, to be greeted by its Shia Muslim inhabitants as liberators. US and British troops will be given roses and pelted with rice – a traditional Arab greeting – as they drive 'victoriously' through the streets. The first news pictures of the war will warm the hearts of Messrs. Bush and Blair. There will be virtually no mention by reporters of the use of DU munitions.

"But in Baghdad, reporters will be covering the bombing raids that are killing civilians by the score and then by the hundreds. These journalists, as usual, will be accused of giving 'comfort to the enemy while British troops are fighting for their lives'. By now, in Basra and other 'liberated' cities south of the capital, Iraqis are taking their fearful revenge on Saddam Hussein's Baath party officials. Men are hanged from lampposts. Much television footage of these scenes will have to be cut to sanitize the extent of the violence.

"Far better for the US and British governments will be the macabre discovery of torture chambers and 'rape-rooms' and prisoners with personal accounts of the most terrible suffering at the hands of Saddam's secret police. This will 'prove, how right' we are to liberate these poor people. Then the US will have to find the 'weapons of mass destruction' that supposedly provoked this bloody war. In the journalistic hunt for these weapons, any old rocket will do for the moment."

Letter to the AP

I WAS sent a letter that Chris Krom, director of the Institute for Southern Studies, sent to The Associated Press. I don't know if the world's top wire service responded although I will say, partially in their defense, that newspapers often come up with their own headlines for wire stories. They are often in conflict with the stories because editors don't read them carefully enough.

"Dear Associated Press, Today, the AP filed a story with the following headline: 'Poll: Bush Has Solid Support for War.' Many readers, of course, will read only that headline, taking with it the message that the U.S. public overwhelmingly supports the Bush Administration's drive to war in Iraq. However, after wading through reporter Will Lester's spin to actually read the poll results, one finds the exact opposite to be true.

"Buried in paragraph six, we find the relevant numbers: The poll found that about half of adults, 47 percent, say they support military action to remove Iraqi President Saddam Hussein from power and disarm Iraq, even without the support of the United Nations Security Council. Almost four in 10, 37 percent, said the United States should do that only with full support of the Security Council; 13 percent said the United States should not take military action even if the Security Council agrees.

"President Bush has resolutely stated he will prosecute a war against Iraq without the 'full support of the [UN] Security Council' – and appears poised to do so. This means that fully 50 percent (37 percent + 13 percent) of those polled OPPOSE the Bush Administration policy on Iraq, as compared to 47 percent in favor.

"Why is The Associated Press afraid to honestly report the poll's findings? What can justify such an astonishingly misleading headline, followed by reporting from Mr. Lester with a similarly suspect message – when the actual facts presented in the article point to precisely the opposite conclusion? I await an explanation, and hopefully, a very public correction." ●

WAR DANCES AND MEDIA COMPLAINTS

GORE VIDAL, the American essayist and novelist who lives in Rome was in the USA recently where he was overdosing on the media coverage of the coming war. It ignited a passionate denunciation: "The media [have] never been more disgusting, every lie out of Washington – they're out there doing war dances."

War dances or not, there clearly is a pattern of coverage that is beginning to attract more dissection and complaint. Andrew Tyndall, who analyzes every U.S. TV newscast, has been keeping track of the tilt in the coverage. USA TODAY found his research newsworthy, reporting:

"Of 414 stories on the Iraqi question that aired on NBC, ABC and CBS from Sept. 14 to Feb. 7, [Andrew] Tyndall says that the vast majority originated from the White House, Pentagon and State Department. Only 34 stories originated from elsewhere in the country, he says.

"Similarly, a check of major newspapers around the country from September to February found only 268 stories devoted to peace initiatives or to opposition to the war, a small fraction of the total number. 'Most editors and reporters think the diplomatic story – the great power narrative – is more real,' NYU's [Jay] Rosen says. 'And people who move into the White House know how to dominate the news agenda.'"

But could they dominate the agenda without the willing cooperation and the promotion of what most media pundits see as the "inevitable." Village Voice media critic Cynthia Cotts, who follows coverage closely, noted, "Last week, journalists were still using phrases like 'a possible war,' 'in the event of war,' 'if war breaks out' and 'assuming there is a war.' Events were unfolding so quickly behind the scenes that results were impossible to predict. But by press time, the subtext that was previously embedded in every newspaper, Internet, and TV war story had become the main thesis: The U.S. is going to attack Iraq. Case closed."

The case seems to be closing against the quality of journalism we are seeing and reading as well. More than two dozen journalism school deans and professors, independent editors, journalists, producers and reporters have signed a letter to the major media indicting the tendency of many media organizations to become a megaphone for the Bush Administration. Their letter cites six specific complaints over the nature of the coverage:

1. The Horserace Syndrome & Highlighting Tactics Over Political Analysis: Endlessly repeated news features with titles like 'Showdown with Saddam' present a grave matter as though it were a high-stakes sports contest," the letter says. It goes on to highlight major news stories the media has failed to cover adequately as they obsess over military tactics.

2. Failing to Protest Government Control of Information: The government has frozen out the media and carefully controlled their access to information. Newspapers and TV news have underreported this freeze out, and failed to contest it aggressively.

3. Failing to Maintain an Arms-Length Relationship with Government: "State-controlled media comes in many garbs," warns the letter, noting the over-reliance of TV news in particular upon government-approved retired military and intelligence consultants.

4. Failing to Question the Official Story: The media should never confuse patriotism with obeisance and a rubber-stamp mentality.

5. Failing to Present a Diversity of Viewpoints: There is a duty to seek out and quote the many experts who express skepticism about claims by the state, rather than simply to rely on the same pundits repeatedly," the letter states. It calls as well on "editors, publishers and producers to see that their op-ed pages, letters-to-the-editor sections and talk shows are open to a vigorous diversity of viewpoints."

6. Radio: Years ago, radio actually acknowledged the concept of orderly debates with widely varying viewpoints. It should do so again.

Influential newspapers like the Washington Post seem to be leading the charge to war. Columnists Russell Mokhiber and Robert Weissman surveyed Post coverage, concluding: "We would say that the Post editorial pages have become an outpost of the Defense Department – except that there is probably more dissent about the pending war in Iraq in the Pentagon than there is on the Post editorial pages.

"In February alone, the Post editorialized nine times in favor of war, the last of those a full two columns of text, arguing against the considerable critical reader response the page had received for pounding the drums of war. Over the six-month period from September through February, the leading newspaper in the nation's capital has editorialized 26 times in favor of war. It has sometimes been critical of the Bush administration, it has sometimes commented on developments in the drive to war without offering an opinion on the case for war itself, but it has never offered a peep against military action in Iraq . . The op-ed page, which might offer some balance, has also been heavily slanted in favor of war."

Even as it appears the bulk of the coverage has joined the march towards war, the public still has not fully enlisted, suggesting a growing gap between what the polls are showing about popular attitudes, and even support for anti-war views, and the mainstream media's enchantment with the spin of the Washington consensus. In an intensifying media war, alternative sources flood the internet as anti war articles from European media circulate in the American heartland.

This battle within the media, between new and old, alternative and independent voices and mainstream pundits is also heating up. At the same time, a culture war is erupting as popular musicians, actors and even athletes take sides. "It's 'Law and Order' versus 'West Wing'" is how one commentator put it. Stay tuned. ●

MEDIA JUMPS ABOARD THE PRESIDENT'S WAR EXPRESS

THEIR pagers are at the ready with new batteries installed. Newsrooms are on higher than high alert. Journalists are at the front. The news industry is as ready to roll as is the military with the specter of war more and more imminent.

The sense of excitement is barely contained in this internal memo sent to a few radio stations by media powerhouse Clearchannel communications. These are the people who sent out an advisory to music DJs after September 11, 2001, suggesting the stations play more patriotic music. (John Lennon's "Imagine" was on a list of songs to avoid.) This new internal memo posted on an internet site shows that many media companies are gearing up while branding war coverage.

"Our Coverage will be called America's War with Iraq. In writing copy please call our coverage, 'LIVE In-Depth Team Coverage of America's War with Iraq.' Branding liners have been produced and are in the system. Mike also make certain that our cross promos on the FMs all address Live in-depth team coverage of the War with Iraq on Newstalk 1530 KFBK,

"Editors, producers get to work on a 'war list' immediately. Make sure it includes local experts, sources, military types, other CC newsrooms around the country, network contacts etc.

"As soon as something happens, notify everyone. As it becomes evident something is approaching, the entire news staff will be placed on standby, even when you're not working. In your off hours listen to KFBK, KGO, and KCBS, watch CNN, MSNBC. Not only will this help keep you posted on war and possible attacks you will find some terrific story ideas. News immersion. Watch, listen, and read! Remember, we ARE or about to be at WAR."

This reference to "news immersion" essentially insures that these stations will just be recycling what their staffers hear and see. No independent analysis. No critical coverage.

Higher up in the media food chain, some media moguls are abandoning all pretense of neutrality. Rupert Murdoch has now openly praised Tony Blair for his courage and endorsed the war as he would a political candidate. Not surprisingly, his newspapers and news troops fall in line and salute. "I think Bush is acting morally," Murdoch told Newsweek.

His Fox News Channel was just acting on February 13 when a reporter in Kuwait staged an urban warfare exercise for viewers back home with heavily armed solders showing how they intend to achieve "dominance" door to door in Baghdad. Unfortunately, the soldiers didn't hear the first command to enter the room so the Fox correspondent had to cue him, giving the whole exercise the aura of obvious staging. He promised his next dispatch would allow viewers to follow the action through "really cool" night vision glasses. This is millitainment in action.

CNN is offering up the same kind of coverage, at least in the USA. They are "outfoxing Fox" says

Robert Wiener, the producer who led CNN's coverage of the Gulf War I back in 1991. He told the Salt Lake Tribune: "The guiding philosophy behind CNN had changed, that the news was no longer the star, and the network became more personality-driven. The people from AOL are not news people and don't give a damn about news. They are really concerned about demographics, ratings." Commented Vince Horiuchi, the columnist who spoke with him: "Sour grapes? Far from it."

The networks can't contain their joy at being encouraged to show some blood and gore this time around. Reuters reports "U.S. television networks are generally enthusiastic about plans to "embed" American and foreign journalists with the U.S. military's air, sea and land units, saying it marks a big step forward in relations between the Pentagon and news media."

Critics note that this letting the viewers see soldiers in all their glory is not the same as granting total and free access as during the Vietnam War. The embedding idea makes media analysts wary, too. "I think the verb itself is enough to make journalists uncomfortable," says Syracuse University TV scholar Robert Thompson. "It implies becoming part and parcel, and really implies in a more glib way going to bed with."

The Pentagon also admits it is seeking to undercut independent journalists in the Arab world. Reports Steve Gorman: "Mindful the public remains deeply skeptical about going to war, Pentagon officials have said it is in their interests to provide Western news media access to combat zones to counteract the potential for Iraqi disinformation that could be distributed by Arab news outlets."

When reference is made to "Arab news channels," officials usually mean the Qatar-based Al-Jazeera. After 9/11 U.S. government officials asked U.S. networks not to broadcast the videos they aired by Osama bin Laden. But earlier this week, in a move that scooped that network's latest scoop, Secretary of State Powell announced that Al-Jazeera would report their latest Bin Laden tape before they actually had done so. Of course, all news organizations picked it up. The Scotsman reported that Powell did so for political reasons, to rally NATO. So much for consistency. That ploy failed.

Meanwhile, the London-based Middle East Broadcasting Corporation (MBC) launches a competitor to Al-Jazeera this month. Variety reports that $200 million has been poured into a new 24 hour Arabic language satellite channel called Al-Arabiya. The magazine did not report who is funding it, but did add: "MBC promises its channel will be perceived by the Western World as more balanced. Variety ran a photo from a Bin Laden monologue under the item, in case the point was missed.

Some media critics in New York plan to picket network headquarters if the police permit. A new "Information Liberation Front" says, "The Corporate Media is the Megaphone for the Bush Administration. The media is the reason this war is going to happen, or haven't you noticed Peter Jenning's new show titled "Are we ready for war?"

Others in the media are speaking out too, The New Yorker magazine's award winning cartoonist Art Spiegelman resigned when his editor supported the war. He told the Italian newspaper Corriere della Sera that he opposes "the widespread conformism of the mass media in the Bush era. I no longer feel in tune with American culture, especially now that the entire media has become conservative and tremendously timid. Unfortunately, even The New Yorker has not escaped this trend."   ●

MARCH 20: WHEN JINGOISM REPLACES JOURNALISM

NEW YORK – I have never seen North Korean TV but I have been told that all it offers is one unending commercial for the government, featuring three channels showing the same programming. We had a dose of that last night as every channel locked on to the same stationary pictures of Baghdad and followed the same format, if not script.

Anchor update. Breaking News. Cut to White House announcement. Anchor update. Military expert. Cut to Presidential message about the ongoing armed "disarmament" of Iraq —which began with the most expensive assassination plot in history: Thirty-six Cruise missiles and two mega bombs at a cost David Martin of CBS estimated at $50 million. The Iraqis claim one civilian was killed, 40 wounded. Of course,we don't know the truth. The New York Post reports "Allies Take Over Iraqi Radio." But this morning, CNN reported that that their correspondent in Baghdad was listening to the radio and nothing had changed.

Waiting to be shocked

THEY tried what they called a "decapitation strike" against a "target of opportunity," later said to be a bunker that Saddam and crew were holed up in. The information came from the CIA, which missed the signals for 9/11. When the strike was reported, all the network guys – and so many look the same, sound the same, and make the same points – were surprised since they had clearly been told when the "real" war would begin. Many seemed disappointed not to be able to see the pictures of Baghdad (they agreed to share) turn into an apocalypse. Tom, Peter, Dan, et. al. were all waiting for the fireworks, the videogame, the promised "shock and awe." On Fox News, Britt Hume stumbled after calling Iraq Al Qaeda and quickly corrected himself. All of the bad guys seem to have merged into one as the crusade for freedom, liberation and more defense spending steps into high gear just like the terror alert that preceded it.

Critic-free coverage

NEEDLESS to say, I saw NO war critics on the air. None. No Iraqis, No Arab journalists.

No one who felt any duty to report the other side, even the multi-sides of the other side. The only critical voices I heard were callers on CSPAN. CBC (Canada) did feature commentary from Eric Margolis, the Toronto Star columnist who explained that the use of the missiles stemmed from an incident in the Afghan War when the U.S. had Mullah Omar in its bomb-sights but did not press the button. The one-eyed epitome of Evil lived and the government vowed never to pass up another such "opportunity."

You could just imagine the scene at the afternoon planning meeting at the White House when these boys with war toys gleefully projected a scenario in which the war could be over before it began with one fatal surgical strike. For weeks now they have been deploying psychological operations to divide Saddam from his gang, and scare the Iraqis into surrender. And scare us at the same time. We have armed National Guardsman in the bus terminal here in New York and one of our staff members said it felt like 9-11 all over again, and that she was near tears.

What is missing?

AFTER watching this wall-to-wall war room for hours, with its videophones, and reporters standing by at the Pentagon, at the White House, in Qatar, in the desert, with the troops, on the ships, I felt a sense of my own decapitation. My own brain was being bombarded with bluster bombs and BS. Needless to say, there was no one standing by with the humanitarian groups, like Doctors Without Borders, which has yet to flee Iraq like the U.N., or for that matter, with the organizers of the anti-war march slated for this Saturday.

These other voices do not exist in the gun sights of the TV cameras. The Bigs are on an endless clock, counting down to war, and, at the same time, counting all the overtime. For them the rest of the world, its crises and issues, seemed to have disappeared into the hole of the ONE BIG STORY, like OJ and Monica before it. For example, there was an escalation in the Afghan War last night that is noted in the press but I did not see covered. Jeanette, my editor, says she saw some CNN and Fox coverage at about 4 a.m.

The commentators seemed to delight in recycling all the Baathist bombast to arouse us all the more. John Burns of The Times reported: "Saddam Hussein exhorted his people to 'draw your swords' against invaders and referred to the U.S. government as 'criminals' and 'Zionists.' But what of the key role of Israel in all this? That was unreported. We saw U.S. troops putting on gas masks, and heard that Israelis have been prepared to do the same. There was no mention of this complaint relayed in the Palestinian Monitor: "Palestinians point out that while Israel is ensuring that its own citizens are provided with gas masks and other equipment in the event of an attack on the region, no such provisions have been made for Palestinians in the Occupied Territories, in contravention of Israel's clear obligations under the Geneva Conventions." On the other hand, Israel says that the Palestinian Authority is in charge of the Palestinian citizenry and its infrastructure and services. It was the PAs choice not to provide for its citizens."

Radio stations rally fans for the war

AS much of the media becomes an outpost for Pentagon pronouncements, some media outlets have stepped outside a broadcast role and are actually ORGANIZING support in the streets. Tim Jones reported in the Chicago Tribune: "Some of the biggest rallies this month have endorsed President Bush's strategy against Saddam Hussein, and the common thread linking most of them is Clear Channel Worldwide Inc., the nation's largest owner of radio stations."

Have you seen any reports on this connection in the rest of the converged and consolidated media? Clearchannel are the folks who circulated a memo to DJs after 9/11 to watch their playlists – as in 'Don't play John Lennon's "Imagine."

Media interests go unscrutinized

JEFF CHESTER of the Center for Digital Democ-racy warns us that "even as the outlets report on the war, their corporate bosses are seeking political favors from the Bush Administration – and the media executives know it.

"The Big Four TV networks, other large broadcasting companies, and most major newspaper chains are currently lobbying the Bush-dominated Federal Communications Commission for new policies designed to promote their corporate interests. They want to end critical rules that limit the number of outlets a single company can control, both at the local and national level. These media giants stand to make untold billions of dollars in profits if the FCC safeguards are eliminated or weakened.

"While the absence of critical analysis, including dissenting voices, on TV news programs, for example, can be attributed to the narrow, commercial mind-set of the U.S. media, viewers and readers should also be aware that these news organizations also have a serious conflict of interest what it comes to reporting on the policies of the Bush Administration. News organizations like to claim that their reporting and commentary are independent of the profit-oriented goals of their parent companies. But it is likely that decisions about how to cover the war on Iraq – especially on television – may be tempered by a concern not to alienate the White House. More so since the FCC is nearing a late spring ruling that may dramatically change the landscape of media ownership in the United States.

"The public deserves to know exactly what the industry is asking for. Here's a thumbnail guide to the lobbying aims by some of the news media's most important companies with regard to the upcoming FCC decision. It doesn't include the many other political favors that the cable and broadcast industry are now seeking, including rules that will determine the future of broadband and the Internet."

The scene at the U.N.

I WAS back at the U.N. yesterday, covering the coverage of the Security Council as it occurred, watching the many TV crews from all over the hold their "stake outs" to catch the 20 seconds it took for Kofi Annan to leave the elevator. There was chief weapons inspector Hans Blix reporting on his work plan, when everyone knew that his moment – and perhaps the U.N.'s moment – has come and gone, at least for now.

"Europe is on Venus, the U.S. is on Mars, and the U.N. is over the moon" is how one British journalist put it to me. Another spoke of the "buzz" and sense of possibility that existed months ago, when the arms inspection process got underway. The U.N. was created to foster peace. It did not fail so much as it too was "decapitated" by the world's No. 1 superpower, which took its marbles and went home. One watched with disbelief as various diplomats talked to themselves and none condemned what is likely to occur, or the U.S. role.

Ian Williams reported: "Reality intruded, briefly, in the form of U.N. Secretary General Kofi Annan, who addressed the Security Council to remind belligerents of their responsibility for the protection of civilians. "Without in any way assuming or diminishing that ultimate responsibility, we in the United Nations will do whatever we can to help," Annan said. The Iraqi Ambassador sensed the "tragic irony of people talking about reconstruction aid for a country that they are in effect, allowing to be blown apart."

J'accuse

THE French Ambassador, the smooth-talking silver-haired Dominique came out to make nice with the press. All the U.N. correspondents started shouting at once, hurling questions his way. "Do you think the criticisms of France are unfair?" Duh. Yes, of course, he does, etc., etc. I caught the eye of a U.N. man picking the questioners. My hand shot up, and to my surprise, I was called upon. I asked him what it means for the U.N. if one nation can make war against the U.N. Charter. He paused, sidestepped the adversarial nature of the question, but then expressed, in most passionate terms, why the U.N. matters. I thought at that moment of how little coverage there is of the U.N. in the U.S., except when Washington is using it or denouncing it.

Why did the U.N. cave?

MANY in the peace movement had put their faith in the U.N., and its inspection process. But when the U.S. demanded that the inspectors leave, the U.N. deferred in a quick second, without any resistance, even verbal, all in the name of staff safety. Could it have done more? Jan Oberg of the TFF in Sweden thought so:

"Thus, it seems that one member issues an ultimatum recommendation and the U.N. obeys and leaves the Iraqi people behind to be intimidated, humiliated, killed, wounded and, in a few weeks, starve. Article 99 of the U.N. Charter states that the Secretary-General may bring to the attention of the Security Council any matter that in his opinion may threaten the maintenance of international peace and security.

"Is that not exactly what the U.S. ultimatum did

– threatening Iraq and threatening the world organization in Iraq?

"Article 100 of the U.N. Charter states that in the performance of their duties the Secretary-General and the staff shall not seek or receive instructions from any government... Well, of course, it was not termed an instruction, it was a recommendation. But what the Secretary-General did on March 17, 2003, was to accept an instruction."

So what happens now? Even before a missile is fired, the U.N. has become the first casualty of this war. ●

MARCH 24: "FICTITIOUS TIMES" ARE HERE AGAIN

WE live in "fictitious times," filmmaker Michael Moore said at the Oscars last night, an event celebrating the dream factory of American culture. To his credit, he took other documentary makers with him to the podium for a collective 15 seconds of fame, to contrast the reality their work is concerned with and the surreal atmosphere that surrounded them and the rest of us. He said, "We love non-fiction but we live in fictitious times, with a fictitious president, providing fictitious reasons for a false war."

A night earlier, he rehearsed these same lines at the Indy Spirit awards on BRAVO when they too honored his movie, "Bowling for Columbine." There, he more directly confronted the media coverage by demanding the withdrawal of the U.S. military in the form of all those military experts from our TV studios where they seem to be an occupying force. TV newsrooms were

invaded long before Baghdad.

TV helped lead to war, critics say

THE disgraceful TV media coverage is finally meriting some discussion in the mainstream media. The New York Times reported in its low-circulation Saturday edition: "Critics Say Coverage Helped Lead to War." Reporters Jim Rutenberg and Robin Toner wrote:

"Critics of the war against Iraq are not reserving their anger exclusively for President Bush. Some also blame the news media, asserting that they failed to challenge the administration aggressively enough as it made a shaky case for war. In an interview, Eric Alterman, liberal media critic and author of "What Liberal Media?"(Basic Books, 2003) argued, "Support for this war is in part a reflection that the media has allowed the Bush administration to get away with misleading the American people."

"The strongest indictment of the press, many of these critics argue, are recent polls that suggest many Americans see Iraq as being responsible for the Sept. 11 attacks," the Times reporters said.

The war is finally on

WHILE the media war and the "war" over the media continues, the shooting war is finally on, as President Bush acknowledged on the White House lawn yesterday. That means both sides are fighting.

All the rest has been prelude and a romp with the weapons fetishists and their media cheerleaders making the U.S. invasion "the" story while leaving the Iraqis, civilian casualties and most of the rest of the world out of it.

The media frame seems to be changing. For days the TV air war was selling the real one, preparing us gleefully for the bombs away "shock and awe" campaign. Even the conservative Washington Times noted this on Friday: "Some correspondents acted as if they were waiting for Fourth of July fireworks, while others seemed giddy as they donned gas masks." One estimate claimed more than $500,000 was spent on the fireworks."

Now it is the U.S. viewers who are shocked and awed by the cruelty of the war, by the graphic images of U.S. soldiers in captivity and worse, on the floor of an Iraqi morgue. Bill Carter and Jane Perlez report in The New York Times that "the networks were in possession of a videotape of captured and killed American soldiers, first aired on the Arab satellite news channel Al-Jazeera." They waited for Al-Jazeera to air it first and for the families to be notified. An Al-Jazeera editor, speaking in English on CNN, told Aaron Brown that they were showing the reality of war and that American-owned networks in Europe, including CNN, were not. They also said they stopped showing the footage after the Pentagon asked them to wait.

The NY Post's "SAVAGES"

"SAVAGES" is the headline on the New York Post, which shows the photo that much of the rest of the U.S. media is censoring, along with other footage being carried by Al-Jazeera, an outlet now being denounced by Donald Rumsfeld and others. (Please note that just last week, The New York Times carried a report quoting American officials praising the channel.) No

sooner had Rumsfeld denounced the footage than CNN announced that it was taking it off the air. To its credit, CNN did briefly show photos of Iraqi casualties, but the network did not shoot them. The Associated Press supplied them. In a media environment where updates seem to be carried every few minutes, I did not see those photos again.

The Post seems to have become an official arm of the Pentagon Propaganda Campaign. Today it carries a column by Harlan K. Ullman, military analyst, described as a distinguished national security expert and a principal author of the military doctrine of "shock and awe." Needless to say, he was given prominence in the paper, which ran 17 pages of pro-war boosterism.

POWs in hell

YESTERDAY, war as a TV game became war as hell. In rapid succession, we heard of a U.S. soldier rolling grenades into the tents of his officers and fellow soldiers. And then screw-ups were reported from what we were being told was a clean mean fighting machine wedded to precision targeting. One of our Patriot missiles shot down a British plane. Two hit Turkey. One blasted a bus in Syria. Another landed in Iran. And soon the casualties started to mount. (Although the number of dead civilians does not seem to be tallied with the same urgency as the number of "coalition" dead and wounded.)

And then we saw some POWs. Last night on ABC radio, Matt Drudge was saying they had been sexually humiliated, a story line no one else has picked up on. Contrast the humility of one American soldier with the hubris of the generals and political leaders who keep saying that "we are on plan," the plan is working. He told his captors: "I only came to fix broke stuff." He was asked if he came to shoot Iraqis. "No I come to shoot only if I am shot at," he said. "They (Iraqis) don't bother me, I don't bother them."

As for POWs and their treatment, the U.S. military was sending around footage to media outlets of Iraqi soldiers surrendering. Many outlets ran it unverified. That was not a violation of the Geneva Convention, apparently. One of our readers, Catherine Kenward, reminded me about how controversial U.S. treatment of prisoners has been in Afghanistan (the Mazar-I-Sharif prison revolt and the more recent reports of prisoners who suddenly died in U.S. custody). Am I the only one who finds it ironic to hear Donald Rumsfeld talking about the Geneva Convention? Don't we still have Afghan prisoners living in cages at Guantanamo? Aren't we the ones talking about how convenient it would be if we could use torture? Haven't we broken every international accord and treaty that hindered us from doing exactly as we please? And suddenly Rumsfeld is talking about the Geneva Convention.

A week ago, the Village Voice reported on the U.S. military shipping prisoners to other countries that routinely practice torture. It makes for 'plausible deniability.'

That chemical plant?

AND then there was the sudden discovery of a chemical plant. To the frat pack on Fox, this was the smoking gun. The GOTCHA! But then the network brought in an ex-weapons inspector who said he doubted it because it was too far south. He was British. An American, David Kay, who double dips as a TV analyst on MSNBC while working for the Uranium Institute of the nuclear industry, was less skeptical. He says that Iraq never declared the plant. We still don't know what is in that plant or what he suddenly discovered there. The Jerusalem Post this morning was saying that U.S. officials confirmed to them that the plant was making weapons. NBC later reported that it was indeed a chemical weapons plant, with huge tanks filled with chemicals. The Iraqi generals and officers in the plant all surrendered.

Please remember that this war, these "serious consequences" as Colin Powell used to call what we are now seeing, were designed to disarm Iraq, to find those alleged weapons of mass destruction. Recall how many times the U.S. government claimed to know where they were, rarely sharing their "intelligence" with the U.N. inspectors. Well, so far – and this could change – we have yet to see this occur. I certainly do not trust Saddam's claims, but it is not surprising that he didn't destroy all his weapons, if that is the case, knowing that nothing he could do would ever satisfy an administration hell bent on invading.

Chemistry lesson

IN the meantime, let's get chemical. Join me in the time machine. Let's go back to 1983 when Iraq used bio-chem weapons 195 times against the Iranians in a war in which the U.S. sided with Saddam. Iran said Iraq killed or wounded 50,000 people, soldiers and civilians.

This is 10 times as many people as in the northern Kurdish area in and around Halabja, a horrific gassing that has been cited repeatedly. (There are some experts who say the Iranians did that, not the Iraqis.) What is of interest is this: How did the United States government react at the time? According to Samantha Power in her brilliant book, 'A Problem From Hell: America in an Age of Genocide':

"The State Department and even the Congress largely let the Iraqi attacks slide. Reports of Iraq's chemical use against Iran first reached Secretary of State Shultz in late 1983. It was not until March 5, 1984, that the State Department spokesman issue a condemnation. It took the UN three more years to "deplore" chemical weapons use. It was this type of response, Power argues, that encouraged Hussein to do it again and to think he could "get away with it."

Even though no chemical weapons have been used yet in this war, we keep seeing reporters in chemical suits. News World reports: A veteran Hong Kong journalist was severely lambasted for his "absurd" TV reports from Kuwait City. Raymond Wong, an assistant director at English-language TV channel TVB, came under fire from viewers about his pieces to camera, including a three-minute stint in which he donned a gas mask and protective goggles. The segment was supposed to show how the Kuwaitis might be subjected to chemical or biological attacks in the advent of a war with Iraq.

Censorship on the rise

CENSORSHIP is rearing its ugly head across the world. Globalvision News Network editor Tim Karr reports: "Danny, Some interesting movements for and against global independent media and their coverage of the War in Iraq:

"Erich Marquardt, the editor of the Amsterdam-based YellowTimes.org. (www/yellowtimes.org) is fighting a shutdown attempt by its hosting provider. The site was temporarily shut down Sunday night after it posted graphic images of Iraqi victims of the war. YellowTimes.org also on Sunday published images of the five captured American soldiers and of dead GIs.

"Without any prior warning YellowTimes.org's hosting provider sent a letter stating: 'Your account has been suspended because of inappropriate graphic material.' Over the weekend, YellowTimes.org acquired several pictures of Iraqi civilian casualties. Since few to none in the mainstream Western media had reported on the civilian toll, Yellow Times posted the images at the site. Marquardt also chose to publish images of captured and killed GIs at a time, on Sunday, when most mainstream American news outlets were reluctant to air these images."

No more anti-war news

MEDIA Guardian reports: "Sir Ray Tindle, the editor-in-chief of over 100 weekly newspapers across Britain, has informed all his editors that they can no longer report any anti-war stories in their newspapers. Sir Ray, who has been knighted for his services to the newspaper industry, wrote: "Everyone knows that Tindle family newspapers have no political bias. Our columns are free. When British troops come under fire, however, as now seems probable, I ask you to ensure that nothing appears in the columns of your newspapers which attacks the decision to conduct the war in which those men are involved, nor, of course, anything which attacks the troops themselves."

The armchair general

MARK LAWSON writes: "We belong to a generation which has largely ceased to be surprised by television, but think about this: those who wanted to, were able to watch an enemy operation live from the banks of the Tigris. This weekend's pictures have widened the eyes like nothing since the moon landings, though with rather greater moral complications. The essential problem is that in seeming to know everything, we know nothing. There are wise old journalists who will tell you that the word "raw" is usually a warning. It is unwise to eat raw meat or smell raw sewage and it may be equally foolish to consume raw news coverage.

"In the triptych of examples given above, what had vividly seemed to be an assassination attempt on General Franks was down-graded later to a gas canister exploding at a car plant over the road. During the Tigris reed-shoot, the western rolling news shows all reported in good faith that the coalition claimed to have no planes missing until Defense Secretary Donald Rumsfeld murmured on NBC that, in fact, the count was short.

"Because we must always doubt the meaning of the scenes we're seeing, following this war on television is like walking around an art gallery in which the pictures dissolve and the captions scramble shortly after you've been admiring them for 20 minutes."

Readers share their media views:

I WAS delighted that my daughter, Sarah Schechter is dissecting your dissector and the media: "I was struck this morning, listening to NPR and the networks, by a couple things. NPR actually cut to CNN which was interviewing a New York Times reporter who is embedded with a military troop to get his feelings about what was happening around him. NPR cutting to CNN seemed strange to me, and trying to understand their justification, I rationalized that they thought it was okay because CNN was interviewing The New York Times. That while CNN may not share the same branding with NPR, The New York Times does. Essentially saying, "don't think we're lazy or just like them but this is The New York Times guys so it's okay."

"As I continued to watch and listen to coverage, I couldn't help noticing that every mainstream media outlet was using the same expression when introducing their correspondents in the Middle East – they all used the word that CNN, NPR and The New York Times had used – 'embedded.' It was almost as if a memo had gone out to everyone instructing them to use the word, it popped up too frequently to be coincidence. I looked up the word embedded this morning and this is what I found:

"1. To fix firmly in a surrounding mass: embed a post in concrete; fossils embedded in shale.

"2. To enclose snugly or firmly.

"3. To cause to be an integral part of a surrounding whole: 'a minor accuracy embedded in a larger untruth' (Ian Jack).

"While they may think of it terms of the first definition, I couldn't help but feel the third was most appropriate. These guys are honorary members – and have in fact become an integral part of the whole of the military complex. What happened to objectivity? How can a journalist remain objective when they are embedded within the very thing they are to report on? How can they remain impartial, and therefore accurate?" ●

15 BUNGLED STORIES

By GREG MITCHELL

THE war is only a week old and already the media has gotten at least 15 stories wrong or misreported a sliver of fact into a major event. Television news programs, of course, have been the prime culprits. Newspapers, while they have often gone along for the ride, have been much more nuanced and careful. Newspaper coverage has not been faultless, as photos and headlines often seem shock-and-awestruck but, compared with TV, newspapers seem more editorially – and mentally – balanced. Some have actually displayed a degree of skepticism of claims made by the military and the White House – what used to be known as "journalism."

On Monday, I received a call from a producer of a major network's prime time news program. He said they wanted to interview me for a piece on how the public's expectation of a quick victory somehow was too high. "But," he hastened to add, "we don't want to focus on the media." I asked him where he thought the public might have received the information that falsely raised their hopes. In chat rooms, perhaps? The problem, I suggested, is that most of the TV commentators on the home front appear to be just as "embedded" with the military as the far braver reporters now in the Iraqi desert.

Surely this is a bipartisan issue. While many on the antiwar side complain about the media's alleged "pro-war bias," those who support the war have also been ill served by overly-positive coverage that now has millions of Americans reeling from diminished expectations.

Here, then, is a list of stories that have been widely misreported or poorly reported so far:

1. Saddam may well have been killed in the first night's surprise attack (March 20).

2. Even if he wasn't killed, Iraqi command and control was no doubt "decapitated" (March 22).

3. Umm Qasr has been taken (March 22).

4. Most Iraqis soldiers will not fight for Saddam and instead are surrendering in droves (March 22).

5. Iraqi citizens are greeting Americans as liberators (March 22).

6. An entire division of 8,000 Iraqi soldiers surrendered en masse near Basra (March 23).

7. Several Scud missiles, banned weapons, have been launched against U.S. forces in Kuwait (March 23).

8. Saddam's Fedayeen militia are few in number and do not pose a serious threat (March 23).

9. Basra has been taken (March 23).

10. Umm Qasr has been taken (March 23).

11. A captured chemical plant likely produced chemical weapons (March 23).

12. Nassiriya has been taken (March 23).

13. Umm Qasr has been taken (March 24).

14. The Iraqi government faces a "major rebellion" of anti-Saddam citizens in Basra (March 24).

15. A convoy of 1,000 Iraqi vehicles and Republican Guards are speeding south from Baghdad to engage U.S. troops (March 25).

– From Editor & Publisher Online.

CHAPTER FIVE

BATTLEFIELD BLUES

IS THE INVASION BOGGED DOWN IN A NEW QUAGMIRE?

The view from Mesopotamia is that trouble's in store

O N Day 6, the rubber is hitting the road, and the road is hitting back. It may be that the special Oscar to Peter O'Toole – the man who played Lawrence of Arabia at the lowest-rated Academy Awards show in recent history – was an attempt to remind us of the joys of the colonial era when British overlords would sip tea at the palaces in Baghdad. Despite the heaviest pounding in history from the air, from the shock and awe that was admittedly AWE-ful, the Iraqis are holding on, fighting back and throwing a curve ball at the Pentagon and forcing a rewrite of the media scripts that forecast a quick rout, with kebab for all.

This is the week of the Q word, the week that media is mesmerized by the Quagmire parallel.

It's true; the war appears, for the moment, to be turning into a quagmire as others have done in the past. You can't abolish history, even when you ignore it. The difficulties are now overshadowing the successes and the Pentagon/Administration is becoming more defensive.

All the focus on Saddam's whereabouts seems to have shifted. We are getting more and more stories like this one from Joseph Galloway of Knight Ridder:

"WASHINGTON – Five days into the war, the optimistic assumptions of the Pentagon's civilian war planners have yet to be realized, the risks of the campaign are becoming increasingly apparent and some current and retired military officials are warning that there may be a mismatch between Secretary of Defense Donald H. Rumsfeld's strategy and the force he's sent to carry it out.

"The outcome of the war isn't in doubt: Iraq's forces are no match for America and its allies. But, so far, defeating them is proving to be harder, and it could prove to be longer and costlier in American and Iraqi lives."

On the tube

ON the TV nets, the generals are working overtime to explain, and explain away, why the Iraqi uprising has not yet occurred, with the proverbial fat lady yet to sing songs of welcome. It is hard to believe that we are getting the full story despite all the embeds and all the expertise. It's hard to know whom to believe.

Last night, CSPAN brought us the Canadian

news from CBC's 'The National', and for the first time, I felt I was back in the land of real information. There was a critically inflected report on the war, with Iraqi voices. There was a feature on an anti-war organizer in Ottawa. There was a report on the debate about Canadian policy, which has, to date, stayed out of the fray. There was a commentary predicting the U.S. would win but worrying about the costs and consequences. In short, there was the kind of TV news Americans used to watch in the age of Cronkite and Chancellor.

Many Americans are turning away from the tube even as ratings soar. What I mean is that they/we are synthesizing our own news input, drawing from many sources including websites overseas. The New York Observer called me yesterday for a comment for a story they are preparing on how many of us are becoming our own editors and personalizing our media choices. For example, as we watch TV news casts that seem more and more like CIA-sponsored briefings, with continuing reports on weaponry and the "wow" factor as expressed by reporters riding in tanks, other news is getting out.

Russian Intelligence vs. Ours

I CAN'T vouch for the accuracy, but it is interesting to find Russian intelligence reports carried on the mediawar.info website about the recent battles that have been portrayed as a big win for the red, white and blue. They quote from Iraqwar.ru:

"The IRAQWAR.RU analytical center was created recently by a group of journalists and military experts from Russia to provide accurate and up-to-date news and analysis of the war against Iraq. The following is the English translation of the IRAQWAR.RU report based on the Russian military intelligence reports. Here is an excerpt from the March 24, 2003, 0800hrs report:

"Other Americans have failed in trying to use their momentum in capturing An-Nasiriya and attempted to encircle the town from the west, where they encountered strong layered Iraqi defenses and were forced to withdraw. The Iraqi forces used this opportunity to attack the U.S. flanks with two brigades, breaking the U.S. combat orders and causing panic among the U.S. troops. The U.S. command was forced to halt the advance of its forces toward An Najaf and once again redirect several tank battalions to support the attacked units. Nearly six hours were needed for the U.S. aviation to stop the Iraqi attack and restore combat order of the U.S. forces.

"During the past day the coalition aviation flew more than 2,000 close support missions in this area [An-Nasiriya]. "We can only thank God for having air dominance," said the commander of the U.S. 15th Marines Exp. Corps Col. Thomas Waldhauser in a private conversation with one of the CNN reporters. Later the CNN journalist cited the Colonel in a phone conversation with his editor. The conversation was intercepted.

"According to the intercepted radio traffic, the U.S. forces have sustained up to 40 killed, up to 10 captured and up to 200 wounded during the fighting near An-Nasiriya. There is confirmed information about one lost attack helicopter and an unconfirmed report about a lost ground attack plane. The U.S. forces have also lost up to 40 armored vehicles, including no less than 10 tanks. Several intercepted reports by the U.S. field commanders stated that their troops are unable to advance due to their soldiers being demoralized by the enemy's fierce resistance and high losses."

Again, I am not accepting all this as fact, just showing how other authoritative accounts can be offered up to challenge all the "authoritative" reports we are hearing. Meanwhile, a debate about the war rages in Russia too. Eurasianet reports: "While most in Moscow believe that an Iraq war will damage Russian interests, a split is developing among Russia's policy-making elite over how to respond to the outbreak of war. One side is ready to continue its opposition to war, while the other says that Russia ought to cooperate with the inevitable."

My point is that even the blow by blow of war reporting can be distorted. That happened in Vietnam with U.S. forces under pressure to exaggerate "enemy kills" and downplay their losses. Last night, former Nixon and Reagan aide Gen. Alexander "I am in charge here" Haig was back on Fox News where he called for "more violence." Honestly, that is what he told Sean Hannity, who sat by approvingly. It was another bloodthirsty performance on the War network.

Better dying through chemistry

LAST night the airwaves crackled with reports that the Iraqi forces may have chemical weapons. According to CNN at 10:46 this morning, Iraqi troops in Baghdad were issued gas-carrying artillery shells and gas masks, and were ordered to use those weapons if the allied troops crossed into the city. No evidence was produced to substantiate the fear, but it appeared in all the promos. Remember, the goal of this war, allegedly, is to disarm Iraq and divest it of its weapons of mass destruction. The seizure of what was described as a chemical plant was cited initially as PROOF. Former inspector and now NBC consultant David Kay suggested he believed that was what the plant was and said the Iraqis have never declared it. The Jerusalem Post also claimed it as a smoking gun. Slowly, some information is trickling out to encourage us to be more cautious. Remember, the initial reports were not making the claims we later heard on NBC or Fox:

"WASHINGTON (CNN) – Pentagon officials on Sunday said the U.S. military has secured a facility in southern Iraq that may have been used to produce chemical weapons. The officials cautioned that it was not clear what suspected materials may still be at the plant, which is located in Najaf, some 90 miles south of Baghdad."

This can be just in a war where propaganda is pervasive. (Digression: Quote of the day from Newsweek's Jonathan Alter: "The popularity of this war so far is at least partly due to the human face of the coverage, a brilliant PR contrast to the antiseptic briefing-room videogames of what is now called Gulf War I." End of Digression.) Leith Elder writes:

"The discovery of the huge chemical weapons factory in Najaf is not a discovery. This facility has been known since about 1991 (document below).

". . . Summary: [deleted] Several sites in Iraq with the capability to produce and store BW weapons. Although the capability exists, no evidence of current production or storage was found. Enclosures. Text 1. Background [deleted] suspected biological warfare sites. Among the sites were the Al-Kindi company, An-Najaf, Taji, the Serum and Vaccine institute, the Agriculture Research and Water Resources Center, and the

Ibn Haithan institute . . ."

The Washington Post reports: "A very important political component is if you find these things, how do you establish the proof of that to the satisfaction of 35 foreign ministries and those of you in the media?" said Jay Davis, who led the Defense Threat Reduction Agency until 2001 and has continued to consult on the Iraqi disarmament plan. "A large number of conspiracy theorists all over the world will say the U.S. government has planted all that stuff."

POW Coverage

WITH two more U.S. airmen in Iraqi custody, the POW issue is back on the news. CNN defied the government this time and did show Al-Jazeera coverage of Iraqi TV pictures. Meanwhile, in England, Guardian columnist George Monbiot challenged what he called double standards by the U.S. government:

"Suddenly, the government of the United States has discovered the virtues of international law. It may be waging an illegal war against a sovereign state; it may be seeking to destroy every treaty which impedes its attempts to run the world, but when five of its captured soldiers were paraded in front of the Iraqi television cameras on Sunday, Donald Rumsfeld, the U.S. defense secretary, immediately complained that it is against the Geneva Convention to show photographs of prisoners of war in a manner that is humiliating for them.

"He is, of course, quite right. Article 13 of the third convention, concerning the treatment of prisoners, insists that they must at all times be protected ... against insults and public curiosity.

"This may number among the less heinous of

the possible infringements of the laws of war, but the conventions, ratified by Iraq in 1956, are non-negotiable. If you break them, you should expect to be prosecuted for war crimes

"This being so, Rumsfeld had better watch his back. For this enthusiastic convert to the cause of legal warfare is, as head of the defense department, responsible for a series of crimes sufficient, were he ever to be tried, to put him away for the rest of his natural life."

Official news

THE media reporting came under fire by TomDispatch.com:

"I caught a fair amount of CNN and MSNBC this afternoon, and NBC Prime Time news followed by the Lehrer NewsHour tonight. What struck me was how much of our periodic 24/7 war extravaganzas are taken up with official and semi-official events. I caught, for instance, an extended performance by Gen. Tommy Franks and various supporting actors and supporting screens at the elaborate Centcom set (sorry, headquarters) in Qatar. I also caught a performance (sorry, news conference) by Ari Fleischer (with a few tough questions from reporters, reflecting perhaps a slight shift in mood) and then a glimpse of Tariq Aziz defiant in Baghdad.

"Each of these four channels also had their semi-official events involving military consultants whose expertise usually lies largely in having directed some aspect of America's last wars. (No former Somalian warlords to offer some vaunted "balance," no less a French or Russian general. Only former American military men or intelligence officers are considered expert enough to comment on an American war.) General Wesley Clark, former supreme allied commander in Europe, NATO commander for the Kosovo campaign, with all his we did this or that today, on I-forget-which-channel sounded distinctly like he was actively engaged in fighting this war as well.

"Of the channels I watched today, most riveted on American casualties and prisoners (and whether or not, or how, or when to show pictures of POWs or dead Americans) – only PBS showed significant footage of Iraqi casualties. Given all those Washington officials, active generals, retired generals, former officials, and anchors and journalists used to negotiating such heady crowds, American television tends to chew over mainly issues of concern to the Bush administration and the Pentagon."

Al-Jazeera in the hot seat

THE love-hate relationship with Al-Jazeera continues. First, the Qatar-based satellite news channel was denounced for carrying Osama tapes. The U.S. networks were urged not to show them by U.S. government officials. Then, Washington decided to try to use the network rather than denounce it and it placed many officials on the channel. Just last week, the U.S. government praised its coverage. This week it is back in the doghouse with the New York Stock Exchange now banning its reporters. Reports the Guardian: "A reporter for al-Jazeera, which has been criticized by the U.S. military for its coverage of conflict, has been barred from entering the exchange while another has been ordered to return his press card. A spokesman for the NYSE said it was limiting access to "responsible" broadcasters and insisted other broadcasters had also been affected."

On the weekend, Jihad Ballout, an Al-Jazeera spokesperson, responded angrily to criticism from Donald Rumsfeld: "Look who's talking about international law and regulations. We didn't make the pictures; the pictures are there," he continued. "It's a facet of the war. Our duty is to show the war from all angles."

Meanwhile, Joe Belden of Asia Times Online reports approvingly of Al-Jazeera coverage from Jordan: "CNN's war coverage had been mocked and overtaken by images that showed the true face of war in all its madness and horror – images that almost invariably bore the label "Al-Jazeera exclusive". These were not scrolling maps or armchair generals – these were scenes of a 12-year-old child with half her head blown off in Basra. This was the sound and fury of the relatives of victims of Tomahawk cruise missile strikes in northern Iraq loudly promising their revenge. This was live coverage of a hundreds-strong posse of armed and delighted Iraqis setting fire to the bulrushes of the Tigris River in search of a Western pilot presumed hiding within.

"This was a guided tour of a roomful of U.S. soldiers in a morgue. This was the fear in the eyes of a captured U.S. soldier as he was asked by an off-screen voice in broken English why he came all the way from Texas just to kill Iraqis. "I follow orders," he answered, a strain in his voice. These were images of war."

And while Western sensibilities might have been spared the trauma of exposure to these images, they went straight into the homes and hearts of 300 million viewers in the Middle East on Sunday. The effect was immediate, and strong.

Protesting media coverage

AS I reported on Sunday, anti-war groups are challenging some media outlets. CNN was picketed in New York and Los Angeles on Saturday, although the network that claims to be the most trusted did not report on its own critics, at least not that I saw. There was a report in the LA News by Rachel Uranga:

"Protesting what they called the broadcast media's uncritical coverage of the Iraq war, thousands of anti-war protesters streamed through the streets of Hollywood on Saturday, on their way to CNN's Los Angeles high-rise.

"Nearly 80 people who sat in the middle of a blocked-off intersection, defying police orders to disperse, were arrested in the demonstration, one of the largest in four days of Southland protests. No injuries were reported.

"Protesters gathered at the 24-hour news agency's Sunset Boulevard office building decried the Bush administration's policy of preemptive strikes in Iraq and railed against the media's 'cheerleading coverage.' 'We feel that CNN and all the major broadcasters act as the information ministry for the government,' said James Lafferty, a lead organizer and executive director of the National Lawyers Guild. Calls to CNN offices in Los Angeles and Atlanta were not immediately returned Saturday."   ●

MARCH 26: THE NETWORK JIHAD ON JOURNALISM

IF you want to get on top of the news, watch the

BBC. I couldn't believe my eyes. I'll take that back. There is little I can't believe after watching the war on TV. Here's CNN reporting from the Pentagon on precision bombing – "authorities here tell us how proud they are of their targeting capabilities," etc. At that very minute, BBC aired a report of two missiles striking a market in Baghdad with a minimum of 15 dead and countless other casualties. BBC did not air any of their more graphic pictures, so we heard about the death of people out shopping but didn't see them, but at least it was reported. Some 15 minutes later, CNN had "new" pictures in from the Iraqi capital. We are not sure what we are showing you," said anchor Carol Costello . . .

MSNBC asks for blessing from on high

TV war coverage in America is becoming routinized, predictable and, at least on the Comedy Channel, a big joke. MSNBC was running new promos to support the troops with an animated "GOD BLESS AMERICA." Fox News has a logo with a plane and an eagle coming out of it. And even as the charade continues, of anchors turning to military generals and approved experts for the interpretation of the war, something is happening and Mr. Jones doesn't seem to know what it is. The answer, my friend, is blowing in the sand. . .

All that sand may be nature's way of singing Dylan's song:

"How many times must a man look up
Before he can see the sky?
Yes, and how many ears must one man have
Before he can hear people cry?"

To learn more about the people crying and dying, check this Iraqi Body count website:

www.iraqbodycount.net/bodycount.htm

"Yes, and how many deaths will it take till he knows that too many people have died?" — Bob Dylan

With experts like these

HERE'S one on those obscene "experts." TomDispatch.com reports on an exchange heard on CNN. I think it must have been NBC because that's where the ex-Drug Czar is busting balls these days, but you can't blame him for confusing the channels because they all tend to meld together.

"I turned on CNN briefly this afternoon and caught their military expert, General Barry McCaffrey (U.S. Army, ret.) answering questions about war strategy from a CNN anchor in a distinctly belligerent tone to interspersed clips of convoys and American foot soldiers moving through blowing sand. Here are a few phrases I managed to jot down: When asked about 'the battle for Baghdad,' he said, 'We gotta get into town, bust their chops, and get outta there.' And a little later he asked rhetorically, 'Do you bust in there, take them down, or do you end up in a 90-day stand-off?' On the subject of sand storms grounding planes, he commented, 'But thank God for the U.S. artillery. Without that we'd be in trouble out there.'

"And so on and so forth, his face perched on a red (and orange lettered) graphic 'Operation IRAQI FREEDOM.' Here, on the other hand, is a telegraphic private note to a friend of mine from a Brit reporter, who in a few well-chosen words , offers a distinctly more realistic vision of this war as it's unfolding: 'had a hairy weekend in southern Iraq since last I messaged. the south,

which was supposed to hate Saddam, has turned out not to be very welcoming.'"

U.N. to meet. Who knew?

THE U.N. Security Council meets today to discuss concerns about the war by the Non-Aligned Movement and Arab League. They will also discuss the need for humanitarian aid, which has yet to flow into Iraq. I found out about this in a rather circuitous manner, while listening to news on the South African Broadcasting Corporation, during an interview with me about media coverage. I had just spent two hours flipping from channel to channel but had not seen any mention of it, a clear sign that the networks have no interest in covering, much less encouraging, efforts to resolve this conflict peacefully.

There doesn't seem to be an embed in with the humanitarian crowd. Kofi Annan has been enraged by the way this issue is treated. Secretary of State Powell was on CBS last night bragging about how "we" now have most of the water supply running again in Basra. The BBC reported that it is the International Red Cross which is trying to fix the water works, which was apparently bombed in one of those precise targetings. The water was, in fact, still off.

At least one CNNer experienced her own shock and awe. Anchor Connie Chung, who had been brought in to tabloidize the network's programming with a steady diet of child kidnappings and sex scandals, is out. Collateral damage. Fired! And that, despite a $2 million contract with one year to run. Reports the Times, "She was very shocked and extremely disappointed," the associate said. "She did the show she was asked to do even though she argued that she wanted to do a different kind of show. But the management changed, and the new management said, 'We don't want that kind of show.' She was not given a chance to do something different for them." I am sure Ted Turner, who made clear his distaste for the show, is a bit happier tonight. What's another million dollars after all the money AOL Time Warner has pissed away?

(My favorite play on the shock and awful scenario was on comedian John Stewart's brilliant nooze show on Comedy Channel where he coined the phrase "stock and awe" to report on the decline in the market in the wake of all the setbacks in Iraq.)

The media war through Arab eyes

HERE'S how Gulf News, one Arab media outlet is reporting on this media war: "The images shown on Arab TV have an explosive impact on Arab public opinion, much to the dismay of U.S. and British officials.

"Western channels, notably CNN, have come under fire for not only following, but also promoting American policy, serving as 'apologists, for a unilateral war on Iraq waged without a UN mandate, and censoring graphic images of the civilian carnage.'

"And then there is the matter of journalists stealing the show.

"No sooner did the U.S. wage their offensive on Baghdad on March 19, 'daredevil' journalists, mainly from the West, had copped a greedy share of the limelight.

"First person accounts of journalists' own experiences in war zones have long been the bane of sober political analysts, who regret that sensationalized tales of adventure should eclipse the reality on the ground.

"As such, critics would argue foreign correspondents reporting on the war in Iraq have broken a cardinal rule of journalism by becoming a part of the story they are sent to cover.

"Their confrontations with the big bad Iraqis, and their subsequent expulsion from the country, have generated more news coverage than the suffering of innocent civilians, including women and very young children."

Back to the drawing board

HOW many times have we heard about the PLAN? The plan is working. We are on plan. Today The New York Times makes it official: The plan is being changed. Why? It didn't work. The unexpected fierce resistance has put a wrinkle in the plan to spend Arabian nights in the Iraqi capital. Washington Post's Howard Kurtz, a mainstream media writer, is now blaming media accounts for misleading viewers and the administration:

Kurtz writes: "Why did so many people think this would be a cakewalk? You'd have to say the media played a key role. The pre-war buildup was so overwhelming that it seemed like the war should be called off as a horrible mismatch. There were hundreds of stories about America's superior weaponry, the Bradleys and Apaches and Mother of All Bombs, the superbly trained forces. There were so many 'shock and awe' stories that Americans could be forgiven for thinking they were in for another video-game conflict. There were stories about how Iraqi units would quickly surrender, how Iraqi citizens would hail the advancing Americans and British as liberators. Some of this was driven by the more than

500 embedded reporters, who naturally reflected the confidence of the commanders and troops they were covering."

Ernie Pyle meets Franz Kafka

JASON VEST picks up on this theme in this week's New York Observer: "With each new report comes a new, contradictory theory, We are conquering. We are not conquering. We are not conquering as fast was we'd expected. The troops are confident. The troops are nervous.

"It is Ernie Pyle meets Franz Kafka. What you are seeing is not the war in Iraq, Donald Rumsfeld said. What you are seeing are slices of the war in Iraq.

"The spectacle was thrilling and clear at first. Those videophoned images of tanks rolling through the desert were stunning – Nintendo of Arabia. Talking to a plucky embedded correspondent in the field named Ted Koppel as the Third Infantry Division rumbled by in the background, ABC's Peter Jennings called the technology astonishing.

"It was only natural that with this astonishing technology came an unvarnished kind of exuberance. Here was our military – live, just like Jimmy Kimmel – and it appeared not only formidable, but also unmolested. Mr. Koppel would later go up in a high-ranking officer's helicopter, and the steel phalanxes he and his cameraman saw below looked invincible. There were pictures of surrendering Iraqis, too. People started getting carried away. Shortly after talking to his network's embed, Fox News' Shepard Smith hailed the forthcoming "liberation of Kuwait." He said it again, before finally correcting himself."

What drives war reporters?

YES, what of the reporters themselves? Veteran war correspondent Sidney Schanberg, Pulitzer Prize winner for his reporting on the killing fields of Cambodia and later purged from The New York Times for his politics, discusses why so many media people are drawn to war, in this week's Village Voice.

"It is a paradox of war that some people who have lived through its slaughter and madness never lose the itch to go back and live through it again. Some soldiers feel the pull, lured by memories of the intense bonding. Medical professionals and relief workers feel it too, still carrying the images of the wounded they saved and lost. And some reporters also have the craving because war is life's most primal story. I, for one, still hear the siren call.

"One modifying remark: Most people who have survived war have little or no or minus desire to relive the experience. Second, I really can speak only about reporters, for it's the only skin I have.

"Why have I chosen to write about this phenomenon of attraction to war? We journalists so rarely explain ourselves to our audience perhaps in fear of letting you see, heaven forbid, our fallibility that a gulf has widened between the public and us. I thought a little self-examination might help people better understand what they'll be seeing and reading in the days of war ahead.

"First though, you probably already know that a lot of the people reporting on the war have no firsthand experience with it, especially those working from air-conditioned television studios an ocean and continent away from the fighting. Probably they should begin their reports with some kind of ignorance acknowledgment, but no matter, they are harmless if you hit the mute button. Reporters in the war zones are, for the most part, quite different. Some are new at it, as we all were, but they won't be innocent for long. War vastly speeds up the initiation process. Clears the mind of flotsam too. Journalists are already among the allied casualties."

Robot reporters in the wings?

SOON we may be able to dispense with human reporters and replace them with robots (if this is not what we have in no short supply.) The AP reports: "Frustrated by what he considers a dearth of solid news from the Afghan conflict, a Massachusetts Institute of Technology researcher has set about trying to build a roving, multimedia reporter. A remote-controlled robot could help journalists troll for news in the world's hot spots, witnessing battles at close range and even conducting interviews, says Chris Csikszentmihalyi, director of the Computing Culture group at MIT's Media Lab. The invention, modeled on NASA's Mars Explorer, would not only help keep reporters out of the line of fire, but could also help overcome the U.S. military's restrictions on press access, the researcher thinks."

Meanwhile, back in a very White House

WE have embeds all over Iraq, but as I have noted, none with Iraqi families. We also have none really in the White House where, nevertheless, some revealing insights are emerging on the Emperor without clothes. Some revealing moments have now come to light. TIME reports the President's nuanced view of his adversary about whom we are not hearing all that much these days: "Fuck Saddam. We're taking him out," said President George W. Bush in March 2002, after poking his head into the office of National Security Adviser Condoleezza Rice, TIME reports. More recently Knight Ridder reported: "Minutes before the speech, an internal television monitor showed the president pumping his fist. "Feels good," he said. Feels GOOD?

Village Voice columnist Richard Goldstein brilliantly takes us deeper in this morass: "As the first bombs fell on Baghdad, George Bush was getting his hair done. We know this because a rogue technician broke protocol by beaming a candid image from the Oval Office to the BBC. Millions of people around the world saw the president primping and squirming, his eyes darting to and fro, for a minute and a half before his here-comes-the-war address. The White House was up in arms. 'This kind of thing has happened more than once,' fumed a senior aide, vowing that it would never happen again.

"It's evident why Bush's hairspray moment was taken so seriously. The blooper must have played like a clip from America's Funniest Home Videos dropped into the middle of Monday Night Football. Not only did the President seem vain and prissy; he looked uncertain, a real blow to the mastery that the White House is determined to project.

"Not to worry: The American networks never picked up the subversive footage. Nothing was allowed to intrude on the spectacle of bombs falling on Baghdad that unfolded before our eyes last Wednesday night."

Put this warning on your TV set

FINAL note on the media coverage. It can be harmful to YOU, reports The Wall Street Journal. I hope the New York Post columnist, who told readers how "addicted" he has become, reads this:

"Studies show regular television exposure to traumatic events can increase risk for stress and depression and it can even weaken our immune systems. Doctors think excessive war viewing before bedtime can cause stress-induced nighttime snacking and interfere with sleep. Even young children who seem oblivious to events on the screen may suffer ill effects simply as a result of leaving the television on throughout the day.

"If you start watching it at 6 p.m. and the next thing you know it's 8:30 and you feel like you've been on the battlefield, then get away from it," says Joseph C. Piscatella, author of 'Take a Load Off Your Heart'. "Excessive watching of TV during these kinds of events can be a major stressor, and it's just as unhealthy as if you spent 2 1/2 hours at a smorgasbord or never exercised." ●

PERSONALITIES TARGETED AS PROBLEMS EMERGE

ON the 7th day, the Lord rested. But the U.S. military can't catch a break. After a week of triumphant coverage, something is bogging down the hoped-for quickie war.

And it's not just the sandstorms, which make Iraq look like the lunar surface. Some of the coverage is over the moon. It is hard not to feel some compassion for all the media embeds who were telling us how swimmingly everything was going until a real war got in their way. If you had read their clips and watched their coverage, our liberators should have been by now welcomed into the Casbahs by the belly dancers of Baghdad. It was in the plan.

Over and over the "coalition" media has been reporting on the plan, the plan, the plan. You have heard and seen it a million times. "We are on plan . . . The plan is working." But now reality has intruded. The New York Times tells us the plan that could do no wrong is being changed. As every psychologist knows, frustration leads to aggression and now there seems to be more bombing of the "non precise" kind. There were more civilian casualties in the Iraqi capital Wednesday morning. We didn't see them but we were told they were there, and that the people who have yet to stage an uprising are "angry." No kidding.

Howard Kurtz, a mainstream media watcher, at the Washington Post is turning critical of media coverage, as are many analysts around the world. Others, including Kenneth Bacon, former Pentagon media chief, says the media is now the military's biggest asset. "The Wall Street Journal revealed that Tori Clark, the military's media czarina, is modeling her operation on the way she used to run media campaigns.

In some ways, the past was prologue in terms of the coverage we are seeing. Back in 1991, much-quoted Republican strategist Michael Deaver, President Reagan's PR spinner, prefigured Bacon with words to the same effect: "If you were to hire a public relations firm to do the media relations for an international event," he said, "it couldn't be done any better than this is being done" At the time, Democrat Hodding

Carter, who handled media for President Carter, said pretty much the same thing: "If I were the government, I would be paying the press for the coverage it is getting."

That was a decade ago. Since then, many believe the situation has deteriorated despite the new technologies, embedded reporters and proliferation of new 24-hour news networks. Richard Goldstein sees almost a merging of interests in an era of media mergers:

"There's more to the collusion between the networks and the Pentagon than ideology. Both parties have an interest in creating a drama, one that draws viewers into a web of associations, producing thrills, chills, and secret delight. These feelings are heightened by the belief that they convey the real meaning of actual events. The French, those weaselly surrender monkeys, call this confluence of the virtual and the vérité hyper-reality. It's the grand illusion of our time.

"Hyper-reality is a fiction that presents itself as fact. Its power is enhanced by churning Chyrons and rolling ribbons of text. These signifiers of "breaking news" are also a landscape that keeps the eye alert and moving. Meanwhile anchors spin the narrative thread. War wipes the usual smiles from their faces, and they must maintain a tone of reverent gravity however mesmerizing the imagery. But every now and then, a burst from the id lights up the commentary"

Lighting up is what U.S. bombs are doing to Iraqi TV, as many news anchors ask, "Why have we waited so long" to "take out" what they see as a propaganda outlet. Journalists in Arab media outlets feel the same way about U.S. stations and and have begun lecturing their western counterparts on what constitutes "real" journalism. (Significantly the right-wing Fox News Channel in America has appropriated that very phrase, "real journalism" as a branding device. Its competitor MSNBC now runs promos saluting the troops with the slogan, "God Bless America." ●

MARCH 27: "A PREPOSTEROUS FACSIMILE OF JOURNALISM"

FIRST, we were shocked but not always awed, now we are getting bored. As TV news appears more and more routine, on a "loop," as one commentator put it with appropriate sarcasm last night, a tune-out is threatening. TV news is up against the very condition that it has fostered over the years – a short attention span.

Perhaps that's why the three U.S. cable news networks this morning took in the feed of a nicely staged press conference with three wounded soldiers from Germany where they are hospitalized. U.S. revenge against German opposition to the war did not include closing this base. So for over a half hour in what is usually a frenetic and well-formatted dash to offer more news in less time, we heard all the details of how they were shot. Being shot "sucks," said one soldier from Long Island who also revealed that he and his unit watched videotapes of HBO's "Band of Brothers" before their work of liberation. Maybe they should have watched "The Sopranos" for a lesson on unconventional warfare.

Up close and personal

FOX NEWS predictably gushed that they were all "profiles in courage" for defending that bridge the way they did. This is a clue that more human interest up close and personal stories are on the way, as a means of sustaining interest. This is another dip into the Hollywood playbook, in which narrative storytelling calls for strong characters. After the press conference, one of those ever-present military experts beamed with pride. As we now know, there seems to be a great deal more that "sucks" about a war plan that keeps being cited but is rarely explained. Another 30,000 troops are being rushed to the front as 1,000 paratroopers "invade" northern Iraq. (Actually they landed in friendly Kurdish territory.)

The BBC did not indulge the drama of the wounded men, and instead did some hard reporting on the shortage of humanitarian aid and the anger in Iraq with the UN which pulled out its western aid workers before the war and left inadequate staffs to cope with what may be the largest humanitarian crisis in history. While there still do not seem to be reporters "embedded" with the humanitarian teams, perhaps because covering the work of peace is not as sexy as reporting on the sands of war, you could see that horror with that snatch of pictures of desperate people clawing for food and water. BBC's correspondent in Baghdad reported that authorities there say their hospitals are well stocked and that are sending a convoy of food and medicines to the south. Such a caravan is likely to be a target, just as the British ship with food aid has been stopped because of mines in the port.

Media war under scrutiny

THE media war is being escalated too, as Lucien Truscott, the Vietnam war vet and author explained in The New York Times: "From the first moments of the war, television screens and newspaper pages around the world have shown and described it with images of exploding palaces and an armored phalanx rolling rapidly toward Baghdad. Reports from the Third Infantry Division do everything but cite highway mile-markers of their progress. Reporters are embedded so deep into the war that they are subsisting on the same dreadful rations eaten by the troops.

"The Pentagon may have been dragged kicking and screaming into its current embrace of the news media. But it is making the most of it. Planners must have contemplated advances in media technology and decided that if they can't control the press, they may as well use it."

Power worshipping

AND use it they are, as Matt Taibbi explains in this week's New York Press: "The preposterous facsimile of journalism that had marked the months leading up to the war vanished, replaced on every network by a veritable blizzard of video gadgetry and power-worshipping bullshit.

"There were so many video effects that it was sometimes hard to see the actual people who were reading the news. Many of the channels (in particular Fox and MSNBC) adopted a two-box format in which the newsreader occupied a smallish hole on the left side of the screen, while the other side contained a live shot of the subject location (Baghdad, Kuwait City). Surrounding the two boxes: a dizzying array of crawls and logos, which from time to time would morph into cutesy, 3-D-rendered graphics of deadly weapons that would literally fly in from the edge of the screen and then stop to rotate proudly in the middle of the video showroom, like the new car on The Price is Right.

"And meanwhile, every network news set was transformed into a boozy officers' club, with a succession of current and former military guest analysts who lined up to be gently fellated on air."

Producers challenged

ON the air, The New York Times reports that producers are struggling to keep up. Jim Rutenberg and Bill Carter are far less critical than Taibbi and portray the TV journalists as sincere, if challenged: "This up-close-and-personal view of the war, including injuries, captures and casualties along with fierce fighting, has given what broadcasters see is a contradiction of the positive progress reports provided in Pentagon briefings. How, then, can they deliver the news fast (and first) without either under- or over-estimating the challenges at hand? 'The process of trying to get it right is weighing heavily on all of us,' said Steve Capus of NBC Nightly News. 'We want to get it right; we don't want to be spun.' Other correspondents blame the military for failing to provide context for the limited yet astonishing images viewers see."

The totality: Missing

CRITICS, on the other hand, blame the TV networks, which have seemed to have merged with the military. Nancy Franklin writes about this in The New Yorker, a magazine published two blocks away from The New York Times bunker: "The totality of the war is bigger than its frontline details, newsworthy though those details are. That totality is something that the news

organizations have so far given scant attention to. We've seen little coverage of the war's opponents or of the global political ramifications, and even after Friday's strikes there was almost no mention of Iraqi casualties. (On Friday night, CNN did show footage of protests around the world and followed it with a segment called "Decapitation 101.") In the days and weeks to come, reporters will have to try not to become intoxicated by the unprecedented access they have been granted, and the organizations they work for are going to have to try to remember that patriotism has nothing to do with slapping an image of the American flag on the screen alongside their logos, and that freedom of the press is ultimately something that can't be taken away or given by the Pentagon."

BBC chief seeks truth

ARE we at least getting the facts? Not necessarily, says the head of the BBC, according to a report carried by the European Journalism Center: "BBC director of news Richard Sambrook has admitted it is proving difficult for correspondents in Iraq to distinguish the truth from false reports, after a series of media claims about the progress of coalition forces turned out to be premature. Nobody, including the media, has the full picture of what's going on. Reporting the war is about putting together fragments of information. We're all trying to work out this jigsaw and what the overall picture is, Mr. Sambrook said. Sambrook is bringing an honesty to this discussion that we have so far NOT heard from U.S. media executives." (Americans do keep hearing from Pentagon briefers with rare challenges from the press corps..)

Reporting or distorting?

HOW do we evaluate the reports we are getting? Are there others we may not be getting? Like this one: "Sanwa ata Mosahra reporting. A film crew from al-Minar TV, a television network of Lebanon, stumbled across the bodies of about 40 U.S. soldiers scattered in the desert outside Naseriah. Ali Fawsua, a cameraman for al-Minar, said, "It was obvious the soldiers had been in a major battle as there were empty ammunition casing everywhere.

"We searched around but could not find any dead Iraqi soldiers and must be thinking they took their dead and injured away from the battle," he added. "We called on our satellite phone to our base camp and told them what we had found and they told the Americans where we were located.

"Soon some American helicopters came to us and the Americans took all our camera and recording equipment and smashed it. They told us to leave the area and say nothing of this finding. When we arrived back at our base to the south there were American military police everywhere and they destroyed all of our equipment and told us to leave Iraq immediately."

"Al-Minar has lodged a complaint with the IJCO and U.S. with a claim for compensation for the many thousand dollars of destroyed equipment."

I haven't seen this report anywhere. Is it true? We need more dissecting. Yes, I am willing to share the role. We have yet to see anything on TV like what The Guardian is doing to analyze the claims and counter claims of what is actually happening in Iraq. This is an important contribution to journalists. Others can do it. Why don't they? Check this out on The Guardian website, MediaGuardian.co.uk.

Sorting claims and counter-claims

THE feature is called "When are facts, facts? Not in a war," by Chris Tryhorn. "'Fog'" is beginning to be the watchword of this war, with the lines between fact and propaganda being blurred on a daily basis. The demands of round-the-clock news means military claims are being relayed instantly to millions without being confirmed or verified. Only to be refuted later by reporters on the ground or by fresh military updates.

"In due course, questions will be asked about the clashing interests of the military and the media and the role of war propaganda in the pursuit of a swift victory against Saddam's regime.

"The worst example of false claims relates to the battle to take control of Umm Qasr, the southern Iraqi deep-sea port and one of the key targets in the early war. On Sunday afternoon, it had been "taken" nine times. By Sunday night there were still ugly skirmishes between coalition forces and irregulars loyal to Saddam operating out of the old town. Umm Qasr was not, in fact, taken until Tuesday."

Chemical weapons factory: Now you see it, now you don't

"MONDAY, March 24, 1:33 am. Reports surface that U.S. forces find first cache of Saddam's chemical and biological weapons, seizing a suspected chemical factory in An Najaf. This would be a significant PR coup for Messrs Bush and Blair who justified their launch of war on the grounds that Saddam had weapons of mass destruction.

"Fox News and the Jerusalem Post, which had a reporter traveling with U.S. troops, both quote unidentified Pentagon officials who said the facility was seized by U.S. forces. About 30 Iraqi troops and their commanding general surrendered as American forces took the installation, apparently used to produce chemical weapons, according to the Jerusalem Post. It was not immediately clear what chemicals were being produced at the facility. Officials caution it is too premature to conclude that forbidden weapons had been discovered but U.S. central command says it is examining several sites of interest.

"Monday, March 24, 2.42 a.m. General Richard Myers, Chairman of Joint Chiefs of Staff, claims U.S. commandos found documents along with millions of rounds of ammunition on Saturday, saying the discovery "might save thousands of lives if we can find out exactly what they have."

"We're not sure"

MONDAY, March 24, 2.44 p.m. General Tommy Franks, head of the coalition forces, claims he "wasn't entirely sure" that it was a chemical factory after all. Fox News forced to back away from the story. Iraq denies it has chemical or biological weapons. Etc.

White House wants to dominate coverage

EVEN as the administration seems to be getting a free ride, it is planning to step up its PR offensive. Douglas Quenqua reports in PR Week, "The eruption of war in Iraq last week set in motion a massive global PR network, cultivated by the Bush administration during the months-long buildup of forces. The network is intended not only to disseminate, but also to dominate news of the conflict around the world.

"Before the attacks began, Suzy DeFrancis, deputy assistant to President Bush for communications, outlined the daily media relations hand-off that was about to begin. 'When Americans wake up in the morning, they will first hear from the (Persian Gulf) region, maybe from General Tommy Franks,' she said. 'Then later in the day, they'll hear from the Pentagon, then the State Department, then later on the White House will brief.'

"The OGC, an office born out of post-September-11 efforts to combat anti-American news stories emerging from Arab countries, will be key in keeping all U.S. spokespeople on message. Each night, U.S. embassies around the world, along with all federal departments in DC, will receive a 'Global Messenger' email containing talking points and ready-to-use quotes. While an obvious benefit to having communicators spread across time zones is the ability to dominate the 24-hour news cycle."

We are under bombardment

WHAT is the effect of all this? I was struck by a cogent critique on a blog called Dave's Web:

"After immersing myself for several days in the world of cable 'news' – an activity that I usually avoid at all costs – I have come to the conclusion that anyone who can watch this parade of fools and not know that they are being lied to has to be a few Freedom Fries short of a Happy Meal.

"A pattern to the coverage of the Iraq war is ridiculously easy to discern: first, a recklessly transparent lie is told; then, it is repeated endlessly by a stable of resident 'experts,' apparently in an attempt to bolster its credibility; this continues until the initial claim is irrefutably revealed as a lie; at which time another layer of spin and lies is added, with no acknowledgment that the initial claim was entirely fraudulent; with the new lies in place, the process begins again."

FAIR demands verification

AND as it does, FAIR has been analyzing its content. It looks at the claims of surgical precision weapons in one analysis at Fair.org. (Interesting in light of the climbing death toll from the bombing of a market in Baghdad, which the NY Post says the Pentagon suspects was planted by the Iraqis. The government there claims 400 dead and 4,000 casualties."

Writes FAIR: "The Pentagon can be expected to claim that its bombing campaign against Iraq is accurate. But without independent verification, reporters should be skeptical about these claims about 'precision' bombing.

"Recent reports on NBC News illustrate the opposite tendency. Correspondent Bob Faw (3/20/03) described a Florida town as 'a community, which very much endorses that surgical strike against Saddam Hussein.'

"Anchor Katie Couric (3/21/03) also referred to 'a series of surgical strikes focusing on Iraq's key leadership' during the first two nights of bombing. Anchor Matt Lauer (3/21/03) agreed: 'The people in that city have endured two nights of surgical air strikes and they've no idea what could come tonight.'

"Pentagon correspondent Jim Miklaszewski (3/21/03) took it a step further, reporting that 'every weapon is precision guided – deadly accu-racy designed to kill only the targets, not innocent civilians.' On the Today show the next morning (3/22/03), Miklaszewski reiterated his point: 'More than a thousand bombs and missiles were dropped on Baghdad, three times the number from the entire Gulf War. And this time, they're all precision-guided, deadly accurate, designed to kill only the targets, not innocent civilians.'

"That same day, reporter Chris Jansing sized up 'the first daylight pictures of severe damage from yesterday's massive and incredibly precise air assault on the Iraqi capital.' But on-the-ground reports from the scene of the bombings would be necessary before making any definitive claims about "surgical strikes.""

From media suite to protest in the streets

WHILE I am up here in my "suite." protesters are out in the streets, just a block away, at Rockefeller Center, home of NBC and parent company GE. Propelled by the slogan "NO BUSINESS AS USUAL," an ad-hoc coalition of anti-war groups is planning massive civil disobedience tomorrow March 27, at 8 a.m. in and around Rockefeller Center. "We target corporate war profiteers and the media/corporate/government collusion that is promoting this war." Note to protesters: Media outlets are being advised that covering protest is bad for business. I kid you not. Harry Jessell writes in Broadcasting and Cable:

"Covering war protesters may be bad for business. That's among the findings of new research from Frank N. Magid Associates, the influential news consulting firm. In a survey of 6,400 viewers on their attitudes regarding Iraq and the media, the news-consulting firm found that the viewers had little interest in anti-war protests. Magid doesn't tell news directors to avoid protests. It just says viewers tend to hate seeing them. "Obviously, you have to give both sides of the story," says Senior Vice President Brian Greif. "But how much time you devote to [protests] and where you place it in your newscast becomes an issue." ●

MARCH 27: WHAT IS THE "VALUE PROPOSITION?"

WHAT is real? What isn't ? When is telling actually selling? Watch the TV coverage of this human disaster in the desert and tell me. The complaints about managed media coverage seem to have started trickling back into media-land. MSNBC, which can, in a nano-second, go live to Doha, can't seem to capture the same immediacy in the streets of New York where anti-war (and increasingly anti-media) protests continued this morning with more arrests.

NBC's Andrea Mitchell was, for the first time that I have seen last night, acknowledging that there is a legitimate dispute about the reliability of the coverage and its impact. Nic Robertson of CNN, reporting now from Jordan also acknowledged that journalists from other countries view developments differently than our merry band of Embeds.

The pulse of propaganda

THE propa-news reached a new low this morning with NBC's Bob Arnot salting the troops by say-

ing they are so much more motivated, brave and patriotic than the actors who play soldiers in the movies. It was almost as bad as a Fox TV special, The Pulse, featuring Bill O'Reilly. It airs on cable and on Fox News savaging Saddam's son with so much rhetorical overkill and bad music that it looked like a World War II propaganda film hatched in Dr. Goebbel's ministry of misinformation. (The word "rape" must have been cited a thousand times, just in case you missed it the first 999 times. When will O'Reilly do a similar trash job on the U.S. Air Force Academy – at which there has been testimony that virtually every female student has been raped?)

After an hour of news that seemed as if it was coming straight out of official military briefings, including detailed descriptions of humongous bunker buster bombs that left a mushroom cloud over Baghdad, no attempt was made to explain WHY these bombs were necessary, or what their impacts were.

Listen to Robert Fisk of The Independent on the bombing of that market in Baghdad that the U.S. government is implying was caused by Iraqi defense missiles. Ask yourself why we never hear anything approaching this angry tone in U.S. journalism.

Outrage journalism

"IT was an outrage, an obscenity. The severed hand on the metal door, the swamp of blood and mud across the road, the human brains inside a garage, the incinerated, skeletal remains of an Iraqi mother and her three small children in their still-smoldering car.

"Two missiles from an American jet killed them all by my estimate, more than 20 Iraqi civilians, torn to pieces before they could be 'liberated' by the nation that destroyed their lives. Who dares, I ask myself, to call this 'collateral damage'? Abu Taleb Street was packed with pedestrians and motorists when the American pilot approached through the dense sandstorm that covered northern Baghdad in a cloak of red and yellow dust and rain yesterday morning.

"We may put on the hair shirt of morality in explaining why these people should die. They died because of 11 September, we may say, because of President Saddam's weapons of mass destruction, because of human rights abuses, because of our desperate desire to liberate them all. Let us not confuse the issue with oil. Either way, I'll bet we are told President Saddam is ultimately responsible for their deaths. We shan't mention the pilot.

"Are we seeing the death and destruction? Word of it is rarely heard at the briefings that get wall-to-wall coverage with all the talk of how we are 'on plan.'

Briefing-based journalism is a joke. Tomdispatch.com explains why: "Let's start with a touch of irony. For thirty years, the men (and lone woman) now running our country have also been running away from Vietnam. In this war, it only took six days for Vietnam to catch up to them. Last night, for instance, here's what I noticed on the CBS and ABC national news, followed by the Jim Lehrer NewsHour. CBS led off with word that the U.S. military in Iraq, where all was going according to plan and on schedule, had nonetheless called for reinforcements from the States to guard exposed supply lines and 700 soldiers from an armored unit were being shipped out immediately.

"As the Vietnam War went on, of course, the military was always offering public reassurances about how splendidly things were going and then asking the President for more men. (DS: the latest is that another 100,000 are being flown in. All according to plan, of course.) PBS also aired clips of the daily Centcom briefing in Qatar. The uniformed briefer seemed distinctly on the defensive! A Canadian reporter was shown complaining that the military never displayed videos of missiles that missed their targets or hit wrong targets and demanded to know when some would be available.

"Then, to my surprise, a CBS correspondent rose to complain fairly vehemently that, while "embedded" reporters were offering many tiny pictures, the "big picture" was supposed to come from Centcom; instead, he commented, all that was being offered were videos of micro-air strikes. In fact, all the Pentagon news conferences of the day managed to look both ridiculous and untrustworthy as spokesmen tried to pin the blame for civilian casualties from the missile-in-the-Baghdad-market on the Iraqis."

Why are we here?

I WAS struck by a question that was raised at yesterday's CENTCOM briefing, which focused on what is happening in the "theater," a great word that explains why we are seeing so many performances. Michael Wolff of New York magazine had the chutzpah to get up and challenge the whole ritual by asking about its value proposition. "Why are we even here, in this million dollar media center?" was his question. It seemed to piss off the briefer because it was a bit pissy, even though he offered it "with respect." Wolff is not a journalist to be messed with.

In many ways the corridor correspondents of

Kuwait are practicing stenography rather than journalism. This mecca of media management also offered up images of some happy kids welcoming the troops and referenced the presence of 500 "Free Iraqi" soldiers who are assigned to civil affairs units, not combat ones. (i.e. talking rather than shooting their way into Iraq.)

RE: The bombing of TV stations

EARLIER, my sometime-bud, Michael Massing popped up to challenge the bombing of the Iraqi TV station, which is prohibited by the Geneva Conventions. We were then told that the bombing was not against the TV station, even though that is how it was described by all the U.S. networks, but against some 'command and control' facility hidden there in some undescribed 'node.' Reader Jackie Newberry, has a point about this: "It is my understanding that bombing a TV station, even though it is state controlled, is against the Geneva conventions. It is still a civilian installation. I heard from sources other than major media that civilians inside the station were killed and injured. That has not been reported here.

"Tonight the U.S. dropped a huge bomb on the information ministry in Baghdad. Despite the reassurance that bombing is precision and surgical, I have heard a number of non-major media reports that there are a number of civilian casualties. All of this bears investigation by the press. I want to know the truth."

Take-out squad

IT is not just the absence of facts that is distressing. It is the gleeful way the news of the destruction of a TV station was treated by U.S. TV sta-

tions. (On Fox this morning, there was a wink and a nod discussion by the morning zoo team about how U.S. programming is likely to be beamed in soon via the hi-tech SOLO aircraft that broadcasts from the sky). That is already happening in Basra, according to this report in The Guardian: "British forces have taken Iraqi state radio and television off the air in Basra, according to unconfirmed reports from the BBC's correspondent in southern Iraq. The report, published today on the BBC's website, claimed transmitters in Basra were destroyed in overnight air raids and coalition forces have taken over a number of radio frequencies. The allied military is now broadcasting its own messages to the people of Basra, effectively isolating Basra from any communication with Baghdad."

The media watchers of FAIR (Fairness and Accuracy in Media) are denouncing the reporting of the bombing of TV and radio stations: "When Iraqi TV offices in Baghdad were hit by a U.S. missile strike on March 25, the targeting of media was strongly criticized by press and human rights groups. The general secretary of the International Federation of Journalists, Aidan White, suggested that, 'there should be a clear international investigation into whether or not this bombing violates the Geneva Conventions.' White told Reuters (3/26/03), "Once again, we see military and political commanders from the democratic world targeting a television network simply because they don't like the message it gives out.'"

The Geneva Conventions forbid the targeting of civilian installations – whether state-owned or not – unless they are being used for military purposes. Amnesty International warned (3/26/03) that the attack may have been a "war crime" and emphasized that bombing a television station "simply because it is being used for the purposes of propaganda" is illegal under international humanitarian law. "The onus," said Amnesty, is on "coalition forces" to prove "the military use of the TV station and, if that is indeed the case, to show that the attack took into account the risk to civilian lives."

Likewise, Human Rights Watch affirmed (3/26/03) that it would be illegal to target Iraqi TV based on its propaganda value. "Although stopping enemy propaganda may serve to demoralize the Iraqi population and to undermine the government's political support," said HRW, "neither purpose offers the 'concrete and direct' military advantage necessary under international law to make civilian broadcast facilities a legitimate military target."

Some U.S. journalists, however, have not shown much concern about the targeting of Iraqi journalists. Prior to the bombing, some even seemed anxious to know why the broadcast facilities hadn't been attacked yet. Fox News Channel's John Gibson wondered (3/24/03): "Should we take Iraqi TV off the air? Should we put one down the stove pipe there?" Fox's Bill O'Reilly (3/24/03) agreed: "I think they should have taken out the television, the Iraqi television...Why haven't they taken out the Iraqi television towers?"

MSNBC correspondent David Shuster offered: "A lot of questions about why state-run television is allowed to continue broadcasting. After all, the coalition forces know where those broadcast towers are located." On CNBC, Forrest Sawyer offered tactical alternatives to bombing (3/24/03): "There are operatives in there. You could go in with sabotage, take out the building, you could take out the tower."

They call it intelligence

NEVER mind thinking about how these tough guys in the "take out" squad would feel if, god forbid, Iraq had the capacity to "take out" their pulpits? What is worse than the showboating and macho messaging is the lack of real perspective on the war itself. It seems as if U.S. intelligence was anything but, just as intelligence on the air is so often missing. Even Murdoch's London Times realizes that the neocons who have been pumping a war for years before Bush was elected, got it wrong. Richard Beeston and Tom Baldwin report:

"British and American intelligence badly miscalculated the level of resistance that coalition forces would encounter in Iraq, with analysts predicting that troops would reach Baghdad in days and defeat President Saddam Hussein in a matter of weeks. As thousands more U.S. soldiers began deploying in the Gulf for what could be a campaign lasting months, there were growing questions in London and Washington over the failure to anticipate the stubborn resistance being encountered.

"At the start of the war, British military officers were confident that the southern city of Basra would fall quickly, that the Shia Muslims in the south would rise up against Saddam and that there would be token resistance on the road to Baghdad. 'The intelligence assessment seriously underestimated what to expect,' one Whitehall source, who briefed Downing Street on the dangers before the war, said. His advice was largely ignored, even though Saddam was openly making careful preparations to defend himself. He armed and trained irregular forces, bribed tribal leaders and used propaganda to portray the looming war as an attempt by America to conquer the country and steal its oil."

This is the old garbage-in-garbage-out problem. The war game exercises that prepared the troops were also fake-outs, as Julian Borger reported last August in The Guardian:

"The biggest war game in U.S. military history, staged this month at a cost of £165m with 13,000 troops, was rigged to ensure that the Americans beat their 'Middle Eastern' adversaries, according to one of the main participants. General Paul Van Riper, a retired marine lieutenant general, told the Army Times that the sprawling three-week millennium challenge exercises, were 'almost entirely scripted to ensure a [U.S.] victory.'"

Embedded sales force

THE embedding-of-journalist policy is also helping the 'coalition' sell the war. The Guardian reports today that "the defense secretary, Geoff Hoon, has claimed a PR victory over the war in Iraq, saying the practice of "embedding" journalists with troops has helped turn around public opinion. Mr. Hoon said TV images from journalists accompanying the British troops were "at least partially responsible, for the swing in public opinion in favor of the war."

Does this policy lead us closer to the truth, despite the glitzy footage that gives the war so much immediacy on TV? Even neocons Cookie Roberts and husband Steve Roberts see a potential problem, stating:

"This is a war for truth," insists Pentagon spokesman Bryan Whitman. "The goal is to have accurate, truthful reporting from the battlefield." We agree. But that means the bad news along with the good, the victims as well as the victories. As ABC's Ted Koppel put it: "I feel we do have an obligation to remind people in the most graphic way that war is a dreadful thing. Young Americans are dying. Young Iraqis are dying. To sanitize it too much is a dreadful mistake."

The contrast is breath-taking

EMBEDDING does lead to many dreadful mistakes, as we hear some reporters recycling military lingo like "the enemy." Here's a report on how Martin Savidge, a CNN- embed, covered one battle and then how the same confrontation was reported in The Age, a newspaper in Australia. First CNN:

"There is a lookout there, a hill referred to as Safwan Hill, on the Iraqi side of the border. It was filled with Iraqi intelligence gathering. From that vantage point, they could look out over all of northern Kuwait.

"It is now estimated the hill was hit so badly by missiles, artillery and by the Air Force, that they shaved a couple of feet off it. And anything that was up there that was left after all the explosions was then hit with napalm. And that pretty much put an end to any Iraqi operations up on that hill."

The focus, as you can see, is on how the military saw it. Here's The Australian newspaper:

"About six hours after marines and their 155-millimeter howitzers pulled up at the border, they opened fire. Safwan Hill went up in a huge fireball and the Iraqi observation post was obliterated."

"I pity anybody who's in there, a marine sergeant said. We told them to surrender."

"The destruction of Safwan Hill was a priority for the attacking forces because it had sophisticated surveillance equipment and is near the main highway that runs from Kuwait to Basra and Baghdad. U.S. and British forces could not attempt to cross the border unless it was destroyed."

"Marine Cobra helicopter gunships firing Hellfire missiles then swept in low from the south."

'Over the next eight hours, the marines opened fire with their howitzers, which have a range of 30 kilometers. They were supported by U.S. Navy aircraft, which dropped napalm."

"The Pentagon has since denied that napalm was used in the attack. A navy spokesman in Washington, Lieutenant Commander Danny Hernandez, denied that napalm – which was banned by a United Nations convention in 1980 - was used."

Embed ex-bedded

ONE of the CNN embeds has been tossed out of Iraq and CNN is pissed. The Christian Science Monitor reports, "Philip Smucker, a contract reporter for the Monitor and The Daily Telegraph of London, was escorted by the U.S. Marines from the front lines of the war in Iraq Thursday. He is being taken to Kuwait, the Pentagon says, because of information Smucker reported in a broadcast appearance with CNN early Wednesday.

"My understanding of the facts at this point from the commander on the ground is that this reporter was reporting, in real time, positions, locations, and activities of units engaged in combat," says Bryan Whitman, deputy assistant secretary of defense for public affairs. "The commander felt it was necessary and appropriate to remove [Smucker] from his immediate battle space in order not to compromise his mission or endanger personnel of his unit."

"Smucker's work in the Monitor is not at issue, but we have read the transcript of the CNN interview and it does not appear to us that he disclosed anything that wasn't already widely available in maps and in U.S. and British radio, newspaper, and television reports in that same news cycle. Of course, the Pentagon has the final say in the field about any threat the information reported might pose."

The skewering of Safire

TOMPAINE.COM features a piece by former CBS 60 Minutes producer Barry Lando vivisecting a recent column by William Safire of The New York Times:

"'France, China and Syria all have a common reason for keeping American and British troops out of Iraq: the three nations may not want the world to discover that their nationals have been illicitly supplying Saddam Hussein with materials used in building long-range surface-to surface missiles.'

'That was the lead of William Safire's recent two part series 'The French Connection' in The New York Times, reprinted in the International Herald Tribune. With the Times' august imprimatur, Safire's charges have been relayed around the globe, in newspapers, magazines and Web sites, fueling the rising storm of outrage against the French.

"But Safire's double broadside is more Francophobia than fact. He is way off-beam; his articles are filled with error and innuendo. What makes matters worse is that editors at both The New York Times and the International Herald Tribune knew there were serious questions about Safire's charges, yet the papers went ahead and published the second part of his series." Lando shows the many errors. See Tompaine.com.

Why we know what we do

THE ultimate test of the coverage is: Is it making us more informed. Editor and Publisher reports the opposite is occurring:

"Somehow, despite the U.S. media's exhaustive Iraq coverage, a very large segment of the American public remained under-informed about key issues related to the Iraqi crisis. In a January poll, 44 percent of respondents said they thought most or some of the September 11, 2001, hijackers were Iraqi citizens. Only 17 percent of those polled offered the correct answer: none. This was remarkable in light of the fact that, in the weeks after the terrorist attacks, few Americans identified Iraqis among the culprits. So the level of awareness on this issue actually decreased as time passed. In the same sample, 41 percent said that Iraq already possessed nuclear weapons, which not even the Bush administration claimed. Despite being far off base in crucial areas, 66 percent of respondents claimed to have a good understanding of the arguments for and against going to war with Iraq."   •

MEDIA SHAKEDOWN AND BREAKDOWN

THERE is a media shakedown underway that may portend a media breakdown as the media war begins to veer "off plan."

While critics on the left can't fulminate enough about the use of media outlets as echo chambers for Pentagon spin-meisters, the administration has been smug and secure with its million-dollar media center in Doha and legion of embedded journalists staying on message.

But now that there are bumps in the road, with more reported casualties and atrocities, new strains are emerging in what has been a military-media mutual appreciation society until now.

First, there have been high profile media casualties that have sparked new controversies where few existed in the past. The right-wing Fox News began to bait MSNBC's Peter Arnett as a traitor. Arnett, apparently unaware of the minefield he was navigating, then appeared on Iraqi TV, saying pretty much what other have been saying about U.S. military strategy across the spectrum. He was axed for being on the wrong venue.

The minions at Murdochville didn't have time to do much gloating because they had their own tempest in this nasty teapot. Star reporter Geraldo Rivera, who vowed to march triumphantly into Baghdad, has had to turn tail and slither out of the appropriately named war "theater." His crime, according to the Pentagon – revealing troop locations. His future among the war boosters at the Fox News Channel is uncertain.

Next, the high command began to lob some shells at the TV generals who had been masterfully offering pro-war analysis and doing more reporting than most of the war reporters. The regiment was skewered by the man at the top, as the New York Post reported in a piece dramatically titled "Fists of Fury." He didn't like what many have been saying.

"An angry Joint Chiefs Chairman Gen. Richard

Myers yesterday blasted critics of the Iraq war plan, charging they are spreading 'bogus' information that is 'not helpful' at a time when U.S. troops are in combat.

"In an astonishing display of emotion at the Pentagon news briefing, the normally reserved Air Force general delivered an impassioned response to the barrage of media reports of internecine warfare at the Pentagon over whether there are enough troops on the ground in Iraq.

"Myers, who didn't name names, said the high-profile carping that's produced a media feeding frenzy may be 'good sport inside the Beltway,' but it is 'not helpful. . .'"

With military problems emerging and political frustration surfacing in a White House whose chief executive is reportedly glued to the tube, the Pentagon is tightening control over its embedded journalists while doing its best to freeze out reporters operating outside the system.

PR Week reports that military spinners are also being embedded to keep their eyes on the spin-ees. "They may not get as much attention as their media counterparts, but dozens of Pentagon public affairs officers are 'embedded' right alongside the reporters in Iraq," PR Week reports. "The Pentagon also maintains the Coalition Press Information Center (CPIC) in Kuwait, a base of operations for public affairs officers not traveling with troops. A 24-hour operation designed to keep up with news cycles in every time zone . . . one of the CPIC's most vital roles is to discourage 'rogue' journalists from venturing into dangerous areas by providing the information they might otherwise attempt to get on their own."

A revolt against these briefers is beginning to find expression too, Michael Wolff of New York magazine, who says he embedded himself at the Press Center in Doha, is disgusted with the quality of information he's been bombarded with.

"It takes about 48 hours to understand that information is probably more freely available at any other place in the world than it is here. Eventually you realize that you know significantly less than when you arrived, and that you are losing more sense of the larger picture by the hour. At some point you will know nothing.

"This may be the plan, of course. There are two kinds of forward reporters: the official embeds with units on the ground in Iraq, who know only the details of the action they see, and those posted to military press centers in Kuwait or Qatar (as close to Franks, the presumptive conqueror of Baghdad, as it's possible to get), who know only what they are told.

"Which happens to be nothing much at all"

These are just the first signs of a polarization and a new fault line in the media war – dissent inside the media and more protest against some media outlets.

Protesters confronted Fox News in New York. Richard Cowen reported on what happened in a story carried on Common Dreams.org. One message reads:

"The news ticker rimming Fox's headquarters on Sixth Avenue wasn't carrying war updates as the protest began. Instead, it poked fun at the demonstrators, chiding them. "War protester auditions here today . . . thanks for coming!" "Who won your right to show up here today?" another questioned. "Protesters or soldiers? Said a third: "How do you keep a war protester in suspense? Ignore them."

It is not doubtful that the protests over the

media and in the media can be ignored much longer. ●

MARCH 31: ONWARD, CHRISTIAN SOLDIERS

ANYONE remember that anthem about praising the lord and passing the ammunition? As Muslims praise their most Merciful and Beneficent God, "whom we forever thank," American soldiers are being advised to praise HE who praises the most holy every time we see Him, to the tune of "Onward, Christian Soldiers." In fact, yesterday was "pray for the President day" in Iraq, a fact I saw reported on nowhere on TV.

ABC is reporting on its web site that "U.S. soldiers in Iraq are being asked to pray for President George W. Bush. Thousands of marines have been given a pamphlet called "A Christian's Duty," a mini-prayer book which includes a tear-out section to be mailed to the White House pledging the soldier who sends it in has been praying for Bush.

In touch

"I HAVE committed to pray for you, your family, your staff and our troops during this time of uncertainty and tumult. May God's peace be your guide," says the pledge, according to a journalist embedded with coalition forces. The pamphlet, produced by a group called In Touch Ministries, offers a daily prayer to be made for the U.S. President, a born-again Christian who likes to invoke his God in speeches.

I'll bet Christian Broadcasting is heavily reporting on this angle of the story. Actually, The New York Times did mention yesterday that the war itself was hatched with evangelic passion. The foregone decision to go to war was made in a formal way, by a President conscious of the history of the moment, in the Situation Room on the morning of March 19. With his closest advisers surrounding him, Mr. Bush spoke to Gen. Franks and the other commanders in the field by videoconference and asked each if they had everything they needed to win. Then the president gave the order, an administration official said, concluding with, "May God bless the troops."

"May God bless America," Gen. Franks replied, as Mr. Powell, the chairman of the joint chiefs during the first Gulf War, reached out and lightly touched the President's hand, said a senior administration official who recounted the scene, "because he's been on the battlefield before."

Hersh roasts Rummy

THAT battlefield remains contested, with U.S. TV focusing on the debate over whether more troops are needed, while the administration regurgitates the mantra that we are on plan. How far we have come from the days of Vietnam when the press challenged the escalation of troop levels. Now the armchair generals on the Sunday talk shows call for more, more and more. Seymour Hersh says that the problem is not with the warriors but with their boss, the Don of Defense, Mr. Rumsfeld.

He writes: "As the ground campaign against Saddam Hussein faltered last week, with attenuated supply lines and a lack of immediate reinforcements, there was anger in the Pentagon. Several senior war planners complained to me in interviews that Secretary of Defense Donald Rumsfeld and his inner circle of civilian advisers, who had been chiefly responsible for persuading President Bush to lead the country into war, had insisted on micromanaging the war's operational details. Rumsfeld's team took over crucial aspects of the day-to-day logistical planning traditionally, an area in which the uniformed military excels and Rumsfeld repeatedly overruled the senior Pentagon planners on the Joint Staff, the operating arm of the Joint Chiefs of Staff. "He thought he knew better,' one senior planner said. 'He was the decision-maker at every turn.'"

Al-Jazeera roasts U.S. media

GEORGE STEPHANOPOLOUS has raised Hersh's point with Rumsfeld on ABC's This Week, which seems even more hawkish than its competitors this week. Rumsfeld denied it, and that was that. No follow-up. And so it goes, as TV shifted to more pictures of Baghdad burning and the light show resulting from a stepped-up bombing campaign. Commentators prattled on about how the Ministry of Information was under assault, and that Iraqi TV had been taken off the air. Imagine my surprise then to click on CNN this morning to see none other than Iraqi Foreign Minister Sabri holding forth from the Ministry of Information, claiming that the foreign invaders were being defeated. An earlier report on the "most trusted" TV news net showed that what you saw depended on where you lived and which TV stations you relied on. The Arab World is watching Al-Jazeera.

And Al-Jazeera,whose website is back in action, says it's doing a better job than its western counterparts. Faisal Bodi offers the station's rationale in The Guardian: "I do not mean to brag – people are turning to us simply because the western media coverage has been so poor. For although Doha is just a 15-minute drive from central command, the view of events from here could not be more different. Of all the major global networks, Al-Jazeera has been alone in proceeding from the premise that this war should be viewed as an illegal enterprise. It has broadcast the horror of the bombing campaign, the blown-out brains, the blood-spattered pavements, the screaming infants and the corpses. Its team of on-the-ground, unembedded correspondents has provided a corrective to the official line that the campaign is, barring occasional resistance, going to plan.

"Last Tuesday, while western channels were celebrating a Basra 'uprising' which none of them could have witnessed since they don't have reporters in the city, our correspondent in the Sheraton there returned a rather flat verdict of 'uneventful' – a view confirmed shortly afterwards by a spokesman for the opposition Supreme Council for the Islamic Revolution in Iraq. By reporting propaganda as fact, the mainstream media had simply mirrored the Blair/Bush fantasy that the people who have been starved by U.N. sanctions and deformed by depleted uranium since 1991 will greet them as saviors."

Peter Arnett back on the hot seat

AS the Arab media challenges western media, some in the western media are targeting one of their own. The New York Post, part of the Murdoch media empire (owners of Fox News) now has Peter Arnett to kick around some more. Arnett, who was the right's favorite target during

Gulf War I for merely reporting from Baghdad, has aroused their ire again for saying U.S. war planners have misjudged the situation, and for thanking Iraqi officials for "the degree of freedom" that U.S. journalists enjoyed. Arnett has now rejoined their axis of evil.

While the NY Post trashed him today, yesterday The New York Times wrote about him sympathetically. Frank Rich quoted him: "It's déjà vu all over again, the idea that this would be a walkover, the idea that the people of Basra would throw flowers at the Marines," he said from Baghdad when I spoke with him by phone last week. Unlike many of his peers, he had been there to see the early burst of optimism in Persian Gulf War I, which he covered for CNN. "This is going to be tough," he said just before it became tough. "When I interviewed Tariq Aziz two weeks ago, it was not put on the network, he said: "You'll have a hard time tearing us down. We're ready to be martyrs. Whatever you think about Saddam Hussein, there is a sense of nationalism here. The Iraqis like American culture and American movies and pop songs. But are they really going to like American tanks?"

For sentiments like this, Arnett is likely to be targeted even more. The Guardian predicted that his comments "are likely to make Arnett a renewed target of Republican lawmakers, many of whom already contend that his reporting is slanted in favor of the Iraqis."

"Nauseating"

IRAQI TV showed the interview at least twice on Sunday afternoon. CNN and Fox News Channel showed excerpts of it last night. Republican Ileana Ros-Lehtinen told Fox News Channel she found the interview "nauseating." She added, "It's incredible he would be kow-towing to what clearly is the enemy in this way." So far, MNBC is sticking with their free lancer.

As for Fox News, I just loved watching convicted perjurer, Ollie North, reporting for Fox from the field. The man who lied to Congress, who sold arranged arms to Iran during the bad old days of Iran Contra, is a correspondent in the field. Fox anchors referred to him reverentially as "Colonel" and "Sir."

Wolff shows no mercy

LAST week I reported on the question raised at the CENTCOM briefing in Doha by New York magazine media columnist Michael Wolff who asked briefer General Brooks why anyone should even go to these briefings. Now Wolff has written about his experiences. The Guardian picked up his report, which will probably also appear in New York, although they don't say so. Wolff calls himself an embed:

"I have embedded myself in the million-dollar press center at General Tommy Franks' central command (CentCom) forward headquarters in Doha, Qatar. Camp as-Sayliya, where the press center is safely stowed, is far enough from the center of Doha that you get a clear and eerie sense of what Qatar was like before it became oil rich and development-happy two generations ago.

"It's pure moonscape. Not a tree, not a bush. Hardly a structure. Just a horizon of flat limestone. And then you come upon the U.S. base – really just a ring of wire and then a no man's land behind which there is the base.

"It takes about 48 hours to understand that

information is probably more freely available at any other place in the world than it is here. Eventually you realize that you know significantly less than when you arrived, and that you are losing more sense of the larger picture by the hour. At some point you will know nothing.

"This may be the plan, of course. There are two kinds of forward reporters: the official embeds with units on the ground in Iraq, who know only the details of the action they see, and those posted to military press centers in Kuwait or Qatar (as close to Franks, the presumptive conqueror of Baghdad, as it's possible to get), who know only what they are told.

"Which happens to be nothing much at all."

Reality is too unsettling

CRITICISM of U.S. coverage is not restricted to the Arab World or the contrarian worldview of Michael Wolff. Roger Franklin writes in The Age in Australia that "America sees no evil."

"What we're seeing in the U.S. are network anchors posing heroically in ruggedly tailored camouflage fatigues as legions of lesser reporters peer over sand dunes to catch the whump of artillery with the microphones of their satellite-phone cameras. That and the Pentagon's greatest hits, each clip featuring a tank or building vanishing in a spout of grainy flame beneath the bombsight's crosshairs.

"The hard stuff – the stone-cold close-ups of the reaper's latest recruits – well, as a talking head on CNN said only the other night, those images are just 'too unsettling for public consumption.' Yes, we viewers get the wide-eyed kids in their hospital bandages and briefly, every now and then, the roadside piles of slumped and crumpled uniforms that contain what once were Saddam's soldiers.

"But those casualties are our side's doing, so that's OK. On the non-commercial PBS network, the closest America gets to a government network, the clips are apt to be followed by sober, serious chats with experts from institutes or think tanks, the talking heads who offer a soundbite or two about the mood in the Arab street or the difficulties of moving a mechanized column through a hostile desert. It's fine, so far as the coverage goes. But sadly, given that death is what war is all about, that isn't very far at all."

Media debate heats up

THE debate over media coverage is now joined at the hip to the debate over the war. Allessandra Stanley reports in The New York Times: "As the conflict in Iraq deepens, so has the debate about television coverage. Secretary of Defense Donald H. Rumsfeld complained on Friday that 'media mood swings' were distorting the depiction of American military strategy. Actually, the movement was less up and down than across the ideological spectrum.

"In the initial phase, the loudest complaints about bias were lodged by anti-war groups frustrated that television gave scant attention to their protests. As casualties mounted, so did conservatives' laments about a liberal bias at the networks. Fox News led the charge. Bill O'Reilly, the network's most popular commentator and most fervent France basher, described the ABC News anchor, Peter Jennings, as an 'internationalist,' which he defined as someone 'who puts foreign countries on the same plane as the United States in the war on terror.'

"On the left, antiwar activists argued that the consolidation of media ownership by corporate giants has led to a 'foxification' of American news shows."

At least the media role in all of this is finally being scrutinized even as Times reporters follow their 'on the one hand, on the other,' middle of the road coverage pattern, which appears neutral, but rarely is.

Media watching – glossary update

IT is not just the images, or the lack of them, that define the coverage. It is also the language. May we praise The Guardian as well for updating our growing glossary of deadening war terminology such as: "Speed bump – Anything that slows down the progress of war – including skirmishes. The resistance at Basra and the protracted resistance at Umm Qasr were nasty speed bumps.

"Effects-based warfare – A nuanced approach to war, combining strategic firepower ('graduated destruction') and psychological operations (or "psyops") – such as leaflet dropping and interfering with TV or radio broadcasts. Some Iraqi commanders have even made 'capitulation agreements' already. The effects-based approach is backed up by the provision of humanitarian aid to create a 'benign campaign.'

"Digital battlefield – The U.S. Army's 4th division is equipped with command and control systems that allow tank movements to be monitored on computers, seen as a first step towards a 'digital battlefield' that involves 'total situational awareness,' i.e., everyone can tell where everyone else is. The idea is to dispel the 'fog of war' that leads to deaths from 'friendly fire.'

"Hammer time – A U.S. admiral was shown invoking the spirit of 90s Christian rapper MC Hammer – albums include 'Let's Get It Started' and 'Please Hammer, Don't Hurt 'Em' – when he declared to his fist-pumping troops that 'hammer time was upon us."

Dissector addendum: Before Gulf War 1, the real Hammer participated in the remake of the song "Give Peace A Chance." The song was suppressed, and Hammer's career was later hammered. Now he's singing in support of the troops. ●

WAR AS ONE BIG JOKE

GEN. BUZZ MOSELEY of Texas, commander of coalition air forces, on retired military critics of 'the plan,' "None of them had seen it, he said, or digested all the considerations that went into its choreography. Their criticism was like "listening to a cow pee on a flat rock."

LAURA INGRAM (on Imus): "Hans Blix couldn't find a stretch-mark on Rosie O'Donnell."

JAY LENO: "War continues in Iraq. They're calling it Operation Iraqi Freedom. They were going to call it Operation Iraqi Liberation until they realized that spells 'OIL.'"

JON STEWART (Comedy Channel) "Yesterday, the president met with a group he calls the coalition of the willing. Or, as the rest of the world calls them, Britain and Spain."

CRAIG KILBORN: "President Bush spent last night calling world leaders to support the war with Iraq — it is sad when the most powerful man on earth is yelling, 'I know you're there, pick up, pick up.'"

JAY LENO: "President Bush spent the day calling names he couldn't pronounce in countries he never knew existed."

DAVID LETTERMAN: "President Bush has said that he does not need approval from the UN to wage war, and I'm thinking, well, hell, he didn't need the approval of the American voters to become president, either."

JAY LENO: "In a speech earlier today President Bush said if Iraq gets rid of Saddam Hussein, he will help the Iraqi people with food, medicine, supplies, housing, and education, anything that's needed. Isn't that amazing? He finally comes up with a domestic agenda and it's for Iraq. Maybe we could bring that here if it works out." ●

CHAPTER SIX

SURROUNDING BAGHDAD

INVADERS FACE SANDSTORMS, BUGS AND CITIZEN SOLDIERS

Invasion slows down as resistance emerges

On the war front itself, it is slow-mo time with ground forces digging in around Baghdad. Marc Crispin Miller passes on two items of interest from a friends overseas: "Yesterday the Hungarian news wire (MTI) carried a story quoting a number of US soldiers who wished to remain anonymous to the effect that the ground war was on hold until the supply problems were solved. They had had their field rations reduced by 1/3 until further notice. I watched CNN, but they didn't report it, just the non-specific denial from the Pentagon." He then sent an update: "The cut ration story did make it (later) onto CNN, as did the "4-6 day delay" story. The question remains, if supplies are short and the most vital supply of all is water, are our people going to face massive dehydration?

"And, what CNN didn't include, however – weather satellites say sandstorms are returning to the area in (you guessed it), 3 days or so. Also didn't include a nugget that came to me from a pal that used to work in oil exploration – April is mosquito season south of Baghdad (swamps). In his words, 'they're thicker than carpets'. In their haste to win before the thermometer hits 120 by 4/15, the ground forces hauled ass faster than their vehicles could carry supplies to them."

Why the surprise?

IT should be noted that asymmetrical warfare challenging conventional forces with unconventional ones is what armies at a disadvantage usu-ally rely on. That was Ho Chi Minh's approach in Vietnam. Writing in Slate, Fred Kapan says: "Much has been made of Thursday's remark by Lt. Gen. William Wallace, commander of U.S. Army forces in the Persian Gulf. Talking about the fierce and guerrilla-style resistance of Iraqi militia groups, Wallace said, "The enemy we're fighting is a bit different than the one we war-gamed against."

"In fact, however, militia fighters did play a crucial role in a major war game designed to simulate combat in Iraq but the Pentagon officials who managed the game simply disregarded or overruled the militias' most devastating moves."

So none of what we are seeing should be surprising including the announcement that more martyr (we call them suicide) bombers are on the way. Iraq created more news with an exploding taxicab than the US did with some of its air raids.

Those oh, so 'precise' bombs

THE NEW YORK TIMES devotes an editorial today praising precision bombing, noting "It is always possible, as American military leaders suggest, that damage was caused by Iraqi air defense missiles falling back to earth or by explosives set off by the Iraqis themselves for propaganda purposes. But whatever the case, the widely publicized civilian deaths have generated anger at the United States and sympathy for Iraq in many nations. The incidents inevitably raise the question: How precise are our much-touted precision weapons?"

Who done it? The irrepressible Mr. Fisk of London's Independent was actually on the scene and reported what he found: "The missile was guided by computers and that vital shard of fuselage was computer-coded. It can be easily verified and checked by the Americans – if they choose to do so. It reads: 30003-704ASB 7492. The letter "B" is scratched and could be an "H". This is believed to be the serial number. It is followed by a further code which arms manufacturers usually refer to as the weapon's "Lot" number. It reads: MFR 96214 09. The piece of metal bearing the codings was retrieved only minutes after the missile exploded on Friday evening, by an old man whose home is only 100 yards from the six foot crater. Even the Iraqi authorities do not know that it exists. The missile sprayed hunks of metal through the crowds – mainly women and children – and through the cheap brick walls of local homes, amputating limbs and heads."

As for what is in those weapons, The Sunday Herald in Glasgow is reporting what I have yet to see in the American press the use of depleted uranium in U.S. ordinance: Neil Mackay reports: "British and American coalition forces are using depleted uranium (DU) shells in the war against Iraq and deliberately flouting a United Nations resolution which classifies the munitions as illegal weapons of mass destruction."

As you can see, making sense of the news in America requires that you leave America, if only through the Internet to seek out information and perspectives missing in the TV News accounts. This daily column is one dissector's attempt at reporting back on what is out there. Happily, your letters and items are fleshing out the picture further. ●

APRIL FOOLS' DAY: THE FALL AND RISE OF PETER ARNETT

THIS patriotic or excitement enhancing music and promotional marketing echoes the advice of radio consultants who are advising clients to go red white and blue all the way. Reports the Washington Post: "Now, apparently, is the time for all good radio and TV stations to come to the aid of their country's war. That is the message pushed by broadcast news consultants, who've been advising news and talk stations across the nation to wave the flag and downplay protest against the war.

"Get the following production pieces in the studio NOW . . . Patriotic music that makes you cry, salute, get cold chills! Go for the emotion," advised McKay Media, a Cleveland-based consultant, in a 'War Manual' memo to its station clients. "Air the National Anthem at a specified time each day as long as the USA is at war."

"The company, which describes itself as the largest radio consultant in the world, also has been counseling talk show stations to 'Make sure your hosts aren't "over the top."' Polarizing discussions are shaky ground. This is not the time to take cheap shots to get reaction . . . not when our young men and women are "in harm's way."

Translation: Keep anti-war voices off the air.

The Phraselator

WHILE the media outlets parade their technology, US soldiers proudly display theirs including, as TIME's Tony Karon explains in his weblog, the Phraselator, a hand-held device used by Marines to communicate with the locals. The user chooses from a menu of about 1,000 stock phrases ("come out with your hands up", "I need to search your car", that sort of thing), and an amplified voice chip barks them out in tinny Arabic. Only problem, as anyone who has ever used a phrase book would know, is that it can't translate the reply. I have the feeling this may be the gadget that best captures the spirit of "Operation Iraqi Freedom." Could there have been a phraselator miscommunication yesterday at that bridge where US forces opened up on Iraqi civilians including women and children.

That Penatgonian CENTCOM spin was immediate. They wouldn't stop their minivan. They wouldn't follow orders. We had no choice. It was not our fault. The Times of London carried the kind of vivid account you didn't see on TV.

Shot by the shell-shocked

"AMID the wreckage I counted 12 dead civilians, lying in the road or in nearby ditches. All had been trying to leave this southern town overnight, probably for fear of being killed by US helicopter attacks and heavy artillery.

"Their mistake had been to flee over a bridge that is crucial to the coalition's supply lines and to run into a group of shell-shocked young American marines with orders to shoot anything that moved. "One man's body was still in flames. It gave out a hissing sound. Tucked away in his breast pocket, thick wads of banknotes were turning to ashes. His savings, perhaps.

"Down the road, a little girl, no older than five and dressed in a pretty orange and gold dress, lay dead in a ditch next to the body of a man who may have been her father. Half his head was missing.

"Nearby, in a battered old Volga, peppered with ammunition holes, an Iraqi woman – perhaps the girl's mother – was dead, slumped in the back seat. A US Abrams tank nicknamed Ghetto Fabulous drove past the bodies.

"This was not the only family who had taken what they thought was a last chance for safety. A father, baby girl and boy lay in a shallow grave. On the bridge itself a dead Iraqi civilian lay next to the carcass of a donkey.

"As I walked away, Lieutenant Matt Martin, whose third child, Isabella, was born while he was on board ship en route to the Gulf, appeared beside me.

"'Did you see all that?'" he asked, his eyes filled with tears. "Did you see that little baby girl? I carried her body and buried it as best I could but I had no time. It really gets to me to see children being killed like this, but we had no choice."

Past is not past

IT was in search for context that I reached back into a book on my shelf, "The Powers That Be," by the great Vietnam War reporter David Halberstam. In it, he writes of two incidents. The first occurred in the spring of 1965, a spring like the one we are living with. Two journalists for the Associated Press, a wire service that specializes in playing it straight down the middle, reported that the US was using poison gas. The reporters had multiple sources. There was a big flap. President Lyndon Johnson personally went on TV to deny it. The Military was enraged. Another story appeared by one of the same reporters on the bombing of a village with a great cost of civilian lives. The military was really pissed off by that one because it quoted an American lieutenant who said, famously, "we bombed the village in order to save it."

"That quote in many ways defined the war, and is its defining epitaph. The reporter on both stories was one Peter Arnett.

Halberstam wrote that reporters like Arnett were never invited on the Sunday talk shows because networks like CBS considered themselves a consensus medium. "In the early days, much of the film seemed to center on action rather than the more substantitive qualities of the war. An emphasis on what the television correspondents for CBS themselves called 'bloody' or 'bang-bang.' There was a group of younger correspondents who felt that that somehow the network was always managing to sanitize the war."

How far have we come? By 1991, Peter Arnett said he had covered 17 wars. Now, he is fighting one of his own.

The resurrection and crucifixion of Peter Arnett

LAST week, TV Guide ran a column on the resurrection of Peter Arnett. It discussed how this Pulitzer Prize winning one-time AP reporter outraged the American right-wing for his reporting during Gulf War I but was getting it right this time. No sooner had the piece appeared than Peter's resurrection imploded, turning into another crucifixion, perhaps a self-crucifixion. One minute the man was on top, reporting every other minute from Baghdad, the envy of all the networks who couldn't or wouldn't have their own man in the hot spot. The next minute, he was being run out of town on a rail, fired, disgraced, and apologizing all over the TODAY show for his "misjudgment." (He has since been hired by the Daily Mirror in London, which features as its headline today: "Fired By America for Telling the Truth." Arnett writes he has not apologized for what he said.)

What Arnett says now

WRITING in the Mirror, Arnett explains his stance: "I am still in shock and awe at being fired. There is enormous sensitivity within the US government to reports coming out from Baghdad.

"They don't want credible news organizations reporting from here because it presents them with enormous problems . . .

"I'm not angry. I'm not crying. But I'm also awed by this media phenomenon.

"The right-wing media and politicians are looking for any opportunity to be critical of the reporters who are here, whatever their nationality. I made the misjudgment, which gave them the opportunity to do so.

"I gave an impromptu interview to Iraqi television feeling that after four months of interviewing hundreds of them it was only professional courtesy to give them a few comments.

"That was my Waterloo – bang!

" . . . I'm not here to be a superstar. I have been there in 1991 and could never be bigger than that.

"Some reporters make judgments but that is not my style. I present both sides and report what I see with my own eyes.

"I don't blame NBC for their decision because they came under great commercial pressure from the outside.

"And I certainly don't believe the White House was responsible for my sacking.

"But I want to tell the story as best as I can, which makes it so disappointing to be fired."

Crime and punishment

WHAT was Peter's crime? Speaking what he believed to be true on Iraq TV. NBC's not just punishing him. The network is punishing us because his reporting is needed now more than ever. NBC recently canned Phil Donahue, in part producers said, for having on too many anti-war guests and it was not about to put up with more corporate unappreciated unauthorized points of view like Peter's. Especially when their competitor Fox News, whom they are trying to clone and beat in the ratings, began bombing Arnett with ideological ordnance of its own.

Once NBC canned him, most of the US media

fell in line praising the decision and, as The Guardian put it, "rounding" on him. Doug Ireland offers an assessment on TomPaine.com:

"What provoked Arnett's defenestration? In an interview he accorded on Sunday to Iraqi television (which an MSNBC spokesperson initially described as a 'professional courtesy'), Arnett allowed as how media reports of civilian casualties in Iraq 'help' the 'growing challenge to President Bush about the conduct of the war and also opposition to the war. The first war plan has failed because of Iraqi resistance. Now they are trying to write another plan.'

"The Americans don't want the independent journalists in Iraq."

Of course, these are rather common sense observations of the sort that can be read daily in the pages of our newspapers, and which even find their way onto U.S. television. Yet when NBC snatched the mike from Arnett's hands, on Monday morning CNN's Jeff Greenfield rushed to endorse the veteran war correspondent's firing. Greenfield dismissed the notion of an anti-war movement whose challenge was 'growing' – as if the millions who have taken to the streets of major U.S. cities and the some 5,000 American civil disobedients who have so far been voluntarily arrested in 'die-ins' and other nonviolent forms of political action – part of the rising crescendo of protest on a scale not seen since the Vietnam war – were not energized by the heart- rending accounts of civilians shredded by American bombs and bullets in an unnecessary and obtusely run war.

Greenfield accused Arnett of pro-Iraqi "propaganda." That was sad to me in light of my once tight 'pal-ship' with Jeff, and the way in which this view seems to be shared by so many in the media mainstream. Yesterday I parried on the issue with Bill Himmelfarb of the Washington Times on Keano's interview program on Cape Talk Radio in South Africa. (I seem to get on the air in South Africa more than in South Jersey.) Bill was blasting Arnett for what he called anti-American coverage during Gulf War I.

Arnett's bias

TO refute this canard, I cited some of my own research based on a book by Major General Perry Smith's, "How CNN fought the War." Smith who now comments for CBS said he originally came on board, in his mind, to counter-balance Arnett's "misleading coverage. I was trying to figure out Peter Arnett," he writes. "Was he biased in favor of the Iraqi government? Was he an anti-war advocate? Was he fundamentally anti-American?"

This TV General for hire decided that he was not ideological after all, "The more I watched the Arnett coverage, the more I talked to people who knew him well, the more I came to believe he was a 'feeler.' In other words, Arnett is someone who empathizes with the people around him."

First the sentencing, then the trial

LEWIS CARROL must be laughing in his grave. Fired for feeling, is it? Actually, Arnett was complimentary of the courtesies extended to him by the Iraqis. He complimented them for it, and was roasted for doing so. Yet the other night on Charlie Rose, John Burns of the NY Times was also praising his minders for treating him courteously as a professional. He said it straight out. No one accused him of treason. It seems that the

NBC brass had bought some its own demonization hype of Saddam. Reports the NY Times today:

"Another NBC executive said that Mr. Shapiro had hoped that the Iraqis pressured Mr. Arnett in the interview and that he would say, 'There was a guy behind this orange curtain with an AK-47.'

"But during a phone call, Mr. Arnett told Mr. Shapiro that he felt no such pressure, a spokeswoman said.

"NBC's decision prompted some debate within journalism circles.

" 'It's regrettable that a news organization feels compelled to fire a journalist for essentially doing journalism,' said Bill Kovach, chairman of the Committee of Concerned Journalists.

"But many others said they supported NBC. 'I would have done the same,' said Alex S. Jones, director of the Joan Shorenstein Center on the Press, Politics and Public Policy at Harvard. 'It would have been to me a very fundamental judgment that you would not go on their state-controlled television.' "

Writing in the New York Times today, Walter Cronkite echoes this view: His argument: "Journalists might recognize a motivation in Peter Arnett's acceptance of an interview with state-controlled Iraqi TV, but they should not excuse it."

Irony: Fired, but never hired

CORPORATE controlled television tethered to the Pentagon is apparently above much criticism, candid disclosure, or self-criticism. MSNBC didn't even have the guts to hire Arnett in the first place, even though he was as good a war reporter as they come. They used a ruse, retaining his services through National Geographic Explorer, which produced his first reports with Camera Planet, the indy news organization. That gave them plausible deniability, or so they believed. NBC later wanted him so bad that they rode roughshod over Camera Planet's contract with Arnett who was all too happy to be back on the air after years of forced exile from CNN.

Do you remember the circumstances of his axing there? The network repudiated a story they investigated alleging the use of nerve gas against US military deserters in Vietnam after a ton of bricks fell on them from the Pentagon. After all the top brass approved the story, they hung some producers and Arnett out to dry. The producers later sued for false dismissal, and CNN, which was so righteous in distancing themselves from the story, gave them big cash payoffs rather than have the issue publicly adjudicated. Arnett embarrassed the network by admitting he had not checked out all the details of the story himself, a common practice among busy network correspondents who rely on producers for most of their reporting. He became the fall guy.

"Outstanding reporting" speaks for itself

AFTER Arnett was targeted this time, NBC at first made positive noises. A spokesperson said that his TV comments "were analytical in nature and were not intended to be anything more," according to a news story on MSBNC.com. "His outstanding reporting on the war speaks for itself," she added. NBC then decided otherwise.

Journalists are debating the ethics of what Arnett did, not what ABC did. There is a discussion between Bob Steele, Kelly McBride and Aly Colu on the Poynter.org web site:

Aly: "I wonder what the reaction from the public, the U.S. government and journalists would have been if Arnett had said on Iraqi TV that the U.S. military had succeeded in its battle plans and that the Iraqi resistance was having no impact on those who oppose the war in the U.S. or on the U.S. government itself. I wonder if the criticism cascading about Arnett now would have been as virulent."

Kelly: "My hope is that journalists as well as the general public will use this conversation to really examine what it is Arnett did wrong. Because his sins, if you will, are common. He revealed his personal viewpoints. He made declarative statements that were beyond his authority to make. He crossed the line that separates reporters from opinion writers. Yet, I'm hearing people call him a traitor for giving aid and comfort to the enemy. That is hardly the case."

Bob: "Peter Arnett had a unique and important vantage point for covering the war in Iraq. He was one of the few reporters remaining in Baghdad. He had the ability – and journalistic duty – to report on what was happening in Baghdad. He could tell meaningful stories. It's a shame that he has wasted this vantage point by stepping out of his reporter's role to express his personal views on how the war is going in Iraq and how it is playing out in the United States . . ."

The de-bedding of Geraldo

ARNETT is not the only correspondent in deep doo-doo. Fox's mighty Geraldo Rivera appears to have stepped on a land mine of his own making. The man who would single-handedly liberate Iraq, if only Roger Ailes at Fox News would give him the nod, may be on his way back to Brooklyn where he went to law school. Geraldo had been talking about the glory that would be his, motor-mouthing: "I intend to march into Baghdad alongside [101st Airborne]." Jason Deans reports in the Guardian, that the G-MAN may be sidelined like Yankee shortstop Derek Jeter who broke a shoulder yesterday: "The US military says that gung-ho Fox News correspondent Geraldo Rivera will be kicked out of Iraq today despite his defiant insistence that he will be staying in the country and marching on Baghdad. He is expected to leave Iraq today after giving away allied troop movements in a TV report, according to US military officials.

"Rivera was still inside Iraq yesterday despite reports – gleefully picked up by Fox News' rivals CNN and MSNBC – that he had already left."

Independent journalists at risk

THE story about the de-embedding of Geraldo in the Guardian was accompanied by a report on what is happening to independent reporters who try to operate outside the warm embrace of the military: "The international press watchdog Reporters Sans Frontiers has accused US and British coalition forces in Iraq of displaying "contempt" for journalists covering the conflict who are not embedded with troops.

"The criticism comes after a group of four 'unilateral' or roving reporters revealed how they were arrested by US military police as they slept near an American unit 100 miles south of Baghdad and held overnight.

"They described their ordeal as 'the worst 48 hours in our lives.'

"Many journalists have come under fire, others have been detained and questioned for several hours and some have been mistreated, beaten and humiliated by coalition forces," said the RSF secretary general, Robert Menard. ●

APRIL 2: PENTAGON TURNS ON ARMCHAIR GENERALS

YOU expect soldiers to refer to their adversaries as the enemy. But now that war term is a media term, increasingly popping up across the dial as journalists, embedded or not, can't contain their enthusiasm for the Battle of Baghdad. It's as if we are moving into the final act of the movie, Act 3, in the mother of all showdowns. It's on. It's not on yet. We ping-pong between military analysts relaying speculation as if it was received truth— all the while shedding a tear that the mighty Geraldo will not be leading the charge. It's official: he's out of there.

The Pentagon is getting testier by the minute in response to criticism within its own ranks, even from the regiment of military officers who have been born again as TV analysts and who made the mistake of offering opinions not cleared by the office of Rumsfeldian reality. I am sure Iraqis may see it as a "degrading" of the US consensus even as the bombs keep falling. The always "feared" Medina Division of the Republican Guard is said to have lost two thirds of its capacity to resist. The Pentagon is no longer wagging the dog. It is wagging the kennel.

Their Master's Voice

YEARS ago, RCA Victor had a little dog as its corporate mascot. "His Master's Voice" was its motto. Today the New York Post plays that role in the media war. Along with Fox, it acts like the official rottweiler on the ideological front. Today the big news is that the news is unfair and that the TV generals have overstepped their bounds and must be spanked publicly. Gen. Richard B. Myers, the nation's highest-ranking military officer, has taken on these "whiners" and complainers. They are hurting the war effort, he says.

The Post Ministry of Misinformation reported: "In an astonishing display of emotion at the Pentagon news briefing, the normally reserved Air Force general delivered an impassioned response to the barrage of media reports of internecine warfare at the Pentagon over whether there are enough troops on the ground in Iraq.

"Myers, who didn't name names, said the high-profile carping that's produced a media feeding frenzy may be 'good sport inside the Beltway,' but it is 'not helpful' when tens of thousands of troops are engaged in dangerous combat missions.

"My view of those reports is that they're bogus. First of all they're false, they're absolutely wrong, they bear no resemblance to the truth, and it's just harmful to our troops that are out there fighting very bravely and very courageously." The newspaper than devoted a full page to pictures and summaries of who all the 'armchair generals' are.

Military, reporters, switch roles

IN a sense this is a delayed reaction to the phenomenon reported by Michael Ryan on Tom Paine.com where he noted that, "As the war grinds on, a strange transformation has occurred: Many of the generals have become more objective and reality-based than the journalists 'embedded' with the troops. Garry Trudeau summed up the problem with [embedded] journalists perfectly in Doonesbury, when his fictional reporter Roland Burton Hedley turned to a company commander and said, "Captain, would you describe our outfit as 'magnificent' or 'mythic?' 'Report it as you see it, sir,' the officer replied. 'It's possible to be objective and still be loyal to the people and organizations that you love.'"

Shhh!

THE military baiting in the media reflects the aggressive putdowns of War Secretary Rumsfeld who Matt Taibbi captures perfectly in The New York Press: "Up until last week, Donald Rumsfeld's press conferences were the hottest ticket in Washington, and the defense secretary was somehow credited by journalists with having a 'charming,' even Wildean, wit. For instance, Rumsfeld has a thing about being interrupted or being asked follow-up questions, and his pissy takedowns of journalists who break his "rules" are often met with warm, approving laughter. A typical exchange:

"Rumsfeld: And we can't tell you if you can't tell how long it's going to last, you sure can't tell what it's going to cost. But now...

"Q: But that budget was based on the war plan

"Rumsfeld: (hissing, raising finger to mouth) Shhh! (laughter) Shhh! (laughter)"

Mugger mugs TV coverage, too

EVEN Taibbi's conservative NY Pressmate Russ Smith, aka "Mugger," a longtime Bush Booster, sees the pro-war TV coverage as over the top: "Maybe you saw the March 28 Pew Research Center poll showing 42 percent of Americans are suffering from "war fatigue" by watching too much television about the rapidly unfolding events in Iraq. In addition, 58 percent find the coverage "frightening." Nevertheless, an overwhelming majority of those surveyed by Fox News claim they tune in at least two hours daily, a certain sign of masochism that one hopes will abate quickly.

"The media's blitz of sensationalizing the Iraqi invasion which obviously boosts ratings and sells newspapers, even more than an abducted child not unexpectedly and crosses ideological lines. But with the exception of MSNBC's Lester Holt, I've lost all patience with the cable stations and just can't stomach the sight of Aaron Brown, Shepard Smith, Dan Rather, Tom Brokaw, Wolf Blitzer, Bill O'Reilly, Larry King, and the hundreds of retired generals and colonels who pop off with conflicting analyses."

Propaganda war misfires

ONE of the leading analysts of war propaganda posing as journalism, Philip Knightly (author of "The First Casualty") writes in The Guardian today that the "coalition's propaganda war is a mess. Iraq is winning the propaganda war against the coalition. The British government admits it. David Blunkett, the home secretary, says we are regarded as the villains. The government's spin specialist Alastair Campbell has called for a media shake-up, and in Kuwait the coalition's Psychological Operations Tactical Group for Special Ground Forces Command (Psyops) is working on an emergency plan to regain the propaganda initiative.

"Everything has gone wrong on the propaganda front. The widespread coverage of the deaths of British servicemen at the hands of their US allies, the shooting by US troops of Iraqi women and children, horrific TV footage from al-Jazeera of Iraqi civilians killed in bombing raids on Baghdad, the contradictory statements from the military briefers, and the failure of Iraqis to turn out to welcome their 'liberators.'"

But the most devastating assessment of the coalition's propaganda failure came in a recent Russian-intercepted secret Psyops report analyzing the effectiveness of the coalition's campaign to win the hearts and minds of Iraqis. Using Iraqi TV broadcasts, intercepted radio communications, interrogations of Iraqi POWs and summaries of British and US media coverage, Psyops concluded that Iraqis were more stable and confident than they were in the last days before the war. The report said that the coalition had little time to change this attitude before what Psyops people call "a resistance ideology" developed, making an eventual coalition victory even more difficult. You have to read this one.

Media worries

MORE controls are being imposed on the embedded reporters. PR Week reports that the Pentagon is embedding staffers among the embeds: "They may not get as much attention as their media counterparts, but dozens of Pentagon public affairs officers are 'embedded' right alongside the reporters in Iraq," PR Week reports. "The Pentagon also maintains the Coalition Press Information Center (CPIC) in Kuwait, a base of operations for public affairs officers not traveling with troops. A 24-hour operation designed to keep up with news cycles in every time zone . . . one of the CPIC's most vital roles is to discourage 'rogue' journalists from venturing into dangerous areas by providing the information they might otherwise attempt to get on their own."

The Wall Street Journal praised the Defense Department's PR Strategy. "The embedded reporters will continue to be a brilliant strategy by the Pentagon – one that should echo in the rules of corporate communications," the Journal's Clark S. Judge writes.

Dehumanization: Order of the day

AS for the content of the coverage, I usually quote the big city press but Pierre Tristam of the News-Journal in Florida has some brilliant insights: "The American war effort is a study in total control, too, of a war positively dehumanized at every level: Politicians, military leaders and their media lackeys, in bed with the military rather than embedded within it, are daily producing a scripted war of advances and virtue more divorced from reality than Max's dream in 'Where the Wild Things Are.'

"News stories from the front (for the most part) are clips for the military's 'Army of One' ads – produced in a void of analytical perspective and brimming with self-important reminders of inflated secrecy ('I can't tell you where we are,' 'I can't tell you where we're going')." Of course not! "These reporters have not only been embed-

ded, they've been captured. A picture is supposed to be worth a thousand words. In this war, a picture is worth a thousand veils. At home the networks' anchored news streams have been closest in kind to porno movies: A little meaningless chatter sets things up, and then money shots of bomb blasts over Baghdad or the Pentagon's latest dirty videos of things being blown up. The human and emotional cost is an afterthought. There is purpose behind the veil. When war is so positively dehumanized, the possibility of defeat is eliminated. Setbacks become narrative devices, stepping tombstones for America's moral superiority. It is war as magical realism. But it isn't real."

Freedom of expression at risk

FROM Canada comes this report: "As the war in Iraq enters its third week, several IFEX members have raised concerns over free-expression violations committed by United States-led coalition forces, including the bombing of an Iraqi television station and the expulsion of four foreign journalists accused of being spies.

"The International Federation of Journalists (IFJ), Reporters Without Borders (Reporters sans Frontiers (RSF), the Committee to Protect Journalists (CPJ), the International Press Institute (IPI), and Canadian Journalists for Free Expression (CJFE) have expressed alarm at the US bombing of Iraqi state television facilities on 26 March in Baghdad. Although US military officials claimed the facility was part of a command-and-control center, IPI and CPJ say the bombing could be a violation of the Geneva Conventions.

"Broadcast media are protected from attack and cannot be targeted unless they are used for military purposes. The broadcast of propaganda does not constitute a military function," CPJ argued. "The attack knocked out the Iraqi station's 24-hour satellite channel, which broadcasts outside the country, for several hours."

What should protesters demand

WHAT should anti-media protesters be demanding? Jeff Chester of the Center for Digital Democracy, addresses this issue on Alternet.org. "The rising tide of protest against U.S. media coverage of the war should also signal the need for a new progressive strategy about the future of the media system. Recent marches across the country protesting the networks, and a new focus by Moveon.org on media issues are vitally important. But they don't address the need to take advantage of fundamental changes taking place and alter how our media system is structured. The time is ripe, given all the activism and commitment now in place, to direct our energy towards achieving long-term positive changes for our media system.

"A major transformation that is underway is reshaping broadcasting, cable, and the Internet. The TV system in the U.S. is being reorganized because of digital technology, which should provide new opportunities for progressives to directly offer channels and program services to the vast majority of television households. But unless progressives and their allies pursue a proactive strategy, they will continue to be as marginalized as we are today."

Attention US networks

WHY not follow the example of BBC News Chief Richard Sambrook who solicits comments from viewers, and responds publicly in the Guardian? Among the questions he is tackling: "Is the BBC biased towards the pro- or anti-war camps? Should the corporation give equal weight to claims by Iraqi and allied military and political sources? Does 24-hour news provide the full picture of what's going on in Iraq? Does 'embedding' reporters with UK and US forces compromise their independence? How safe is it for journalists working in the war zone?" How about it? Which US media execs have the guts to do the same? Also, Anna Kaca, a Mediachannel advisor, writes from Finland that TV channels there are raising questions about the media coverage. We hope to have more from Helsinki soon. ●

APRIL 3: BAGHDAD BRACES, SAY TV FACES

O' SAY can they see Baghdad in the springtime, rising mirage-like from the desert where the temperature is also rising and the media and the government seem to be getting more and more eager to get "it" over with? American forces are reportedly near the airport, liberating the suburbs and getting in position for a "final" push. The bulls on Wall Street are bullish and the Irish Studies professors in the Mission District of San Francisco are laying odds of a cease-fire within 1-3 weeks. The Iraqis are fighting furiously, even taking down a plane here and helicopter there but the technology-and-weapons divide is so huge that it makes this one of the most lopsided wars in history. Roll on, O' Roman Legions. Sail On, O' Ship of Fate.

What are we seeing? Last night Aaron Brown of CNN had former Times war reporter Sidney Schanberg on to discuss coverage. He wrote about that last week in The Village Voice. This week he offers a "dissection" of government lies. He told Brown that the structure of constantly updated TV News scrambles all understanding. He compared the coverage to keeping score of a sports event. (The BBC's news chief apologized for a similar comment that aired there) Brown praised Schanberg as a journo great and acknowledged that it is challenging to keep up. Over on Nightline, at the same time, General Ted Koppel was war-gaming his marine division's next moves.

Murdoch: get it done!

THE GUARDIAN reports: "Referring to the American people as 'we,' Mr. Murdoch said the public was far too worried about what the rest of the world thought of the US's declaration of war on Iraq. He said he believed Americans had an 'inferiority complex' about world opinion and that Iraqis would eventually welcome US troops as liberators.

"Mr. Murdoch told a conference in California it would be "better to get war done now" rather than have a longer conflict that could prove more damaging to the world economy. "We worry about what people think about us too much in this country. We have an inferiority complex, it seems," he said at the Milken Institute Global Conference yesterday." Michael Milken, the convicted stock fraudster who funded the Institute, was one of the financiers of the Murdoch Empire and a key advisor until a federal court ordered him to cease and desist. He later paid millions in fines for dealing with/advising Rupert, contrary to a court order . . .

War fatigue claims TV viewers

THE Networks are hoping to get the war over with. In England, it is being reported that viewers show signs of war fatigue. "Audience figures for the BBC1 and ITV late evening news bulletins dipped yesterday," according to the Guardian. The Onion jokes about this with a simple headline: "NBC Moves War To Thursdays After Friends." The networks have already bailed out of wall-to-wall coverage and now report war news mostly on less watched cable networks.

Even as the volume of network coverage declines, the level of media bashing is going up. Yesterday, I reported on the denunciations of media skepticism by the top brass at the Pentagon. Today, there is a report that Tony Blair's home secretary Mr. Blunkett has been tasked to rein in the reporters in Baghdad because "progressive and liberal" opinion believes them. Earlier in the week, Blair's spin-doctor in chief, Alastair Campbell, was even nastier.

"Saddam Hussein can go up and do a broadcast, and how many of our media then stand up and say what an amazing propaganda coup that was. (Osama) Bin Laden can sit in his cave and throw out a video and you get BBC, CNN, all these other guys, saying 'What a propaganda coup'."

He's mad at the media, too

BEHIND all of these attacks on the press seems to be growing anxiety in the White House. Unfortunately we have no real embeds there (You have to give big political contributions to get into bed in the Lincoln Bedroom). USA Today gave us a rare portrait yesterday of a President who is losing it. "News coverage of the war often irritates him. He's infuriated by reporters and retired generals who publicly question the tactics of the war plan. Bush let senior Pentagon officials know that he was peeved when Lt. Gen. William Wallace, the army's senior ground commander in Iraq, said last week that guerrilla fighting, Iraqi resistance, and sandstorms have made a longer war more likely." He has a special epithet for members of his own staff who worry aloud. He calls them "hand-wringers."

And then there was this: "He can be impatient and imperious. On March 17, before he delivered a 48-hour ultimatum to Saddam, Bush summoned congressional leaders to the White House. They expected a detailed briefing, but the president told them he was notifying them only because he was legally required to do so and then left the room. They were taken aback, and some were annoyed. Bush copes with anxiety as he always has. He prays and exercises."

The media massage

OVER at the Pentagon, Tori Clarke has to keep the Pentagon press corps in line. According to today's New York Times, now that the news media has better access to the troops, she is being peppered almost hourly with queries from the battlefield about topics as varied as checkpoints, rations, rescues, and killings of civilians. More troubling, she faces a growing chorus, including several retired generals, questioning whether the war plan of Mr. Rumsfeld and his lieutenants was ill advised and whether the

administration fueled unrealistic expectations that Iraqis would welcome American troops with open arms.

Episodes like the news briefing on Tuesday are part of the most difficult trial yet for Ms. Clarke, 43, who has devoted her career in politics and public relations to working with clients in tricky situations. As a campaign aide, she defended the first President Bush as his popularity evaporated in the polls. She later represented the cable industry when it infuriated consumers with rising rates and poor service.

This article goes on to report how well she is doing in winning hearts and minds from the media and the military. Maybe it is her colorful clothes, which rated a fashion spread in the Post the other day.

Iraq mistreats reporters

YESTERDAY two Newsday reporters freed from prison in Iraq discussed their harrowing experience at a press conference in Jordan. Their newspaper reports: "Newsday staffers Moises Saman and Matthew McAllester were recently held in Iraq's Abu Ghraib prison for eight days with two other Western journalists and an American peace activist. They described seeing a man being beaten: 'Journalists are meant to bear witness. That's rather the point of our job. We watch and record and tell other people what we have seen, perhaps in the hope that an account, a witnessing, could eke away at badness. But I turned away and chose not to see a thing.'

"Eventually the beating stopped, and the man was dumped into his cell. The big guard seemed to have exhausted his fury. The block echoed as it always did when the iron bars of the prisoner's cell door was closed and the click of its padlock confirmed that he would not be leaving his 6- by 10-foot room that night. With each breath he made a sort of crying sound. Sometimes he broke that rhythm to exhale his pain with more force, and the otherwise silent block filled up with what I wondered might be the man's last gasp."

U.S. mistreats reporters

THIS tearful and horrific account was given lots of airtime on all the channels, as it should. An interview with non-embedded foreign journalists detained by U.S. military forces was aired on Amy Goodman's Democracy Now yesterday, but not, as far as I know, picked up by any of the majors. It involved the experience of four so-called unilaterals. I reported on this last week.

One of them was Dan Semama who describes meeting some U.S. soldiers who suspected they were spies. "They took away our cameras. They took away our ID cards. They took away our money. They took our phones. They put their guns towards us. They forced us to lie down on the floor. To take our shirts up to make sure we didn't have any explosives on our bodies and were arrested."

At that point a Portuguese reporter asked the soldiers to phone home and tell his wife he was ok. Semama continues, "Five soldiers went out of the camp, jumped on him and started to beat him and to kick him. We ran to his direction. They all put bullets inside the cannons of their guns, and they said if we move forward they shoot at us. We were standing like stupid guys. We saw our friend lying on the ground crying, hurting. They tied his hand behind his back. They took him into the camp. And after half-an-

hour, they let him go, and came back to us all crying. And then came this Lieutenant Scholl. And he told us, 'Don't mess with my soldiers. Don't mess with them because they are trained like dogs to kill. And they will kill you if you try again." They were held for 36 hours.

Reporting on the content of the coverage

THE Project On Excellence in Journalism has issued a report on the embedded journalists. Here's what they report: "The embedded coverage, the research found, is largely anecdotal. It's both exciting and dull, combat focused, and mostly live and unedited. Much of it lacks context but it is usually rich in detail. It has all the virtues and vices of reporting only what you can see."

In an age when the press is often criticized for being too interpretive, the overwhelming majority of the embedded stories studied, 94 percent, were primarily factual in nature. Most of the embedded reports studied were live and unedited accounts. Viewers were hearing mostly from reporters, not directly from soldiers or other sources. In eight out of ten stories we heard from reporters only.

This is battle coverage. Nearly half of the embedded reports (47 percent) described military action or the results. "While dramatic, the coverage is not graphic. Not a single story examined showed pictures of people being hit by fired weapons.

"Over the course of reviewing the coverage, project analysts also developed a series of more subjective impressions of embedding. Often the best reports were those that were carefully written and edited. Some were essentially radio reporting on TV. Technology made some reports stand out but got in the way when it was used for its own sake. Too often the rush to get information on air live created confusion, errors, and even led journalists to play the game of telephone in which partial accounts become distorted and exaggerated in the retelling."

Roy: "Taking revenge"

INDIAN author Arundhati Roy comments on the embeds in her most recent essay: "On March 21, the day after American and British troops began their illegal invasion and occupation of Iraq, an embedded CNN correspondent interviewed an American soldier. 'I wanna get in there and get my nose dirty,' Private AJ said. 'I wanna take revenge for 9/11.'

"To be fair to the correspondent, even though he was 'embedded,' he did sort of weakly suggest that so far there was no real evidence that linked the Iraqi government to the September 11 attacks. Private AJ stuck his teenage tongue out all the way down to the end of his chin. 'Yeah, well that stuff's way over my head, he said.'

"According to a New York Times/CBS News survey, 42 per cent of the American public believes that Saddam Hussein is directly responsible for the September 11 attacks on the World Trade Center and the Pentagon. And an ABC news poll says that 55 per cent of Americans believe that Saddam Hussein directly supports al-Qaeda. What percentage of America's armed forces believe these fabrications is anybody's guess." ●

WORDS OF THE WISE

"Just as weapons have gotten 'smarter,' so too has the military gotten more sophisticated about how to use the media to meet military objectives." – **LT. COL. JERRY BROECKERT, public affairs, U.S. Marine Corps.**

"A chill wind is blowing in this nation. Journalists can insist that they not be used as publicists by this administration…You have, whether you like it or not, an awesome responsibility and an awesome power: the fate of discourse, the health of this republic is in your hands, whether you write on the left or the right. This is your time, and the destiny you have chosen." – **TIM ROBINS, National Press Club, April 15, 2003**

"There's an entertainment factor that's huge in television in creating this drama. It's about them." – **PHIL BRONSTEIN, editor, San Francisco Chronicle**

"Within six months of the end of the first Gulf War, Iraq disappeared from the daily coverage. The Tyndall Report shows 1,177 minutes of network reporting on Iraq in January 1991, when the war started, but just 48 minutes in August 1991. The war in Afghanistan received 306 minutes of coverage on the newscasts in November 2001, but that dropped to 28 minutes by February 2002, and last month it was one minute. – **ANDREW TYNDALL, Media Monitor, April 16, 2003**

"While the Inquirer ran 20 stories a day during the war – about a third more than usual for foreign news—when that statue [of Hussein] came down, the space began to contract pretty rapidly. Given the brutal nature of the combat, people are wanting to hunker down and get as far away from it as they can. I was hearing readers say, 'Enough! Enough!' – **NED WARWICK, foreign editor, the Philadelphia Inquirer.**

"The buildup to this war was so exhausting, the coverage of the dash to Baghdad so telegenic, and the climax of the toppling of Saddam's statue so dramatic, that everyone who went through it seems to prefer that the story just end there. The U.S. networks changed the subject after the fall of Baghdad as fast as you can say "Laci Peterson," and President Bush did the same as fast as you can say "tax cuts." – **THOMAS FRIEDMAN, columnist, New York Times** ●

CHAPTER SEVEN

WAR KILLS JOURNALISTS

DEATH TOLL MOUNTS AS WAR TRAGEDY INVADES NEWSROOMS

Horror of war comes home as journalists become part of story

I t has been a week when the horror of war came home to the media – home to stay. Suddenly the war was not just another big assignment, or an adventure, or a chance to score points. Suddenly it was not a game of action and reaction, or mission and maneuver. It became a real world horror show as journalists who traditionally seek distance from the news they report became part of the story.

In just three weeks, the war in Iraq (or on Iraq, if you serve many outlets in the Arab world) has already claimed more than the number of journalists killed during Gulf War I in 1991. Only four journalists are known to have died then.

Death lurks everywhere on today's battlefield, It can take the form of auto accident like the one that took the life of editor-columnist Michael Kelly who was overconfident that he would survive a conflict that he boosted in print. It could take the form of a friendly fire incident like the bombing of a military convoy that pulverized BBC translator Kamaran Abdurazaq Muhamed and wounded the BBC's star correspondent John Simpson. Terry Lloyd of Britain's ITN died in similar circumstances after being shot by "Coalition" gunfire near Basra on March 22.

NBC's David Bloom was struck down by a pulmonary embolism that could have been linked to the vehicle he created that allowed him to broadcast while barreling across the desert. The action shots of him were captivating, but he may not have paid attention to his immobilized legs, which were attacked by a blood clot.

Australian freelance cameraman Paul Moran, was on the scene of suicide bombing by people who make little distinction between embedded journalists and the armies they travel with. Kaveh Golestan, another freelance cameraman, an Iranian, was on assignment for the BBC. He stepped on a landmine.

A German and a Spanish journalist were at a US base when it was rocketed by Iraqi forces.

Others suffered accidents, like Gaby Rado of Britain's Channel 4 News, while two more colleagues are missing: Fred Nerac, and translator Hussein Othman, both part of Terry Lloyd's crew, disappeared. And there are others. A German and Spanish journalist died April 7 during an Iraqi missile attack on a US base. Gone also are Wael Awad, a Syrian reporter working for the Dubai Arabic TV station al-Arabiya and his partner Talal Fawzi al-Masri, a Lebanese cameraman and Ali Hassan Safa, a technician.

Add the captured to the list including: Peter Wilson, London correspondent for The Australian, his photographer John Feder and their translator Stewart Innes. And let's not forget Marcin Firlej, Polish journalist with news channel TVN 24, captured south of Baghdad, or Jacek Kaczmarek, journalist with Polish public radio.

I am not sure this is whole roster but they all deserve our support. Unfortunately, protecting journalists is higher on the media agenda than protecting journalism. And journalism is rarely as equally outraged by the deaths of civilians and even the massacring of combatants.

Everyone who knows Gulf War I remembers the "turkey shoot" on the road out of Kuwait when US jets strafed and slaughtered fleeing soldiers. Many remember the bulldozers that were used to bury "enemy" soldiers alive. We won the war but lost the peace. When the parades ended, Saddam was left standing. Could it happen again? Don't bet against it. Let us not forget that the war we fight today has been underway for at least a decade. This is only the latest phase. What will be its legacy?

Will there be a resurgence of Gulf War syndrome that was denied for years by the Pentagon but caused so much pain and misery for all those who were inflicted? You barely hear any reference made to the sanctions that went on for ten years, robbing so many Iraqi children of their futures, even if the regime was complicit as well in their deaths.

Remember, too, the use of depleted uranium in "coalition" weapons that defiled a land that is the cradle of western civilization. Remember also how the gassing of the Kurds, so widely cited as grounds for invasion today, barely rated a condemnation in its immediate aftermath, even by a Republican Administration.

We forget this history at our peril.

We didn't see many of Iraq's faces then, and we are not seeing them now. Iraq became a geopolitical abstraction for most Americans until this Administration decided to wage war there. Before shock and awe, only 13% of the young people now fighting could even find it on a world map, according to a National Geographic survey.

War may kill but it also desensitizes. When we get into them, they get into us. We may escape alive or even prevail but the images and the experience stamp our lives forever. For many, the trauma will lead to sleepless nights for the rest of their lives. And that goes for journalists too, as hard-nosed as many of us believe we are.

As NY Times journalist Chris Hedges explained to Editor and Publisher: "The real 'shock and awe' may be that we've been lulled into a belief that we can wage war cost-free. We feel we can fight wars and others will die and we won't. We lose track of what war is and what it can do to a society. The military had a great disquiet about the war plans, as far back as last fall. The press did not chase down that story."

I cite all of this not to score some cheap political points because war is always a tragedy, usually a lose-lose proposition even when you "win."

Journalists are mourning for their own this week as you do when you lose a member of your family. But we can't turn our back on all the other families in pain and in grief because of this war. Journalism without compassion, without empathy, and without consciousness is but stenography by another name. ●

APRIL 4: WHAT WOULD DR. KING SAY ABOUT ALL OF THIS?

IRONIC isn't it, that the anniversary of the death of Dr. Martin Luther King Jr., that apostle of non-violence, is being commemorated in a country mesmerized by all the violence all the time. Peace coalitions of the kind that Dr. King once marched with will be devoting this weekend to a range of anti-war activism. While they march for peace, military units continue their march on Baghdad, the first target in what many believe is a crusade for "region change," even global change. (The term regime change is likely to be dropped now that John Kerry is using it in reference to the Bush Administration.)

All flights out of Baghdad's Saddam Hussein (oops, strike that name) airport have been cancelled due to invasion. The city is being spooked. The lights are out. The US military may soon be in. Bear in mind that what you are watching on both sides is less a military campaign than a psyops operation. Already Washington is broadcasting into Baghdad while its soldiers mow down a far more poorly equipped Iraqi force. The Arab press now speaks of the country as a "killing field." You know this is real because Ted Koppel is among those checking in (but not out) from the airfield. Unlike US airports, security there was, shall we say, light.

It would be wrong to see this Psyops dimension only in military terms. It is also being directed at the American people and world public opinion with constant events staged for media consumption.

Yesterday, President Bush did one more photo-op and tough-guy speech with thousands of soldiers saluting like synchronized swimmers behind him at Camp LeJeune. It had a certain Nuremberg feel to it. These events are held to fortify the President's mental health as well as convince us that he is still presidential and actively commander-in-chiefish. The networks dutifully carry them.

On TV there is as much competitive sniping as there is on the battlefield, with dueling promos between Fox and MSNBC and the NY Post targeting The New York Times in an ideological battle aimed at further polarizing our politics by delegitimizing the center.

What are we fighting for?

REUTERS reports that the priorities, they are a shifting: "When Defense Secretary Donald Rumsfeld spelled out the eight U.S. objectives in Iraq on day two of the war, he said the first was to topple Saddam Hussein and the second to locate and destroy Iraq's alleged weapons of mass destruction."

On day 10 of the war, Pentagon spokeswoman Victoria Clarke restated those eight objectives: Ending the Iraqi president's rule remained top of the list, but finding Saddam's suspected chemical and biological weapons had slipped to fourth place, while destroying them dropped to fifth. Have you see this widely reported?

What's in store? World War IV!

CNN reports that the Bush Administration is now talking about fighting World War IV. "Former CIA Director James Woolsey said Wednesday the United States is engaged in World War IV, and that it could continue for years. In the address to a group of college students, Woolsey described the Cold War as the third world war and said, 'This fourth world war, I think, will last considerably longer than either World Wars I or II did for us. Hopefully not the full four-plus decades of the Cold War.' Woolsey has been named in news reports as a possible candidate for a key position in the reconstruction of a postwar Iraq."

Woolsey's worldview spiced with threats towards Syria and even US ally Egypt echoes the imperial ambitions of the takeover-the-world cabal around Bush. They convinced themselves that they, and they alone, have been appointed by history. Now they are trying to convince us – with lots of media support.

TomDispatch.com notes: "Our present ideologues spent the last decade mustering strength (academic as well as governmental) and convincing themselves as much as anyone else that only one country was capable of creating a 'new world order,' that it would have to dismantle the old international order (of which the UN is but a hated symbol) to do so, and that it could bring untold benefits to the very region that most had to be remade and so controlled, the world's economic lifeline, the source of its energy bloodstream, the Middle East. If we are now dealing with a regime of true believers, in their years out of or at the edges of power, they managed, first and foremost, to indoctrinate themselves."

Chomsky: Iraq is a trial run

NOAM CHOMSKY, in an interview with the Indian publication Frontline, says that what we are watching is far MORE than a pre-emptive war: "This should be seen as a trial run. Iraq is seen as an extremely easy and totally defenseless target. It is assumed, probably correctly, that the society will collapse, that the soldiers will go in and that the U.S. will be in control, and will establish the regime of its choice and military bases. They will then go on to the harder cases that will follow. The next case could be the Andean region, it could be Iran, it could be others.

"The trial run is to try and establish what the U.S. calls a 'new norm' in international relations. The new norm is 'preventive war.' Notice that new norms are established only by the United States. So, for example, when India invaded East Pakistan to terminate horrendous massacres, it did not establish a new norm of humanitarian intervention, because India is the wrong country, and besides, the U.S. was strenuously opposed to that action."

Words of war

EVERY day seems to bring a new term, a new word, and another stab at media spin. The military has taken the term 'attrition,' as in people whose jobs are abolished or never filled when they are laid off and fired, and turned it into a war word. They are now talking of soldiers being "attrited," another way of saying killed, or even evaporated. Antonia Zeribisas of the Toronto Star wrote yesterday about neo-con pundits on US TV (are there any other kind?) defending carpet-bombing as humane.

She writes: "For a few interesting – at least for news junkies – days over the weekend, when the war seemed bogged down by unexpected resistance, bad weather and vulnerable supply lines, the right was on the run, defending the Pentagon's 'humane' bombardments, even as civilians going to market were being blown to smithereens."

Ashamed of being a journalist

ACROSS the globe, veteran Israeli journalist Uri Avnery is sounding the same alarm. He, too, has coined a word, but you won't hear it on TV. It is "presstitute." He explains: "In the Middle Ages, armies were accompanied by large numbers of prostitutes. In the Iraq war, the American and British armies are accompanied by large numbers of journalists. I coined the Hebrew equivalent of "presstitution" when I was the editor of an Israeli newsmagazine, to denote the journalists who turn the media into whores. Physicians are bound by the Hippocratic oath to save life as far as possible. Journalists are bound by professional honor to tell the truth, as they see it.

"Never before have so many journalists betrayed their duty as in this war. Their original sin was their agreement to be "embedded" in army units. This American term sounds like being put to bed, and that is what it amounts to in practice."

He says he is ashamed to be a journalist: "I am ashamed when I see a large group of journalists from all over the world sitting in front of a many-starred general, listening eagerly to what is called a "briefing" and not posing the simplest relevant question. And when a courageous reporter does stand up and ask a real question, no one protests when the general responds with banal propaganda slogans instead of giving a real answer."

Oh, the horror

LET'S go back to that whole issue of civilian casualties, hardly a subject of much media focus. Yesterday, I noted that reference is made to the use of cluster bombs without any descriptions being offered of these lethal weapons. We have all seen the graphics detailing the various planes and their specs. But what about the bombs and their consequences? As it turns out, Pepe Escobar wrote about this yesterday on Asia Times Online (not The New York Times off-line.)

He writes: "Reports from the Hilla region of Iraq, 80 kilometers south of Baghdad, say that scores of civilians, many of them children, have been killed and hundreds more injured by cluster bombs. Gruesome images of mutilated bodies are being shown on Arab television stations. But for Western viewers, this ugly side to the war has been sanitized.

"Roland Huguenin-Benjamin, a spokesman for the International Committee of the Red Cross (ICRC) in Iraq, describes what happened in Hilla as 'a horror, dozens of severed bodies and scattered limbs.' Initially, Murtada Abbas, the director of Hilla hospital, was questioned about the bombing only by Iraqi journalists – and only Arab cameramen working for Reuters and Associated Press were allowed on site. What they filmed is horror itself – the first images shot by Western news agencies of what is also happening on the Iraqi frontlines: babies cut in half, amputated limbs, kids without their faces, a web of deep cuts caused by American shellfire and cluster bombs. Nobody in the West will ever see these images because they were censored by editors in Baghdad: only a 'soft' version made it to worldwide TV distribution."

What Europe reads

SOURCES like these are being believed more than US TV news reports, according to USA Today: "Channel-surf from Britain's BBC to Germany's ZDF, or flip through newspapers from Spain to Bangkok, and one finds stories that tilt noticeably against the war and in favor of besieged Iraqi civilians. Often, these are emotional first-person accounts of visiting hospitals or bombed-out apartments, accompanied by graphic photos of the dead and dying that would never appear in U.S. outlets.

"'Most Europeans do not support this war, and so the coverage is simply a reflection of that,' says Giuseppe Zaffuto, project director at the European Journalism Centre in Maastricht, the Netherlands. For now, it seems much of the world's media still need to be convinced of Washington's position."

We still don't know why al-Jazeera was booted from Baghdad and according to them, at least officially, they don't either. An official statement says: "The Iraqi Information Ministry told al-Jazeera office in Baghdad its decision to ban Diar al-Omari, al-Jazeera's Baghdad correspondent, from practicing his journalistic duties. The decision also said that Tayseer Allouni should leave Iraq as soon as possible. The ministry did not provide any reasons for that decision. Al-Jazeera network is sorry for this unpredictable and unreasonable decision by the ministry."

It helps to have friends in high place

GUESS who is going back to the front? The well politically connected Faux News Network seems to have made a few calls and Geraldo Rivera is

going back. Reports the NY Post: "The Pentagon says Geraldo Rivera is welcome to go back into Iraq with U.S. troops now that he's 'learned his lesson.'

"It was a stunning turn-around for Geraldo, who appeared just 24 hours ago to be on the verge of a career meltdown. Rivera's latest gaffe infuriated U.S. war commanders who – at one point Tuesday – threatened to remove him physically from the battle zone if he did not "voluntarily" agree to leave." There were anti-war, anti-media protests yesterday at Fox News HQ in San Francisco.

What the polls show depends on what polls you read

HOW does the public feel about the war coverage? TV Guide's Max Robins cites a poll that says they can't get enough. The Gallup people meanwhile offer an opposite conclusion: "A poll shows a sharp decrease in the percentage of Americans who rate media coverage as "excellent" since the wargasm coverage began. Say the pollsters:

"Interestingly, those Americans who support the war with Iraq are most likely to rate the media coverage positively.

"At the same time, war supporters are also the most likely to have downgraded their views of news coverage since the war began, suggesting that this group is most sensitive to how the war is being portrayed."

What should we call it?

ON the Language Front, Larry Piltz from Austin, Texas, offers his own lexicon to differ with the conventional view.

It's an invasion, not a war.

It's fomenting terror, not fighting terror.

It's using weapons of mass destruction, not suppressing them.

It's using uranium ammunition, not suppressing uranium weapons.

It's practicing fascism, not promoting democracy.

It's Anglo-American colonialism, not a willing coalition.

It's classic hegemony, not charity.

It's backwards logic, not forward defense.

It's another racist hate crime, not a noble just war.

It's an organized lynch mob, not leadership decapitation.

They're homicide bombs, not guided bombs.

They're the natives, we're the cavalry.

Déjà vu all over the place.   ●

APRIL 5: TV IS BOMBED TO CURE THEIR PROPAGANDA

IF we ever needed a clearer demonstration of the power of media, we have it now. The battle for media control has moved into the center of the war. Despite the violation of international law associated with bombing a television station, the US forces continue to try to do it in Iraq. Suddenly we are back in the Romania of 1989, or the Russia of 1991 as a fight against a TV station becomes a centerpiece in the campaign to delegitimize a regime.

US forces have been targeting the TV towers in Baghdad the way they did in Belgrade. And they still haven't taken it off the air, despite all the

cruise missiles, smart bombs, bunker busters, (JDAMs) and who knows what else, they have thrown at them. At the CENTCOM briefing this morning, comfortably televised from the million-dollar air conditioned media center in Doha by another type of controlled TV, there were suggestions that the Iraqis had built redundant systems anticipating just such an attack. They have also leased time on satellites.

Propaganda front and center

THE media war has moved centerstage with briefers describing their own propaganda initiatives, i.e. taking over Channel 3, and launching radio stations that Clear Channel Communications are likely to pick up for a song when the war ends. Meanwhile, the American TV commentators buzz about whether or not that was the "real" Saddam we saw in the streets with cheering supporters yesterday.

(As for the briefings, here's a disturbing side bar. Last week we cited NY Magazine columnist Michael Wolff's report lambasting the phoniness of the whole Doha disinformation enterprise. When he returned to New York, he reportedly discovered that radio talk show host Rush Limbaugh had been blasting him on the air and calling on his listeners to bombard him with emails. Rush gave out his email address and his ditto heads dutifully overloaded his computer. So much for freedom of expression.)

No one commented on the contrast between President Bush flanked by cheering soldiers in North Carolina and the Iraqi leaders being embraced by his people in the streets. The Iraqis are showing tapes of what they call martyrs – most recently women with rifles calling for more resistance. Our media calls them suicide bombers as if they are ending their lives for personal, not political reasons. At CENTCOM briefings, the Major General of the moment characterizes the entire Iraqi resistance as suicidal because of the disparity in firepower.

He, along with most US TV, sees the war only in military terms. The Iraqis and much of the world view it politically. Oddly enough, the US administration views it politically too but in much more self-interested terms as The New York Times reports today: "The invasion of Iraq has accelerated with stunning speed in less than a week, taking some of the political heat off President Bush." He knows that "winning" the war is a key to winning reelection.

CNN and Al-Jazeera cover different wars

THIS contrast of images is also seen on TV when you compare CNN's antiseptic and sanitized coverage to Al Jazeera's depiction of a far bloodier conflict. (Al Jazeera is now back in Baghdad after shutting down when a reporter was ousted.) The Wall Street Journal led with a story about this media war yesterday. Emily Nelson reports:

"The two networks, with unprecedented access to the battlefields of Iraq, are playing a powerful role in shaping perceptions of the war. The gulf between the two views could even have an impact on U.S. policy in the Middle East. A look at 24 consecutive hours of programming on CNN and al-Jazeera reveals the many differences, both dramatic and subtle.

"CNN offers human-interest features with the families of U.S. POWs. Al-Jazeera keeps updating the war's death toll. CNN refers to 'coalition forces,' al-Jazeera to 'invading Americans.' CNN viewers expect the latest technology, such as lipstick cameras and night vision, and they get it. Al-Jazeera has had unusual access in places such as Baghdad and Basra, so it could offer its audience a street-level view of the war's impact on Iraqis. CNN's correspondents were all either pulled out or kicked out of Baghdad.

"Many Arabs and Americans believe the other audience is being fed propaganda. But there is more than ideology at work at the two networks. Both are business operations competing for viewers and advertisers against increasingly aggressive rivals and avidly seeking to please their target audiences."

Arab world unconvinced by the US 'Sellathon'

THE NY Times is reporting that US propaganda to win over the Arab world is not working. At the same time, the Times op-ed page yesterday showed some news papers in the Arab world along with a piece by Lebanese journalist Rami G. Khouri who argued that "the Arab press, while predominantly in opposition to the allied attack on Iraq, is neither monolithic nor uniformly anti-American." (The Times did not carry his reporting. The Globalvision News Network (gvnews.net) actually ran the full story that is referenced three days earlier. The prominent conservative columnist and magazine editor Michael Kelly who called for the war was claimed by it yesterday, killed in a Humvee accident. He edited the Atlantic Monthly. The White House offered its condolences, as did many colleagues.

Arnett back on the air

PETER ARNETT is also back on the air from Baghdad. AP reports on its former staffer: "Within days of being fired by the U.S. network NBC, Arnett found an unlikely new audience Thursday: the Dutch-speaking and hopefully English-comprehending citizens of northern Belgium. 'Thanks Peter Arnett, we are proud to have you on our team,' said VTM news anchor Dany Verstraeten after Arnett finished his first report for the private Belgian TV network.

"VTN said it will have daily reports from one of the world's most famous reporters until the end of the war. Also Thursday, a state-run TV channel in Greece said Arnett would soon be providing nightly dispatches for it, too. 'This story also shows how TV networks around the world do not share the values and viewpoints of the US based cable news networks.'

"Arnett, who apologized for his 'misjudgment,' told VTM he was a casualty of the information war. 'There are two wars taking place. You have the war of bullets and bombs, then you have the information war,' he said. He complained he was making 'just obvious statements' about the war that should not have backfired the way they did. 'This caused a firestorm in America. I was called a traitor,' he said, adding NBC 'let me crash and burn.'"

Pro-war media relentless

ON the pro-war side of the media war, we have an assessment to share from Steve Johnson of the Chicago Tribune, who explains what Fox News is doing right. (I used that word knowingly.)

"They report. We deride.

"We deride Fox News Channel for saying 'us' and 'our' in talking about the American war effort, a strategy that conjures images of gung-ho anchor Shepard Smith, like Slim Pickens in 'Dr. Strangelove,' riding a Tomahawk straight into Baghdad.

"We deride Fox for playing ratings politics with the news, turning Joint Chiefs Chairman Richard Myers' public call Tuesday for media to be 'fair and balanced' into a back-door endorsement, pointing out frequently afterward that the general had echoed a Fox News marketing slogan.

"This, the folks in the bunker at Fox would argue, is due to the rest of the media's liberal agenda, an agenda Fox News slyly re-alleges with every repetition of 'fair and balanced' (the others aren't) and 'we report; you decide' ('they' don't give you that chance).

"A less calculatedly paranoid worldview would recognize that scrutiny is the price of success, of the channel becoming, in a sense, the Scud stud of this Persian Gulf conflict. Ratings during the war have confirmed that Roger Ailes' and Rupert Murdoch's upstart operation has become the clear leader in cable news popularity." (Should that be 'cheer leader?')

"Fox News has held the lead it built in peacetime by following its well-established and fairly simple recipe: dollops of news reported by comely anchors and correspondents tossed atop a main dish of attitude and argument led by charismatic and right-leaning hosts."

This piece is worth studying because Steve is right. Knocking Fox or dismissing it is too easy. We need to study its formula and understand its appeal.

Breaking news is hard to believe

FOX is not the only offender of journalistic practice, as FAIR points out in a dissection of one incident in which subsequent accounts in newspapers that I cited in an earlier column contradicted the initial TV report and the impression it fostered.

"A recent Washington Post article describing the killing of civilians by U.S. soldiers at a checkpoint outside the Iraqi town of Najaf proved that 'embedded' journalists do have the ability to report on war in all its horror. But the rejection by some U.S. outlets of Post correspondent William Branigin's eyewitness account in favor of the Pentagon's sanitized version suggests that some journalists prefer not to report the harsh reality of war.

"The Pentagon version was the one first reported in U.S. media sometimes in terms that assumed that the official account was factual. 'What happened there, the van with a number of individuals in it . . . approached the checkpoint,' reported MSNBC's Carl Rochelle (3/31/03). 'They were told to stop by the members of the 3rd Infantry Division. They did not stop, warning shots were fired. Still they came on. They fired into the engine of the van. Still it came on, so they began opening fire on the van itself.'

"Fox's John Gibson (3/31/03) presented the story in similar terms: 'We warn these cars to stop. If they don't stop, fire warning shots. If they don't stop then, fire into the engine. If they don't stop then, fire into the cab. And today some guys killed some civilians after going through all those steps.' But later on the night of March 31, the Post released its story on the shooting that would appear in the April 1 edition of the paper.

Branigin's report described U.S. Army Capt. Ronny Johnson's attempts to avoid the incident as he directed his troops via radio from the checkpoint:

"'Fire a warning shot,' he ordered as the vehicle kept coming. Then, with increasing urgency, he told the platoon to shoot a 7.62mm machine-gun round into its radiator. 'Stop [messing] around!' Johnson yelled into the company radio network when he still saw no action being taken. Finally, he shouted at the top of his voice, 'Stop him, Red 1, stop him!'"

In short what happened, according to close observers is not quite what was first reported and rationalized.

Clear Channel has no agenda. Repeat, none

MEANWHILE on the radio front, Clear Channel Communications continues to organize rallies to support the troops. I went to the ABC news website and did a search "Pro troop rally" and got the link about who is organizing this, Clear Channel Radio stations, across the country. Keep in mind that our local peace rallies are not sponsored or paid for by anyone. My understanding is the various local peace rallies (which also support the troops) are a grassroots movement rising directly from the people, church groups, veterans for peace, and various groups interested in social justice such as United Voices for Peace . . . A reader sends this from an unidentified local newspaper:

"Clear Channel has a reporter embedded with a Marine unit in Iraq, leading one expert to question whether the company's support for the rallies creates at least the perception that its news report is compromised."

"When a media company takes an advocacy position on a significant public policy issue, it can certainly undermine the credibility of that media company's journalists," said Bob Steele, director of the journalism ethics program at the Poynter Institute in St. Petersburg, Florida.

But Ami Forester, a spokeswoman for Clear Channel subsidiary Premiere Radio Networks, whcih syndicates their shows, said, "There is no hidden agenda here." . . .

She's right: it is not hidden and she was also correct to note that some of their competitors are now staging similar events.   ●

APRIL 7: DECAPITATION STRIKES TARGET SADDAM

SURPRISES, "strategic" and otherwise, seem to be the order of the day as spring takes hold. In Baghdad, US Marines staged one of their raids into the center of town because it was there, and so were they. Its point: to demonstrate the weakness of the town's defenses, to prod and to probe, and to score more psychological warfare points by strutting through one of the palaces and hanging out on the lawn. Sadly eight died in this demonstration. A soldier called Flip told his buddy Greg of Fox News that it "showed we are here to stay."

Eyewitness to hell

LIFE, like war, is chaotic and sometimes it is hard to tell friends from foes. Sometimes friends are foes. I was watching Michelle Martin on ABC's This Week mentioning that 25% of the US casualties in Gulf War 1 came from friendly fire. It seems to be happening again. BBC warhorse John Simpson and team were traveling with Kurdish fighters and US Special Ops troops when the skies exploded overhead. He described the hellish scene on BBC online:

"I saw two F-15 American planes circling quite low overhead and I had a bad feeling, because they seemed to be closer to us than they were to the tank. As I was looking at them – this must sound extraordinary but I assure you it is true, I saw the bomb coming out of one of the planes – and I saw it as it came down beside me. It was painted white and red. It crashed into the ground about 10 or 12 meters from where I was standing.

"It took the lower legs off Kamaran, our translator, I got shrapnel in parts of my body. I would have got a chunk of shrapnel in my spine had I not been wearing a flak jacket, and it was buried deep in the Kevlar when I checked it. Our producer had a piece of shrapnel an inch long taken out of his foot.

"The planes circled round. I shouted out at the American special forces, 'Tell them to go away – tell them it's us – don't let them drop another bomb.' It was a mistake. They were so apologetic afterwards."

News addiction

INCIDENTS like these were observed and reported on. But the full extent of other casualties, including the US war toll, is buried (some say deliberately in that ever present fog of war.) CENTCOM commander Tommy Franks brags: "We don't do body counts." IraqBodyCount.net does. They claim there is a maximum of 1,050 civilian dead, but that has to understate the overall carnage which is psychologically traumatizing a population as well as the men fighting. The psychological drama here is just being noted. A New York Times report on viewers who can't sleep because of their addiction to the coverage resonates with my own experience:

"Mr. Angelo, the sleep-deprived telephone worker, said he had given up reading about the war in his favorite newspapers, including The Philadelphia Inquirer, because he has often found that much of the news compiled the previous day has gone stale by the following morning.

"In place of the printed page, he says, he has become addicted to the news crawls that stream across the bottom of his 27-inch Sony when he is watching CNN or Fox News.

"In contrast, J. C. Alonsoperez, 55, a molder at a glass factory off Main, says he has sworn off the very news channels on which Mr. Angelo relies. He says he craves the more 'in-depth' analysis of the war that he finds in The Inquirer, as well as on National Public Radio and the BBC.

"After being captivated at first by the war, Mark Roszkowski, 49, a financial planner from nearby Wildwood Crest, said he now permitted himself to watch only a few minutes of television coverage – 'til I get the gist of what happened today' – because, he explained, 'I don't really like to dwell on it.' "His reasons are at least partly political. 'It's upsetting to watch,' he said, 'because the more the war goes on, the bleaker our future becomes. We're getting into something as a country that's going to be hard to get out of.'"

Remembering 'The Bloomster'

REPORTS of the death of two more western jour-

nalists are coming in. Fox says one is German, the other French. Others report they are Russian . . . NBC is still mourning the loss of its media star David Bloom, a.k.a "The Bloomster." Everyone watching the US coverage was impressed by his inventiveness and conversational reporting style. His Today Show training served him well, but his own enterprise may have sealed his fate. According to his colleague Tim Russert, he had built that open-air platform he rode, like a modern day Lawrence of Arabia across the desert. He has even made sure that the people who engineered it for him would not make another one for a competitor.

Colleagues like John Simpson admired his pluck and style: "During this war he had frequently pushed the line dividing news from show business, ducking rocket fire and broadcasting live from a specially adapted M-88 tank retriever known to colleagues as the 'Bloom mobile,' while troops fought northwards. Bloom and his cameraman were able to produce 'jiggle-free' video even while racing through the desert, by using a gyrostabilized camera."

The Steadicam effect made him look great but it also immobilized his legs, perhaps contributing to the pulmonary embolism that was to claim his life at age 39. He left a wife and three kids.

Michael Kelly, the conservative commentator who perished in a Humvee accident left two kids. All of their colleagues spoke about these children as they should. As a father myself, I can understand, and feel for both of their families. Yet it made me sad to think of all the Iraqi children being victimized in this war – half of Iraq's population is under 18 – who are all but forgotten by a media focus on the US military.

Red Cross horrified

IT was in the Canadian press that I found a Red Cross report I have yet to see referenced on American TV: "Red Cross doctors who visited southern Iraq this week saw 'incredible' levels of civilian casualties including a truckload of dismembered women and children, a spokesman said Thursday from Baghdad. Roland Huguenin, one of six International Red Cross workers in the Iraqi capital, said doctors were horrified by the casualties they found in the hospital in Hilla, about 160 kilometres south of Baghdad.

"'There has been an incredible number of casualties with very, very serious wounds in the region of Hilla,' Huguenin said in an interview by satellite telephone. 'We saw that a truck was delivering dozens of totally dismembered dead bodies of women and children. It was an awful sight. It was really very difficult to believe this was happening.'"

Also unbelievable was this quote in the US Times re-quoted in The Guardian: "from a Marine who had shot at an Iraqi soldier in a civilian crowd and watched a woman fall instead. 'I'm sorry', said the Marine, 'but the chick got in the way.' Now, how does that make you feel?"

Questions about casualities

WHAT about military casualties? Wayne State University professor David Fasenfast raises questions about the coverage on this score, questions you rarely see or hear being raised by the anchors or correspondents:

"It strikes me as people discuss this war no one mentions the strange nature of the reporting on casualties. I saw a report the other night that lists total deaths about 71 with about a third due to friendly fire. On the same day I saw a report that 'enemy' dead from one engagement was up to 2,000 and the daily numbers are always real large.

"Old enough to remember, I am skeptical. First, during Vietnam the US regularly inflated the numbers engaged and killed. Second, it turns out that many of the dead "combatants" ended up being civilians presumed to be combatants for the simple reason that they were killed during the battle (much later the reports of atrocities tempered those estimates). Why is there no commentary on what is now easily (by the reports) tens of thousands dead. Even if they are all soldiers, there is something obscene about (alright, even more obscene than) this war. Where is the sense of more than battle testing weapons – but rather testing them in a kill zone environment."

Conflicting reports

HERE is an example of the problem. Following are two reports from AP, the first on April 2, the second three days later:

"U.S. Marines describe ambush outside Nasiriyah that wounded 31 troops.

" . . . The Marines are among 221 combat wounded who have been treated at Landstuhl, in southwestern Germany, since the war began March 19. Ninety-four troops and a civilian remain at the hospital, the American military's largest hospital outside the United States, Landstuhl spokeswoman Marie Shaw said."

US war toll rises to 75

"APRIL 5 – The number of U.S. service members killed in action since the war began March 20 stands at 75, U.S. officials said Saturday. Seven service members had been captured, seven were missing and 154 had been wounded."

Where are the Iraq defenses?

ALSO confusing is just what the Iraqis are doing and not doing to defend Baghdad. Erudite commentator George Will, who usually claims to know everything about everything, admitted to doubts and confusion on ABC Sunday. (He also approvingly read us a quote from Michael Kelly urging pundits on TV to shut up. Clearly he didn't realize that he is among the most offensive of the chattering classes.) So what is happening? During the Vietnam War analysts used to say that the US was playing the western game of chess while the Vietnamese were playing the Asian game of GO. What goeth on?

Mark Crispin Miller passes along a provocative analysis by Mark Gery, an independent Iraq analyst of the non-armchair-general variety. He writes: "Saddam and most of the Republican Guard will probably lay low in Baghdad and elsewhere and let the Fedayeen and other paramilitary units harass us as we try to move about the city. (We have yet to secure even one major city in Iraq). The Guards have already discarded their combat uniforms and apparently dispersed into several locales.

"At some point, when temps near 100 and the sandstorms begin again, thousands of Iraqi troops now in hiding will strike in mass at a few choke points in our supply lines, which extend all the way into Kuwait. They may even still blow the bridges over the rivers. Our forces will become isolated from each other, and within a few weeks will be short on water, food, and gasoline. Vehicles and men will have to come into Iraqi cities for clean water, and again be subject to commando attack. In short, weather and logistics will win the war for Saddam."

Dubya: "Good"

"MR. BUSH smiled a moment at the latest example of Mr. Rumsfeld's brazenness, recalled the aide. Then he said one word – 'Good' – and went back to work," reports the Independent.

"It was a small but telling moment on the sidelines of the war. For a year now, the president and many in his team have privately described the confrontation with Saddam Hussein as something of a demonstration conflict, an experiment in forcible disarmament. It is also the first war conducted under a new national security strategy, which explicitly calls for intervening before a potential enemy can strike."

This war is also a selling exercise – a way to showcase and field-test US weaponry. During the Gulf War, Guy Trebay called CNN a "home shopping channel" for military recruitment officers who are watching with checkbooks at the ready. It is happening again. Sir Timothy Garden, a British expert wrote about this in March in The Guardian: "With war seemingly inevitable, weapon designers will be looking forward to another opportunity for field-testing new products."

Media hatred

AS for the media war being fought alongside the

military conflict, it is getting uglier by the minute. As Peter Preston writes in today's Guardian: "So, who's winning the loathing campaign? The lower echelons of the empire Rupert built produced some wonderful haters. The Post hates The New York Times. It dissected a Times front page, story by story, and labeled the result 'News by Saddam.' It hates the 'vermin' of Iraq, the 'euro-weasels' of Brussels, and the failed, 'irrelevant' UN. It even quite despises Murdoch's London Times for printing damp little pieces about British public opinion based on one interview with a 'market gardener.'

"Some of the vituperation, though, reaches pitches of bitterness, which can only betoken sincerity. See Matthew Parris in the Times diagnosing 'the Madness of King Tony' in grim clinical detail. See Nick Cohen (of this parish) taking a New Statesman cleaver to Andrew Murray of the Stop the War Alliance: 'A living fossil from the age of European dictators is heading the biggest protest of the new century.' See our great farceur, Tom Sharpe, writing an incensed open letter to Tony Blair, which ends 'yours in despair, and disillusionment.'"

The word "Coalition:" how true?

WRITING from Baghdad, The Independent's Robert Fisk blasts the BBC for speaking of "coalition" troops: "Why do we aid and abet the lies and propaganda of this filthy war? How come, for example, it's now BBC 'style' to describe the Anglo-American invaders as the 'coalition.' This is a lie. The 'coalition' that we're obviously supposed to remember is the one forged to drive Iraqi occupation troops from Kuwait in 1991, an alliance involving dozens of countries almost all of whom now condemn President George Bush Junior's adventure in Iraq. There are a few Australian special forces swanning about in the desert, courtesy of the country's eccentric prime minister, John Howard; but that's it. So who at the BBC decreed this dishonest word 'coalition?' True, there's a 'coalition of the willing," to use Bush's weird phrase but this is a reference to those nations which have given over flying rights to the United States or have given political but not military support. So the phrase 'coalition forces" remains a lie." ●

APRIL 8: COMICS MAKE FUN OF THE CONFLICT

WHAT was billed as the war of liberation began with an attempted decapitation and remained focused on execution in all realms. This time, thanks to an intelligence intercept and a tip on the ground, a B-1 bomber was dispatched to finish the real job – the annihilation of Saddam and company, one of the most expensive assassinations in history – that is, if it was as successful as the gleeful TV anchors and their "high-level" sources were hoping. Three "bunker buster" bombs were used this time to leave an enormous crater in a residential Neighborhood. Reportedly it happened at 6 a.m. our time yesterday but the news was withheld for over twelve hours.

Throughout it all, the demonization continues; "Butcher and evil sons may have died plotting escape," reads one headline in today's New York Post, a facsimile of a newspaper published in New York. As I tuned in for the latest this morning, before the briefers showed up to tell us what to report, the news nets were still recycling the big story. The Post must not have heard or believe the banter about who is supposed to be controlling Iraq when it captioned a photo of US soldiers having a smoke yesterday in one of Saddam's palaces. "MEET THE NEW OWNERS," it says. Funny, how reality creeps through the fog of "journalism."

The latest: Bush doesn't know

AS of 8 a.m. EDT today, CNN was reporting: Bush said "Saddam Hussein will be gone. It might have been yesterday, I don't know."

"Central Command: Marines attack, seize Rasheed military airfield in southeastern Baghdad.

"Abu Dhabi TV: Firefight near presidential compound in Baghdad; Coalition tanks take up position on nearby bridge."

Al-Jazeera bombed (again!)

THE war against Al Jazeera has claimed a life, CNN reports. "Al-Jazeera TV says one of its journalists was killed Tuesday when a U.S. air strike hit a building housing Arab media, the Arab network said. The reporter, identified as Tariq Ayoub, was carried along the street in a blanket before being placed in the back of an Abu Dhabi TV vehicle and being rushed off for medical treatment.

"An Al-Jazeera reporter on-air said he felt, as did his colleagues, the U.S. strike was a deliberate attack against the network, since two missiles hit the building, not one, and that the raid happened at about the same time Abu Dhabi TV offices were hit." A US missile also previously hit al-Jazeera offices in Afghanistan by "mistake."

A media freedom group in Jordan condemned the attack and "criticized the US expression of regret and excuses over its attacks on journalists and media, describing what took place as a "crime against humanity and a clear violation of international law," adding that those who committed them should not be allowed to avoid punishment.

"The organization demanded the international community and international bodies defending human rights to establish committees to investigate into those violations.

"In the same context, CDFJ criticized the media coverage carried out by some of the US media outlets describing it as being "biased" and failing to respect objectivity and ethics while turning into entities that advocates for war as well as defending violations that U.S. and British troops are committing against innocent victims."

More journalists targeted

ALSO this morning, Ann Garrels of NPR reported from the Palestine Hotel, the media headquarters in Baghdad, that a US tank shell was fired into the 15th floor, with at least four media colleagues wounded. This is preliminary information phoned into the Media Channel. A US soldier reportedly said he saw people with binoculars in the hotel and thought they were being fired on. Garrels said she heard no gunfire, but noted that many reporters were watching the battle with binoculars.

Is this a a war?

HERE'S Hendrik Hertzberg of the New Yorker to

offer a useful framework to integrate all the "Breaking News" that keeps pouring in: "There is one way in which it is misleading to classify what is happening in Iraq as a war at all. Like Dunkirk, Midway, and the Bulge, it is only part of a larger enterprise. That is how it has been justified; that is how it must be judged. The aim of that larger enterprise is not to overthrow the Iraqi regime, however devoutly that is to be wished; it is to minimize the chances of another September 11th. The success of what might more properly be called the Battle of Iraq must ultimately be measured by whether it brings us closer to that larger aim or leaves us farther away from it. The longer the fighting continues, the greater the suffering inflicted upon Iraqi civilians, the solider Arab and Muslim (and European and Asian) anger toward the United States becomes, the bigger the pool of possible terrorist recruits grows – the more these things happen, the higher becomes the cost of victory, until, at some unknowable point, victory becomes defeat."

The WMDs: Missing in action

WHAT happened to the hunt for Weapons of Mass Destruction, as in the prime rationale for the war? Agence France-Press is reporting: "A facility near Baghdad that a US officer had claimed might finally be 'smoking gun' evidence of Iraqi chemical weapons production turned out to contain pesticide, not sarin gas as originally thought.

"A military intelligence officer for the US 101st Airborne Division's aviation brigade, Captain Adam Mastrianni, told AFP that comprehensive tests Monday determined the presence of the pesticide compounds. Initial tests had reportedly detected traces of sarin – a powerful toxin that quickly affects the nervous system – after US soldiers guarding the facility near Hindiyah, 100 kilometers (60 miles) south of Baghdad, became ill.

Mastrianni said: "They thought it was a nerve agent. That's what it tested. But it is pesticide."

Where is the chemical war?

WRITING on this issue, George Monbiot notes today in The Guardian, "When Saddam Hussein so pig-headedly failed to shower US troops with chemical weapons as they entered Iraq, thus depriving them of a retrospective justification for this war, the American generals explained that he would do so as soon as they crossed the 'red line' around Baghdad. Beyond that point, the desperate dictator would lash out with every weapon he possessed.

"Well, the line has been crossed and recrossed, and not a whiff of mustard gas or VX has so far been detected. This could mean one of three things. Saddam's command system may have broken down (he may be dead, or his troops might have failed to receive or respond to his orders); he is refraining, so far, from using them; or he does not possess them.

"The special forces sent to seize Iraq's weapons of mass destruction have found no hard evidence at any of the 12 sites (identified by the Pentagon as the most likely places) they have examined so far. As Newsweek revealed in February, there may be a reason for this: in 1995, General Hussein Kamel, the defector whose evidence George Bush, Tony Blair, and Colin Powell have cited as justification for their invasion, told the UN that the Iraqi armed forces, acting on his instructions, had destroyed the last of their banned munitions. But, whether Saddam Hussein is able to use such weapons or not, their deployment in Iraq appears to be imminent, for the Americans seem determined to do so."

Depleted uranium: Words we never hear

AMONG the weapons being used are anti-tank shells coated with depleted uranium. The US insists they are safe. Critics contest that. The LA Times, a winner of yesterday's Pulitzer Prize, noted on March 30th:

"Although the potential human cost of the war with Iraq is obvious, not many people are aware of a hidden risk that may haunt us for years.

"Of the 504,047 eligible veterans of the 1991 Persian Gulf War, about 29% are now considered disabled by the Department of Veterans Affairs, the highest rate of disability for any modern war. And most are not disabled because of wounds.

"These guys were rough, tough, buff 20-year-olds a decade ago. The vast majority is ill because of a complex of debilities known as the Gulf War Syndrome.

"These vets were exposed to toxic material from both sides, including numerous chemicals, fumes, and weird experimental vaccines. But the largest number of the more than half a million troops eligible for VA benefits – 436,000 – lived for months in areas of the Middle Eastern desert that had been contaminated with depleted uranium."

"We kicked the crap out of them"

TOMDISPATCH.COM writes on this issue, too: "It

is worth remembering that the army of 100,000-plus young men and women who will occupy Iraq for who knows how long – and of course the Iraqis who have nowhere else to go – will all be putting their health on the line so that we can create a certain degree of greater target penetration with our weaponry. As the LA Times piece suggests, the famed epitaph for the Punic Wars might apply: "They made a desolation and called it Peace."

Our response? According to Col. James Naughton, director of munitions for the U.S. Army Material Command, as quoted in a recent Article in the Pittsburgh Post-Gazette: "The Iraqis tell us terrible things happened to our people because you used it last time ... They want it to go away because we kicked the crap out of them – OK? There's no doubt that DU gave us a huge advantage over their tanks."

You can check in, but you can't check out

SOME embeds want out, as Joe Strupp reports in Editor and Publisher: "At least 10 embedded journalists have left their assigned slots with U.S. military units in Iraq, according to a Pentagon spokesman, who said twice as many people have requested to leave but chose to stay after being told their news organizations would lose the slots for good if they departed. Meanwhile, the Pentagon says they 'won't change the rules that bar news organizations from replacing embeds who leave or switching them from one military unit to another.'

"Col. Jay DeFrank, director of press operations for the Department of Defense, said he understood that some newspapers may need to move reporters and photographers out of their embed assignments, especially if the war takes more than a few weeks, but stressed that the rule still stands. "When our forces are engaged in ground combat, it is no time to bring in a new journalist to the environment," he said this week. "Having a journalist there complicates the situation already. Having a new person does it more so."

Follow the money

SOME new information about political donations by US media companies has come out. Where? In England, not in the US. You haven't seen this on Fox or CNN. The Guardian reports: "Political donations by U.S. television and radio stations have almost doubled in the last year, research has shown.

"And the Bush family's association with many media organizations runs deep and is reflected by the hefty handouts from the likes of NBC network owner General Electric and Rupert Murdoch's News Corporation, both trenchant supporters of the war.

"The amount of money ploughed into party coffers by Rupert Murdoch's Fox TV, NBC, and radio giant Clear Channel (among others) has gone up to £7.56m in 2001/2002, compared with just £4.6m in 2000, the latest figures reveal."

Press reunion

THEY have been talking about the press up at Yale as the Yale Daily News celebrates its 75th anniversary. Former Media Channel Managing Editor Larry Bensky, an alumnus of that venerable organization, is on hand. The newspaper reports that "panelists discussed the changes

necessitated by the 24-hour news cycle, where cable news can provide up-to-the-minute access and print journalists scramble to compete. Washington Post White House correspondent Dana Milbank said the Bush administration has been especially clever in using this demand for immediate news by sending out small bits of information.

"There's no time to question it, or Fox or MSNBC are going to have it," Milbank said. "By the time we catch up and say, 'Maybe that's not true,' we're already on to something else."

Can you trust the polls?

CNN trotted out new polls showing 80 percent of the people see President Bush as a strong leader (what other leader are they seeing?) 65 percent of the people think that he "cares about people like them." The LA times reports "Some 95 percent of Americans say they are following news coverage closely and 61 percent approve of the coverage," says a Los Angeles Times poll. In his book, 'The New Crusade,' Rahul Mahajan says most polling is deceptive. He writes: "Polls are notoriously volatile – they vary greatly on the background information given, on the way questions are phrased, and on the alternatives given. Responses also have no requirement of logical consistency. So to draw on very specific conclusions from these numbers would be a mistake." There is no doubt that public opinion is affected by what people see – and don't see – on television." ●

APRIL 9: AMNESIA STALKS THE AIRWAVES

THIS week the horror of war came home to the media, home to stay. Suddenly the war was not just another big assignment, or an adventure, or a chance to score points, or get ratings. Suddenly it was not a game of action and reaction or mission and maneuver. It became a real world horror show as journalists who traditionally seek distance from the news they report became part of the story.

In just three weeks, the war in Iraq (or "on Iraq," if you serve outlets in the Arab world) has already claimed more journalists than the number killed during Gulf War 1 in 1991. Only four journalists are known to have died then.

Death for media people lurks everywhere on today's battlefield – even when you are not on it. Al Jazeera's offices and the Arab Media Center in Baghdad were bombed yesterday, clearly not a move that will endear the US war to the Arab world, which relies on the reporting from there. One Al Jazeera correspondent was killed. US soldiers reportedly rocketed the Palestine Hotel, home to most correspondents in Baghdad. As I write, the toll of dead and injured is not known. It seems like it's open season on journalists.

The way death comes

DEATH can take the form of an auto accident, like the one that took the life of editor-columnist Michael Kelly who was overconfident that he would survive a conflict that he boosted in print. It could take the form of a friendly-fire incident, like the bombing of a military convoy that pulverized BBC translator Kamaran Abdurazaq Muhamed and wounded the BBC's star correspondent John Simpson. Terry Lloyd of Britain's ITN died in similar circumstances after being shot by "Coalition" gunfire near Basra on March 22.

NBC's David Bloom was struck down by a pulmonary embolism that could have been linked to the vehicle he created that allowed him to broadcast while barreling across the desert. The action shots of him were captivating, but he may not have paid attention to his immobilized legs, which were attacked by a blood clot.

Australian freelance cameraman Paul Moran was on the scene of a suicide bombing by people who make little distinction between embedded journalists and the armies they travel with. Kaveh Golestan, another freelance cameraman, an Iranian, was on assignment for the BBC. He stepped on a landmine.

A German and a Spanish journalist were at a US base when it was rocketed by Iraqi forces.

Others suffered accidents, like Gaby Rado of Britain's Channel 4 News, while two more colleagues are missing: Fred Nerac and translator Hussein Othman, both part of Terry Lloyd's crew.

Missing and captured

AND there are still others. A German and Spanish journalist died April 7 during an Iraqi missile attack on a US base. Missing are Wael Awad, a Syrian reporter working for the Dubai Arabic TV station al-Arabiya; his partner Talal Fawzi al-Masri, a Lebanese cameraman; and Ali Hassan Safa, technician.

Add the captured to the list, which includes

Peter Wilson, London correspondent for the Australian, his photographer John Feder and their translator Stewart Innes. And let's not forget Marcin Firlej, a Polish journalist with news channel TVN 24, captured south of Baghdad, or even Jacek Kaczmarek, a journalist with Polish public radio. I am not sure this is the whole roster but they all deserve our support.

Memories and amnesia

EVERYONE who knows Gulf War 1 remembers the "turkey shoot" on the road out of Kuwait when US jets strafed and slaughtered fleeing soldiers. Many remember the bulldozers that were used to bury "enemy" soldiers alive. Amnesia seems to have taken hold because these incidents are rarely mentioned. We won the war but lost the peace. When the parades ended, Saddam was left standing. Could it happen again? Don't bet against it.

Let us not forget that the war we fight today has been underway for at least a decade. This is only the latest phase. What will be its legacy? Will there be a resurgence of Gulf War Syndrome that was denied for years by the Pentagon but caused so much pain and misery for all those who were afflicted. You also barely hear any reference made to the sanctions that went on for ten years, robbing so many Iraqi children of their futures, even if the regime was complicit in their deaths.

Remember, too, the use of depleted uranium in "coalition" weapons that defiled a land that is the cradle of western civilization. Remember also how the gassing of the Kurds, so widely cited as grounds for invasion today, barely rated a condemnation in its immediate aftermath, even by a Republican administration.

Will we repeat history?

WE forget this history at our peril. We didn't see many of Iraq's faces then, and we are not seeing them now. Iraq became a geopolitical abstraction for most Americans until this administration decided to wage war there. Before shock and awe, only 13% of the young people now fighting could even find it on a world map.

War may kill but it also desensitizes. When we get into them, they get into us. We may escape alive or even prevail, but the images and the experience stamps our lives forever. For many, the trauma will lead to sleepless nights for the rest of their lives. And that goes for journalists too, as hard-nosed as many of us believe we are.

We lose track of what war is

AS NY Times journalist Chris Hedges explained to Editor and Publisher: "The real 'shock and awe' may be that we've been lulled into a belief that we can wage war cost-free... We feel we can fight wars and others will die and we won't. We lose track of what war is and what it can do to a society. The military had a great disquiet about the war plans, as far back as last fall. The press did not chase down that story."

I cite all of this not to score some cheap political points because war is always a tragedy, usually a lose-lose proposition even for the "winners."

Journalists are mourning for their own this week as one does upon losing a member of your family. But we can't turn our back to all the other families in pain and grief because of this war. Journalism without compassion, without empathy, and without consciousness is but stenography by another name.   ●

185

ANOTHER WAR OF WORDS

THE Terror Era has not only radicalized our domestic politics and foreign policies, but it has infected our language. Our vocabulary has undergone a paradigm shift along with government policies. Academics call it "social construction."

Conversations are now peppered with terms we rarely heard or thought much about before 9/11. (Before 9/11, no one even marked dates that way. Sure there was 24/7 but that's not the same.) Few of our "new" words are new – but the frequency of usage certainly is. Words are weapons or their extensions and often used as such. Many are the lethal offspring of an alphabet of anguish, a lexicon of slanted war speak. Orwell would have been right at home, but for the rest of us, it is often uncomfortable finding these terms bubbling up almost involuntarily from within. "News language" has a way of fusing with our own language in the same way that babies absorb the lingo, accents and phrasing of their parents. What we hear again and again in the media embeds itself in the inner voice. We recycle what is repeated. Pavlov understood this more than Orwell, but never mind.

So here is an armchair linguist and news dissector's A-Z in progress. Help me fill in the blanks.

A – Allah, Axis, Assets, Alert; ABC-Atomic Biological Chemical, Anthrax, Aluminum Tubes, Al Samud Missiles; Al-Jazeera, AAR (after action report), amphetamines, (supplied to exhausted pilots who bomb Canadian allies in friendly fire incidents in Afghanistan).

B – Breaking News, Bio-Terror, Baghdad, Basra, "Black Hawk Down," Box Cutter, Botchilinum, Burka, Ba'ath Party, Bush "Doctrine".

C – Caves, Condoleeza, cells (of the sleeper and awake varieties), CC (Central Command); Centriguges, Clash of Civilizations, Crusade, CNN-effect, Collateral Language (or damage, collateral), Combatants, illegal, Chicken Hawk, C2 - command and control, Civil Liberties (Huh?).

D – Duct Tape, Desert Spring, Delta Force, Detainees, Dirty Bomb, Democracy (in Iraq, not the U.S.), Drones, Daisy Cutters, (not be confused with the country called Cutter but spelled Qatar), Dead or Alive, Disarmament (them, not us).

E – Embed, Embedded, Evil, Evildoer, Evil, Axis of, E-bomb.

F – Fundamentalism, Foreign Fighters, Friendlies (the soldiers we like), Fights Back (as in America), Franks (Tommy), Food for Oil, Freedom Fries (in lieu of French fries).

G – Ground Zero, Gitmo, Guantanamo Bay, Geneva Conventions (now irrelevant), Geraldo (see force of nature).

H – Homeland, Homicide Bombers, Hamas, Hizbollah, Holy War, House to House, HinduKush, Hazmats, Haj, Halliburton (rarely mentioned), Human Rights (no longer relevant).

I – Infidel, Inspections, IAEA, IO (Information Operations as in "Information is the Currency of Victory"), IDF, Imam, Interrogate, Interrogation, Islamabad, ISI (Pakistan Intelligence), Intifada (again), Infant Mortality, Imperialism (word not used on television).

J – Jihad, Jihad Junkie, Journalists (endangered species), "Just War" (no longer in quotes).

K – Kurds, Kurdistan, Kabul, Kunduz, Kandahar, Kashmir, KC-10A Extender jets.

L – Likud, Laconic, Liberation (of Iraq, not U.S.), Love (forget it).

M – Muslim World, Madrassa, Mullah, one-eyed, Mastermind, Material Breach, Mobile Labs, Mustard Gas, Mazer I-Sharif, Mujahadeen, Mecca, Mistake (not used).

N – Northern Alliance, No Blood for Oil, Not in My Name, Non-permanent members.

O – OBL, Omar, Operation Mountain Lion, Operation Anaconda, Operation Infinite Justice, Operation Enduring Freedom, Old Europe (as opposed to New).

P – Perception Management, Profiling, P5 or Perm 5 (once the Big Five on the Security Council), Patriot Act, Patriotically Correct, Pens (Demonstration Areas), Preemptive War, Preemptive Strike, Proxies, Poodle (see Blair, Tony), Prisoners of War (quaint term, seldom used), Peace (term no longer used), "Power of the Blood" (Hymn often cited).

Q – Qaeda, Al; Quran, Queasy.

R – Regime Change, Rummy, Radiological Weapon, "Real" Journalism (Fox News slogan), Republican Guards (Special), Racin, Ro-Ro (Roll-on and Roll-off transport ship), The Raven (Bush's favorite book about fellow Texan Sam Houston).

S – Sarin, Sheikh, Saddam (as in Showdown with Saddam), Soft Targets, State Sponsored, Suicide Bombers, Satellite channels, Security Alerts (High, Elevated, Highest, Yellow, Orange, Red), Settlements, Smart Bombs, Smallpox, Smoke 'em out, Stealth (B2 bombers, fighters, technology), Spin Cycles, Sunni, Shiite, Shock and Awe, Subs, SecDef (Secretary of Defense), Sanctions, Impact of (rarely mentioned in media).

T – Tape, Duct (again), Terror, Terrorist, Terrorism, Taliban, Terminators (anti-Taliban), Tora Bora, (as opposed to Japanese War cry "Tora" and not to be confused with the Israeli Hora), TIA (Total Information Awareness), Twin Towers, Tribunal, Traitors (Whoever Fox News Disagrees With), Torture (word never used on television), This Just In (now used interchangeably by CNN with Breaking News), Truth (first casualty of war).

U – UAV (Unmanned Aerial Vehicle), UNMOVIC, UNSCOM, U-2 (sans Bono), Urban Warfare, USCINCCENT (Commander-in-Chief, United States Central Command).

V – Veto, VX, Vigilance, Virgins, as in 70 or 99 or the magical number of maidens waiting in Paradise to reward martyrs, Virtual March.

W – Warlords (ours and theirs), Weaponize, WTC, WMD, WUF (Weapons Unaccounted For), War on Terror, War on Iraq, Willing (our friends in coalition).

X – Exterminate, X-filtrate, X-journalist.

Y – You Decide (They Distort).

Z – Zalmay Khalilzad, U.S. envoy to Kurdish opposition, was U.S. envoy to Afghan opposition, was U.S. oil company envoy to Taliban; Zerbisias, Antonia, media columnist, Toronto Star, who dis-

CHAPTER EIGHT

SO, THIS IS VICTORY?

LOOTING ERUPTS, BAGHDAD IN CHAOS AS SOLDIERS WATCH

Questions arise as law and order collapses

"OVER," proclaims the NY Daily News. "Liberty" counters the New York Post. "US Forces Take Control in Baghdad," explains The New York Times. Each of these headlines is for the most part wrong, as is the new promo on that news channel MSNBC, copping Dr. King's phrase, "Let Freedom Ring." So far, the only freedom in Iraq is the freedom to loot and create chaos. Even Donald Rumsfeld is saying that it's not over yet and – 'deploying' my favorite sound bite of the day – "there's still more killing to do." The continuing resistance proves how un-over this war is. Yes, a statue was pulled down as we saw over and over again on television as some Iraqis danced for the cameras, a scene that could not have been more perfect had it been scripted. Having shed no tears for Saddam myself, I am sure much of the joy is genuine. His ouster is overdue. But there is a sense of foreboding about what happens next.

Oh say, does that Star Spangled Banner still wave?

POOR Cpl. Edward Chin is straight 'outta' the Republic of Brooklyn, NYC. He's the soldier who wiped Saddam Hussein's concrete face with an American flag, a flag that reportedly was flown at the World Trade Center. He (and the administration) was trying to make a connection between the fall of the twin towers and the fall of Baghdad. (Many blame 9/11 on Iraq, despite the lack of evidence). Today there will be a victory rally at the World Trade Towers site to celebrate the payback, real or invented. (It will not be massively attended!)

Osama bin Laden and much of the Arab world was delighted to seize on the symbolism of that U.S. flag going up. Many Arab newspapers ran that photo to suggest that occupation, not liberation is the real agenda. (The NY Post ran it with a caption calling the flag a "Burqa for the Butcher.") Someone must have told Cpl. Chin to knock it off because an Iraqi flag conveniently materialized to replace Old Glory, that is, until they drove the statue down. Arab journalists interviewed on U.S. TV made the point that we were only seeing one part of Baghdad. Shortly afterwards, there were major fire fights at a university and a mosque. Last night Colonel Ollie North was exulting on Fox News that some

Ba'ath Party officials were being hung from lampposts in Baghdad. Much of this sounds as if it is straight out of a Special Forces play book. (One soldier interviewed on CNN last night expressed disappointment that the Iraqi army had disappeared and "didn't want to play," as if this is all a game.)

Freedom to loot

THE Red Cross and aid workers are demanding that the U.S. and the Brits restore law and order to let humanitarian supplies through. (CNN's newly "dis-embedded reporter" Walter Rodgers arrived in Baghdad and quickly announced, on the basis of a few chats with residents, that there is plenty of food and water in the city, and nothing like the crisis many fear.) That was hardly the case, but typical of the way a reporter's impression is projected as fact.

This morning BBC showed a confrontation between a group of Iraqi professionals and British soldiers in Basra. the Iraquis were pleading for protection from the thugs who are menacing their homes and offices. The Royal Marines said they are there to fight a war, not to police the area. Could it be that restoring order is just not part of the much-vaunted plan – or could that be the plan? Let chaos ring for a few days so that the international community and the Iraqis will clamor for the new U.S. administration to step in to restore order? (Ironically, the Taliban was initially welcomed in Kabul because of its promise to restore order.)

What next?

THE oil fields around Kirkuk have been seized as

the Iraqi military "melts away." Could this be a maneuver to regroup or a "rope-a-dope" strategy like the one Muhammad Ali used in the ring to confuse his opponents? And what, if anything, will the Turkish army do as the Kurds consolidate their power in Kirkuk and Mosul? More importantly, will the war spread to Syria, as many analysts are now suggesting with the argument that "region change," not regime change, has always been the Bush plan. Already MSNBC is telling us that the massive 21,000-ton MOAB bomb is now in the region and ready to be dropped. Let's see. Where will it be field-tested? Tirkut? Damascas? Fill in the blank. Strap in. This is not over by a long shot.

TomDispatch.com wrote yesterday: "So we are, it seems, at the moment of 'liberation' (the word 'occupation' having been declared taboo) – really the moment of victory, of triumph, not for the Iraqis but for the men of this administration and for the president himself. It's the moment they have long awaited for beginning the cleansing of the Middle East. Syria, as a start, is now like meat in a sandwich, and who plans to take the first bite . . . Only today John Bolton, undersecretary of state for arms control and international security, promptly warned countries [the U.S.] has accused of pursuing weapons of mass destruction, including Iran, Syria and North Korea, to 'draw the appropriate lesson from Iraq.'"

For many Iraqis released from decades of oppression, how could there not be something euphoric in this moment, whatever the state of their homes and country, however it was brought to them? For them, post-liberation tristesse is likely to come soon enough. The problems to be faced in Iraq are monumental, if not insurmountable, under the present circumstances.

Was this even a war?

THE ever skeptical Mick Hume of Spiked On-line asks, "Was there a war at all? There were certainly plenty of bombs dropped, guns fired and Iraqis killed by the American and British forces. But there has not been one single clash with Iraqi forces that could remotely be described as a battle. Compared to the major wars of the past, the entire campaign adds up to little more than an extended skirmish. The Big Battle to Come was always the one just around the corner – in Basra, or Baghdad, or Tikrit – that somehow never quite came.

"The 'surprisingly stiff resistance' that coalition forces claimed to be facing from a few irregulars at various times over the past three weeks has been largely a product of their own anxious imagination. By the time of the first armored raid into Baghdad last weekend, the coalition seemed to be wildly exaggerating the scale of Iraqi military casualties, almost as if to prove that there really had been a proper fight. 'One thousand' killed in a three-hour shooting trip along a Baghdad boulevard quickly became 'two thousand' or more. Who was counting?

"But then, remember, this was supposed to be a war against a dictator who held the world to ransom, a regime the like of which, according to the Pentagon only last week, 'the world has not ever seen before.' Having launched a war on the risible basis that Saddam the tin-pot dictator was a bigger monster than Stalin and Hitler, they could hardly afford to admit that he had turned out to be a pantomime villain with a cardboard army . . .'"

An Iraqi voice

SOMEONE forwarded a letter to me from an Iraqi woman named Yasmin who says that her country now has to pick up the pieces, as TV News celebrates the great victory. She writes: "In Basra, I saw kids throwing rocks on soldiers and tanks . . . does it bring any memories to your mind?

"Palestine, perhaps? So . . . no dancing . . . no flowers!

"The hospitals are suffering severe shortages in medical supplies, and doctors have also complained, of not having clean water, to wash their hands before handling the patients . . . "

Exploding ordnance

ESSAM AL-GHALIB, Arab News War Correspondent, reports that unexploded ordnance litters the landscape: "Six days after the "liberation" of Najaf, Iraqis of all ages continue to pack the corridors of Saddam Hussein General Hospital. They are mostly victims of unexploded munitions that are strewn throughout various residential neighborhoods, along streets, in family homes, in school playgrounds, in the fields belonging to farms . . .

"U.S. forces have been using cluster bombs against Iraqi soldiers, but the majority of the victims are civilians, mostly children curious about the small shiny objects which are the same size as a child's hand. Cluster bombs have been dropped by the hundreds, explained an administrator at the hospital." They are supposed to explode on impact. However, many do not, and lie on the street exposed to the elements.

"A young Iraqi in Najaf told Arab News yesterday: 'They are everywhere, and they are going off periodically. We don't even have to touch them – they just go off by themselves, especially as the temperature rises throughout the day.'"

Why do Iraqis resist?

WHY would some Iraqis not be jubilant, or put another way, why has there been continued resistance despite reports and rumors of Saddam's demise by decapitation strike. United Press International (UPI) carries this report from an Indian businessman who knows Iraq well. File this report in the department of unexplored news angles: "Why should the Iraqi people feel any gratitude or loyalty to President Saddam Hussein? You would not know it from anything that has been written in the U.S. or British media, but there are very good reasons.

"I was commercial counselor and deputy chief of mission at the Indian Embassy in Baghdad from 1976 to 1978. During the interregnum between two ambassadors, I was also for a while the Indian charge d'affaires. This explains why I had more than one occasion to stare into Saddam's expressionless grey-green eyes – straight out of 'The Day of the Jackal' – while shaking his hand at various official banquets and other ceremonial occasions.

"Saddam ran a brutal dictatorship. That, however, caused no concern to the hordes of Western businessmen who descended in droves on Iraq to siphon what they could of Iraq's newfound oil wealth through lucrative contracts for everything. Everything – from eggs to nuclear plants. Because technically, from the end of the Turkish Empire over Iraq in 1919 through the British mandate, which lasted till 1932, and the

effete monarchy masterminded by Anthony Eden's buddy, Nuri es-Said, right up to the Baath Party coup of 1968, there was virtually no progress at all.

"It was Saddam's revolution that ended Iraqi backwardness. Education, including higher and technological education, became the top priority. More important, centuries of vicious discrimination against girls and women were ended by one stroke of the modernizing dictator's pen." Etc. Etc.

Were journalists murdered?

JOURNALISTS in Iraq continue to steam at the U.S. officials who expressed "regret" at the killings of reporters and cameramen and then moved on. Robert Fisk asks: "Was it possible to believe this was an accident? Or was it possible that the right word for these killings – the first with a jet aircraft, the second with an M1A1 Abrams tank – was murder? These were not, of course, the first journalists to die in the Anglo-American invasion of Iraq.

"The U.S. jet turned to rocket al-Jazeera's office on the banks of the Tigris at 7.45 am local time yesterday. The television station's chief correspondent in Baghdad, Tariq Ayoub, a Jordanian-Palestinian, was on the roof with his second cameraman, an Iraqi called Zuheir, reporting a pitched battle near the bureau between American and Iraqi troops. Mr. Ayoub's colleague Maher Abdullah recalled afterwards that both men saw the plane fire the rocket as it swooped toward their building, which is close to the Jumhuriya Bridge upon which two American tanks had just appeared.

"On the screen, there was this battle and we

could see bullets flying and then we heard the aircraft," Mr. Abdullah said.

"The plane was flying so low that those of us downstairs thought it would land on the roof – that's how close it was. We actually heard the rocket being launched. It was a direct hit – the missile actually exploded against our electrical generator. Tariq died almost at once. Zuheir was injured.

"Now for America's problems in explaining this little saga: Back in 2001, the United States fired a cruise missile at al-Jazeera's office in Kabul – from which tapes of Osama bin Laden had been broadcast around the world. No explanation was ever given for this extraordinary attack on the night before the city's 'liberation.' The Kabul correspondent, Taiseer Alouni, was unhurt. By the strange coincidence of journalism, Mr. Alouni was in the Baghdad office yesterday to endure the USAF's second attack on al-Jazeera.

"Far more disturbing, however, is the fact that the al-Jazeera network – the freest Arab television station, which has incurred the fury of both the Americans and the Iraqi authorities for its live coverage of the war – gave the Pentagon the co-ordinates of its Baghdad office two months ago and received assurances that the bureau would not be attacked . . ."

Press freedom groups demand investigation

PRESS freedom groups are pressing for an investigation. The Committee to Protect Journalists comments: "While U.S. officials have expressed regret for the loss of life in these attacks and stated that they do not target jour-

nalists, they have left the impression that they bear no responsibility for protecting journalists operating independently in Iraq. We remind you that journalists are civilians and are protected under international humanitarian law and cannot be deliberately targeted."

This comment from Reporters Without Borders: "We are appalled at what happened because it was known that both places contained journalists. Film shot by the French TV station France 3 and descriptions by journalists show that the neighborhood was very quiet at that hour and that the U.S. tank crew took their time, waiting for a couple of minutes and adjusting its gun before opening fire.

"This evidence does not match the U.S. version of an attack in self-defense, and we can only conclude that the U.S. Army deliberately, and without warning, targeted journalists. U.S. forces must prove that the incident was not a deliberate attack to dissuade or prevent journalists from continuing to report on what is happening in Baghdad."

The 'standards' of MSNBC

MSNBC came in for a trashing from Michelangelo Signorile in this week's New York Press. "The way MSNBC responded to Peter Arnett, on the other hand, is indicative of why that network is on the bottom of the cable-TV trash heap. Rivera was right about one thing in his otherwise paranoid claims that his former employer, NBC, was 'spreading lies' about him: 'MSNBC is so pathetic a cable news network they have to do anything they can to attract attention.' That includes hiring and firing anyone at whim, so long as there's a remote chance of seeing those sagging ratings lift.

"For sheer inconsistency, in both wartime and peacetime, you really can't beat the desperate souls at MSNBC. It was amusing to watch honcho Erik Sorenson and the higher-ups at NBC scramble to figure out what to do about Arnett's Iraqi TV interview. Arnett merely repeated what just about every former general was then saying to the rest of the planet via every other television network: that Bush's war plan was flawed. After first issuing a statement supporting Arnett and defending his decision to give the interview, the network brass turned around and axed him, deciding sanctimony to be the better path.

"It's just inappropriate and arguably unpatriotic," Sorenson solemnly declared about Arnett's actions. He told the Washington Post that, while watching the interview, he was hoping "there was a guy with an AK-47 behind the curtain" so as to justify Arnett's actions."

Voice: Honest journalists abound

WRITING in this week's Village Voice, Cynthia Cotts is praising some journalists for gutsy coverage: "Before the war started, the Pentagon told its embedded reporters not to dig for dirt or conduct their own investigations – just sit back and let the 'truth' set them free. Even so, during the week ending April 6, some correspondents stayed honest by covering not only American victories and losses, but also the dark side of war, excesses that are unlikely to win the loyalty of Iraqis. Never mind what the Arab media are saying. Some of the most unflinching stories have been written by reporters from the U.S. and U.K."

Government propaganda escalates

THE U.S. government continues to invest millions in getting its media message out–with great success. Bob Kemper of the Chicago Tribune reports: "The Office of Global Communications, a controversial agency created by President Bush in January, has blossomed into a huge production company, issuing daily scripts on the Iraq war to U.S. spokesmen around the world, auditioning generals to give media briefings, and booking administration stars on foreign news shows. The communications office helps devise and coordinate each day's talking points on the war. Civilian and military personnel, for example, are told to refer to the invasion of Iraq as a 'war of liberation.' Iraqi paramilitary forces are to be called 'death squads.'

"According to Kemper, "Critics are questioning the veracity of some of the stories being circulated by the office and deriding it as a propaganda arm of the White House." Administration officials rebut the charges, saying they "serve a crucial purpose." The Tribune reports that OGC chief Tucker Eskew told Washington Foreign Press Center journalists, "Our executive order insists that we deal with the truth." (Thanks to P.R. Watch for this.)

The legalities of assassination

SOCIOLOGIST Michael I. Lichter is calling for a probe into the legality of military assassination operations. The NYTimes.com headline right now is "U.S. Blasts Site in Effort to Kill Hussein," and the teaser to the story "CIA Tip Led to Strike on Baghdad Neighborhood" reads "American military forces in Iraq dropped four bombs in an attempt to kill Saddam Hussein, administration officials said in Washington.

"It's appalling that The New York Times is (again) willing to report these extremely blunt assassination attempts as if they were routine and clearly justifiable.

"An executive order approved by President Ford in the mid-1970s and affirmed by President Reagan in 1981, states: 'No person employed by or acting on behalf of the United States government shall engage in, or conspire to engage in, assassination.' Ford issued the order after extensive hearings that exposed CIA assassination plots."

The prohibition is not limited to assassination against heads of state, said Steve Aftergood of the Federation of American Scientists, a Washington-based watchdog group that follows intelligence matters.

The legalities of killing a specific person in a military strike are less clear. "I don't think the prohibition applies if you're undertaking a military action," said Sen. Arlen Specter, R-Pa.

Arab media coverage

BBC Monitoring offers a flavor of the reporting on pan-Arab TV channels: "Many pan-Arab TV channels carried live footage of the prolonged attempts by Iraqi civilians to topple the statue of Saddam Hussein in Baghdad's Al-Fardus Square. Commentators were united in saying that the event was history in the making.

"Syrian TV, which has followed a distinctly pro-Saddam line in its coverage of the conflict, ignored the event completely, screening instead a program on Islamic architecture. Other state-run TV channels in the Arab world – including Algeria, Morocco, Tunisia and Sudan – chose not

to broadcast the event live.

"Excerpts from how the commentators described the scene: Abu Dhabi TV: 'This is a moment of history. Baghdad people must be feeling sad at witnessing the fall of their capital... Baghdad has been offered on a silver plate.'

"Al Jazeera – Qatar: 'This scene suggests something which does not leave any room for doubt, namely that the rule of the Iraqi president, Saddam Hussein, has now collapsed in Baghdad ... This is a banner saying "Go home." Despite their obvious welcome of the U.S. troops, they, as Iraqi people, are demanding the departure of these troops, maybe after a short period.'"

The role of The New York Times

BOSTON PHOENIX media critic Dan Kennedy went after Johnny Apple of The New York Times who had been under attack from pro-war journalists for suggesting that there was a quagmire. He seems to buckling under the pressure. Writes Kennedy: "Well, today Johnny Apple weighs in with something that should disturb those who might be called patriotic antiwar liberals – a group that includes Media Log and, one would have thought judging from his previous pieces, Apple himself. He writes: 'The antiwar forces, who have had to contend from the start with the widespread belief that their position is unpatriotic and unsupportive of American troops engaged in deadly combat, must now bear the additional burden of arguing with success. American losses are relatively small: 96 dead to date, compared with 200 a day at the height of the Vietnam War.'

"As Greil Marcus once said, 'What is this shit?' Responsible war critics never thought the U.S.

was going to lose, or even suffer many casualties. Rather, the danger was that we would unleash chaos in Iraq, inflame the Arab world by inflicting civilian casualties (which we have certainly done), and cause terrible problems for ourselves down the road, such as creating a new generation of revenge-seeking terrorists.

"But 'arguing with success?' Please. Johnny Apple's problem isn't just that he's consistently wrong. It's that he tries on a persona-a-day, and expects us not to remember or care what he wrote just days before. Today's Apple feature on The Times's front page celebrates the victory in Baghdad. The headline: 'A High Point in 2 Decades of U.S. might.'"

Fox News is winning Israel

IF Washington is winning the war, Fox News (which has tied its brown nosing and brain washing wagon to the Bush Administration) is scoring some victories, too. Roger Alper writes in the Israeli newspaper Ha'aretz: "America's Fox News network has been demonstrating since the start of the war in Iraq an amazing lesson in media hypocrisy. The anchors, reporters, and commentators unceasingly emphasize that the war's goal is to free the Iraqi people from the tyranny of Saddam Hussein. The frequency, consistency and passion with which they use that lame excuse, and the fact that nearly no other reasons are mentioned shows that this is the network's editorial policy . . .

"Fox looks like part of the propagandistic campaign of systematic disinformation by the Bush administration, while it accuses the Iraqi regime of disseminating false information about the situation on the battlefield . . . Like CNN, it presents

to the globe the face of America and its perception of reality, and it exports its dark side, the infuriating side that inspires so much hostility: the self-righteousness, the brutality, the pretension, hubris, and simplicity, the feverish faith in its moral superiority, the saccharine and infantile patriotism, and the deep self-persuasion that America is not only the most powerful of the nations, but also that the truth is always American.

"For some reason, ever since Fox showed up on Israeli cable, the other foreign networks have become unnecessary. CNN was nearly removed, BBC World has been thrown out of the cable package, and both are suspected of hostility to Israel. Fox, for whom Israel's enemies are 'the bad guys,' is the perfect alibi for the new fashion of censorship. Who needs BBC when there's Fox?" ●

APRIL 11: LIBERATION FESTIVAL FOR THIEVES AND TERROR

STATUES are relatively easy to demolish. Lies and false impressions are far more difficult to undercut. For three weeks now, we have heard about a war organized according to "plan," a paint-by-numbers plan that no one has been allowed to see or scrutinize. Now we are being told that that plan was based on a more spontaneous "opportunistic response," as in "we will see what's happening and take advantage of any opportunities." It's a form of military situationism. There may be command but there is no control. Let it rip and then we pick up the pieces when we get around to it. It sounds mad, but could this all be part of the plan? When you let a society fall apart, you will soon hear mighty calls for law and order, as you are beginning to. There is nothing that occupiers like more than market demand–an invitation to rule by command.

Is Bush a secret anarchist?

COULD the chaos and looting and anarchy be part of it? Is President Bush a secret member of some "black block" – the name the anarcho street-trashing brigades called themselves when they sought to wreak havoc in places like Seattle or at other global justice marches? Their anarchism was a no-no, but what we are seeing now is being treated almost approvingly by news networks who do a bit of "tsk-tsking" and explain away and rationalize the lack of response to calls by Iraqi citizens to stop the Visigothian pillaging of their communities. "Our soldiers were not trained to be policemen," said Martin Savidge on CNN this morning. Robert Fisk reported in the Independent:

"As tens of thousands of Shia Muslim poor, from the vast slums of Saddam City, poured into the center of Baghdad to smash their way into shops, offices, and government ministries in an epic version of the same orgy of theft and mass destruction that the British did so little to prevent in Basra – U.S. Marines watched from only a few hundred yards away as looters made off with cars, rugs, hoards of money, computers, desks, sofas, even door-frames."

If this was happening in New York, would the military stand by? No way. Martial law would be instituted at once as it has been in uprisings in American cities during various insurrections . . . In one sense, therefore, America occupying the capital of an Arab nation for the first time in its history was helping to destroy what it had spent so much time and money creating. Saddam was "our" man and yesterday, metaphorically at least, we annihilated him. Hence the importance of all those statue-bashing mobs, of all that looting and theft. I was struck by all the interviews with poor Iraqis who compare their lot to the opulence of the palaces they are now trashing. Couldn't the same thing be said about the gap in living standards between the poor and super rich in the USA or anywhere else?

Humanitarian law flouted

MEANWHILE over on the BBC, a representative of the International Red Cross says the conditions created by the invasion make it impossible for them to provide humanitarian aid, an obligation under the Geneva Conventions. You will recall how many times we heard about violations of the conventions when a handful of U.S. prisoners of war were shown on TV. Now Washington is silent even as UN Secretary General Annan pleads that the "coalition," as the occupying force, fulfill its responsibilities. The Red Cross says it cannot even estimate the number of civilian casualties. There are no journalists that I know of "embedded" in Iraqi hospitals or with humanitarian agencies. Beatriz Lecumberri of the Sydney Morning Herald reported:

"The southern Iraqi city of Basra is sinking into anarchy, with rampant looting, murders, and petty crime. 'Let's say I had a problem with someone in the past. Now I come with a gun and kill him. Nobody's there to do anything about it. That's the situation we're in,' explained Aya, a housewife.

"We're getting patients who were hurt in the looting, stabbed by their neighbors, hit by bullets in squabbles between members of (Saddam's) Baath Party and their rivals," said Muayad Jumah Lefta, a doctor at the city's largest hospital. "The British are responsible for this," he seethed. He said even the hospital was targeted, with the doctors themselves fending off the thieves until a group of British soldiers arrived yesterday and took up a position on the roof. . .

"Where are the soldiers when we need water?" she said. "They look at people heaping up everything they can and they just laugh. It's awful . . . The British have only brought freedom to the thieves, not to the people," she said.

Towards Freedom TV

WHILE all this was going on President Bush and Tony Blair launched their own media war as a new "Towards Freedom" TV station began broadcasting from a plane into a city with no electricity, so few could actually see it. (I wonder how the folks in Vermont who publish the radical magazine Toward Freedom feel about the appropriation of their name?)

More people in the West saw the broadcasts than in Iraq, I am sure. Dr. Mohammad T. Al-Rasheed was watching for Arab News. His review: "Watching George W. Bush deliver his speeches is becoming more alarming as his diction and body language become ever so transparently arrogant."

When it comes to body language, Bush speaks volumes. The fixed stare in his eyes is boyish, as he declares something as Biblical as, "The day of reckoning is near." He awaits the applause from the "safe" crowds of servicemen and women as a little child awaits the teacher's commendations. The posture seems to say, "How did I do in this recitation of my Sunday school homework?" Not bad, Mr. President.

Warnings were baseless

STEVEN SHALOM offers an assessment of this war of liberation on ZNET: "The relative ease of the U.S. military victory confirms how little threat Saddam Hussein's regime posed beyond its borders. Where in 1990 Iraq had substantial armed forces, it was clear well before the start of this war that the Iraqi military was no longer a formidable force, even by Middle Eastern standards. The Bush administration claim that Saddam in 2003 was a danger to his neighbors was not taken seriously in the region and has now been shown to have been baseless.

"Despite Bush's constant repetition that there was no doubt that Iraq had massive supplies of chemical and biological weapons, no such weapons, or even prohibited missiles, were used by the Iraqi forces. Indeed, it seems the only time U.S.-U.K. troops needed to wear their chemical warfare suits was when recovering a body from a friendly fire incident to protect themselves from the radiation given off by U.S. depleted uranium ordnance – which, of course, the Pentagon claims is absolutely harmless.

"Nor, despite many fevered media reports, have any hidden stores of Iraqi proscribed weapons come to light. Since Iraq's alleged possession of banned weapons was the official explanation for the war, their absence is rather embarrassing for the administration."

Off the charts

IN FACT, there was another false alarm yesterday in terms of those weapons of mass destruction. Some radiation detectors went "off the charts" near a nuclear plant. Another "GOTCHA," assumed a press corps eager to relay the news until experts in Washington said it was probably low-grade uranium not immediately useful for the manufacture of weapons. Meanwhile speaking in Spain, Hans Blix, the chief UN weapons inspector, is sounding more and more cynical.

News24.com reported: "The invasion of Iraq was planned a long time in advance, and the United States and Britain are not primarily concerned with finding any banned weapons of mass destruction, the chief UN weapons inspector, Hans Blix, said in an interview on Wednesday. "There is evidence that this war was planned well in advance. Sometimes this raises doubts about their attitude to the (weapons) inspections," Blix told the Spanish daily, El Pais.

Penetrating the fog

I NOW believe that finding weapons of mass destruction has been relegated to fourth place, which is why the United States and Britain are now waging war on Iraq. This is pretty obvious but why has it taken so long for him and others at the UN to start telling the truth? Robert Fisk cuts through some more of this oft-cited "fog of war."

"Of course, the Americans knew they would get a good press by 'liberating' the foreign journalists at the Palestine Hotel. They lay in the long grass of the nearest square and pretended to aim their rifles at the rooftops as cameras hissed at them, and they flew a huge American flag from one of their tanks and grinned at the journalists, not one of whom reminded them that just 24 hours earlier, their army had killed two Western journalists with tank fire in that same hotel and then lied about it.

"But it was the looters who marked the day as something sinister rather than joyful. In Saddam City, they had welcomed the Americans with 'V' signs and cries of 'Up America' and the usual trumpetings, but then they had set off downtown for a more important appointment. At the Ministry of Economy, they stole the entire records of Iraq's exports and imports on computer discs, with desktop computers, with armchairs and fridges and paintings. When I tried to enter the building, the looters swore at me. A French reporter had his money and camera seized by the mob."

Professional looters in the wings

LOOTING can be organized and government approved. Truthout reports: "U.S. plans to loot Iraqi antiques." Here's part of the story: "Fears that Iraq's heritage will face widespread looting at the end of the Gulf war have been heightened after a group of wealthy art dealers secured a high-level meeting with the U.S. administration.

"It has emerged that a coalition of antiquities collectors and arts lawyers, calling itself the American Council for Cultural Policy (ACCP), met with U.S. Defense and State Department officials prior to the start of military action to offer its assistance in preserving the country's invaluable archaeological collections.

"The group is known to consist of a number of influential dealers who favor a relaxation of

Iraq's tight restrictions on the ownership and export of antiquities." Translation: give us the valuable antiquities to sell, all in the name of preservation.

The sound of statues falling

YESTERDAY, I cast a skeptical eye at the big story on all the TV News – the toppling of the big Saddam statue. We all saw it, complete with scenes of dancing mobs and young men with hammers beating up on what had been Saddam's head. Many networks showed that dramatic "hammering" over and over. They milked the scene, which seemed to rationalize and justify the invasion. American officials gushed about the pictures. If there is one thing this war has taught us all, it's that we can't believe what we're told. As an indy media site explained: "For Donald Rumsfeld these were 'breathtaking.' For the British Army they were 'historic.' For BBC Radio they were 'amazing.'

BUT – and there is always a big But. "A wide angle shot in which you can see the whole of Fardus Square (conveniently located just opposite the Palestine Hotel where the international media are based), and the presence of at most around 200 people – most of them U.S. troops (note the tanks and armored vehicles) and assembled journalists."

Run that by me again? Another IMC reader adds: "Oddly enough . . . a photograph is taken of a man who bears an uncanny resemblance to one of Chalabi's militia members . . . he is near Fardus Square to greet the Marines. How many members of the pro-American Free Iraqi Forces were in and around Fardus Square as the statue of Saddam came tumbling down?

Picture this

"THE up-close action video of the statue being destroyed is broadcast around the world as proof of a massive uprising. Still photos grabbed off of Reuters show a long-shot view of Fardus Square . . . it's empty save for the U.S. Marines, the International Press, and a small handful of Iraqis. There are no more than 200 people in the square at best. The Marines have the square sealed off and guarded by tanks. A U.S. mechanized vehicle is used to pull the statue of Saddam from its base. The entire event is being hailed as an equivalent of the Berlin Wall falling . . . but even a quick glance of the long-shot photo shows something more akin to a carefully constructed media event tailored for the television cameras."

Kim Sengupta reported another fascinating detail yesterday from Baghdad: "It was, by any measure, an astonishing coincidence. As the biggest statue of Saddam Hussein in Baghdad was pulled down 'spontaneously' in front of the world's media, the Stars and Stripes which flew on the Pentagon on 11 September was at hand to be draped over its face.

"The U.S. army denied that the toppling of the 20-ft edifice by a tank tower was stage-managed. It was a coincidence, they said, that Lt. Tim McLaughlin, the keeper of that flag, happened to be present. And, it has to be noted, the commander of the U.S. marines who completed the capture of Baghdad did express concern at the time that the use of the Stars and Stripes smacked of triumphalism. It was later changed to an Iraqi flag. But not before acres of TV footage had been shot."

The CIA role: Out of sight, not out of hand

IN my experience as a longtime CIA watcher, who personally spent years investigating covert activities of the kind dramatized in "The Quiet American," the movie about Vietnam that was briefly released and pulled from theaters by Miramax even after Michael Caine was nominated for an Oscar, this operation smells of so-called "special ops," a propaganda operation.

Richard Sale of UPI reminded us yesterday that the CIA has had a long history in Iraq as well as an association with the man whose regime they are now helping to topple. "U.S. forces in Baghdad might now be searching high and low for Iraqi dictator Saddam Hussein, but in the past Saddam was seen by U.S. intelligence services as a bulwark of anti-communism and they used him as their instrument for more than 40 years, according to former U.S. intelligence diplomats and intelligence officials."

United Press International has interviewed almost a dozen former U.S. diplomats, British scholars and former U.S. intelligence officials to piece together its investigation. The CIA declined to comment on the report.

Where is Saddam? Was there a deal?

IF the CIA has been dealing with Saddam over all these decades, why not now? While the media keeps focusing our attention on the "where is Saddam?" question, the Tehran Times is reporting rumors of a deal between the U.S. military and Hussein. Here's the story by Parviz Esmaeili:

"Almost 10 days ago, there was a halt in U.S.-British operations in Iraq. However, U.S. Defense Secretary Donald Rumsfeld and the chief of the U.S. Central Command, General Tommy Franks, in their interviews with the media never elaborated on the issue but instead tried to mislead world public opinion in order to hide a greater secret decision from them.

"Suspicions rose on the same day when U.S. troops, that had been stopped at the Euphrates, immediately were able to advance toward the heart of Baghdad without any significant resistance by Iraqi forces . . . Or why when the elite Iraqi forces arrived in eastern Iraq from Tikrit, the pace of the invaders advancing toward central Baghdad immediately increased. Also, it has been reported that over the past 24 hours, a plane was authorized to leave Iraq bound for Russia. Who was aboard this plane?

"All these ambiguities, the contradictory reports about Saddam's situation, and the fact that the highest-ranking Iraqi officials were all represented by a single individual – Iraqi Information Minister Mohammed al-Sahhaf – and the easy fall of Baghdad shows that the center of collusion had been Tikrit, where Saddam, his aides, and lieutenants from the Baath Party had been waiting for al-Sahhaf to join them so that they could receive the required guarantees to leave the country in a secret compromise with coalition forces."

This possibility was confirmed by the Al-Jazeera network, which quoted a Russian intelligence official as saying that the Iraqi forces and the invaders had made a deal. The Russian official told Al-Jazeera that the Iraqi leaders had agreed "to show no serious resistance against the U.S.-British troops in return for a guarantee that Saddam and his close relatives could leave Iraq unharmed."

If this explosive story has any truth to it, it offers one more example of the total unbelievability of the news we have been watching around the clock.

Media Tenor: War as entertainment

IF truth is being sacrificed on the altar of news daily, who is benefiting from all the exposure? MediaTenor, the international media monitoring organization based in Bonn, Germany, has issued a new report on coverage:

"It started with entertainment shows such as Big Brother, Survivor, and Idols – it's the new buzzword in media, albeit printed or television, and preferably should be combined with entertainment: Reality. With an added plus, however cruel or inhumane, reality always seems to carry with it an entertainment value. Now media have stumbled across the ultimate in reality: war. And it is now available on worldwide television, uncensored and uncut. Well, then at least only as far as new journalistic ethics define reality. It must be sensitive to its viewers when showing the 'good guys' and repellent when depicting 'the enemy.'

"The U.S.-led war against Iraq with its 'embedded' journalists, is turning to be the biggest PR machine yet for President George W Bush. The war offers Bush the best opportunity to position himself as a leader with integrity as trailing opinion polls suggested last year. All those issues that may have caused concern in the past, such as environment, the rejected Kyoto Agreement and ailing health system are unnoticed by the media. A staggering 40% of all statements in U.S. television (of a total of 3135) on Bush in the first quarter of 2003 focus on foreign affairs, a mere 29 on education, 90 on health, and 27 on environment. International television seemed to have picked up on this trend even before the outbreak of the conflict. In Germany, 91% of all reports on Bush focus on foreign affairs, in Britain 93%, and in South Africa 82%. And approval seems to be the fruit reaped from the strong focus on the war and foreign affairs."

Cronkite calls Bush 'arrogant'

ON the media front, the Washington Post reports that "nearly two-thirds of Americans who oppose the war say there is too much coverage, while only a third of war supporters feel that way. In a college appearance, former CBS news anchorman Walter Cronkite called President George W. Bush "grossly arrogant" for invading Iraq without the approval of the United Nations. Cronkite also said that the major networks have far less editorial control of their newscasts than before. The 86-year-old news veteran said the proliferation of cable news channels has advantages, but has harmed CBS, ABC and NBC.

FCC: Giveaway on the horizon

THE Hollywood Reporter said yesterday: "The odds seem to favor that the FCC will ease the restrictions on who can own what media company and where." Reuters reports that "FCC Chairman Michael Powell said yesterday that he supports adopting an empirical method for assessing diversity in individual media markets. Speaking to the National Association of Broadcasters at their national convention, Powell reported that a mathematical formula seemed more desirable than having to individually assess each market whenever a company proposes to buy another property. Fellow Commissioner Kevin Martin expressed concern over incorporating complex mathematics versus using "simple rules" to measure voices."

Meanwhile, the Center for the Creative Community notes that all this could be illegal. The FCC's plan to issue final rules in its media ownership limits proceeding by June 2nd violates the Regulatory Flexibility Act, writes the Small Business Administration's Office of Advocacy in a letter to FCC Chairman Michael Powell. Prior to issuing final rules, the FCC must first analyze the impact of those rules on America's small businesses and then allow small businesses to comment on that analysis.

"The SBA Office of Advocacy intervened after a request by the Center for the Creative Community, a nonprofit 501(c)(3) organization providing research, public education, and policy development on behalf of the tens of thousands of individual writers, directors, producers, performers, and other talented people who give life to America's popular and literary works of art and entertainment."   •

APRIL 16: WAR WOWS THEM IN THE HEARTLAND

I AM writing from the library of Washington State University in Pullman, just up the road from the wheat fields of Moscow, Idaho. I clicked on to CNN this morning but got the wrong channel. I was misled by the title "IRAQ: The Final Days" at the bottom of the screen. It looked like one of those familiar news graphics, but this one

floated under a sermon by a Reverend Bill Hagee, who was describing the war on Iraq as the beginning of the apocalypse, raving and ranting about the need to drive out Satan beginning with Saddam (sounds like Sodom, doesn't it?) and praising President Bush who has a "backbone, not a wishbone." I realized that I was now in a foreign country called the YOUnited States where I came face to face with the evangelical message that our Messiah from Midland has unleashed. His audience loved it. For only $69, you can buy all three videotapes blasting the UN, the Nazis, the Commies and the Saddamites as one. Hallelujah.

TIME Magazine must have been given an early preview of his tapes because they simply put Saddam on the same cover they used to announce the demise of Adolph the fuhrer. What a way to drive home the comparison that the Bush Administration has been pounding into the ground from day one.

The shark bite stories are back

YOU know the war is over when CNN starts returning to shark bite stories, missing kids, and the new Madonna video. (She, like many artists was intimidated into sealing her lips and videos on the war.) Happy Times are almost back again. FORTUNE offers the case for "optimism," reporting that "Contrary to popular belief, 2002 was one of the most profitable years ever for corporate America." That should make you feel much better. The Seattle Times was headlining the bright profit picture announced by the hometown heroes at Microsoft. In the back of the paper, there is a report on boycotts worldwide against Starbucks, another star in the firmament here in Washington State. The Washington Mutual Bank is also gloating because it has now broken the billion-dollar quarterly profit barrier. Folks in New York City (where city services are poised to be slashed) know the bank on the basis of an advertising campaign that promises to "liberate" us from checking account fees. There are giant bill boards in Times Square promising LIBERATION, a word we have been hearing about in government and in the media that echoes its message of the day.

Quote of the day

SPEAKING of Liberation, it is a word that has been used before. Here is my quote of the day: "Our armies do not come into your cities and lands as conquerors or enemies, but as liberators. Your wealth has been stripped of you by unjust men . . . The people of Baghdad shall flourish under institutions which are in consonance with their sacred laws." (General F.S. Maude, commander of British forces in Iraq, 1917)

We don't do body counts

AS one who has been looking for data on civilian casualties, I was not surprised to see that the Pentagon now says it wasn't counting, won't count, and has no plans to release figures. This latest diktat flows from Commander Tommy Franks' mantra: "WE DON'T DO BODY COUNTS." Of course, you don't. We will have to wait a long time before all the damage caused by the U.S. military is "assessed" and added up. By then, we will be moving on "preparing" the next battlefield. I noticed that the cluster bomb story that I have been citing is getting some pick up

with a Newsday account on how the deadly ordnance is still claiming lives of kids who pick up the shiny bomblets. Newsday had a good story on this that was picked up in these parts.

The people in Iraq are already being forgotten now that ABUL ABBAS, once the world's most wanted terrorist, was captured. We in the media prefer to focus on individuals, not whole populations. It appears that he has been moving around for years, and may have been covered by the 1993 peace agreement that precluded persecutions of killers on all sides of the Israeli-Palestinian divide. The terms of that treaty won't mean much in this case of a well-known terrorist. I cry no tears for his capture but with him grabbing the headlines, other more important stories are ignored.

The death toll from SARS is now at 150 and growing, to cite but one example.

The shades of Fox

BILL O'REILLY'S radio show wanted me to come on last night to defend CNN which admits it didn't disclose some of Saddam Hussein's crimes against its staffers in Iraq for fear of harming them. When I wasn't available, they asked Norman Solomon, the great media writer. Norman told me over lunch yesterday that when he told them he considered it a gray area, Fox dumped him. They only deal in black and whites over there, never grays. I was on Capitol radio, though. In Rome, Italy. What does that say about access to the airwaves for media critics in the home of the free?

I am out at Washington State University to speak on war coverage at the Edward R. Murrow School of Journalism. Ed was my mentor although we never met. It was his broadcasts that turned me on to journalism. As kid, I memorized one of his I CAN HEAR IT NOW records. Hear them if you can. •

APRIL 18: NETWORKS DECIDE TO CHANGE THE SUBJECT

SOMEONE in network-land has decreed that people have had enough of Iraq. Having contributed for eons to cultivating the incredibly short attention span that characterizes so many Americans, it seems as if the word has gone out to wean us off the breaking news parade, and shift us back into a more tranquilized state. And so CNN led this morning with the death of Dr. Atkins, of health diet fame (He never said that eating no carbs means you live forever), the stroke suffered by musical great Luther Vandross and then the Iraq aftermath. They later featured U.S. POWs invoking the God Bless America mantra.

Welcome and go home

TONY KARON leads his weblog this week with these words: "Welcome to Baghdad, Now Fuck Off." He writes: "Less than a week after the momentous toppling of a Saddam statue outside Baghdad's Palestine Hotel, Iraq's self-styled liberators appear to have become the address for all manner of Iraqi grievances. Whether the issue is the looting of Mesopotamian antiquities, the prevailing anarchy in many parts of the country (even the capital) or the demand to be included in the decision-making over the future,

there's suddenly a torrent of anti-American rhetoric pouring out of the mouths of Iraqis."

Moneyline

SOME real news is trickling out. First, there is the report that that politically connected Bechtel Corporation, which serves as the construction arm of Pentagon planners on many continents, has been pressed into action once again with the juicy contract to rebuild what we have just destroyed. Reports The New York Times on its front page: "The award will initially pay the Bechtel Group $34.6 million and could go up to $680 million over 18 months."

Ah yes, the coalition for the drilling of many a dollar is just being put together. In other lands, this news is greeted, shall we say, with more skepticism since irony seems to have become a casualty of this conflict, at least in the press.

It takes a humorist like Terry Jones of Monty Python to cut through the 'coalition' chatter as he did in the pages of London's Observer: "Well, the war has been a huge success, and I guess it's time for congratulations all round. And wow! It's hard to know where to begin.

"First, I'd like to congratulate Kellogg Brown & Root (KBR) and the Bechtel Corporation, which are the construction companies most likely to benefit from the reconstruction of Iraq. Contracts in the region of $1 billion should soon come your way, chaps. Well done! And what with the U.S. dropping 15,000 precision-guided munitions, 7,500 unguided bombs and 750 cruise missiles on Iraq so far and with more to come, there's going to be a lot of reconstruction. It looks like it could be a bonanza year.

"Congratulations, too, to former Secretary of

State, George Schultz. He's not only on the board of Bechtel, he's also chairman of the advisory board of the Committee for the Liberation of Iraq, a group with close ties to the White House committed to reconstructing the Iraqi economy through war. You're doing a grand job, George, and I'm sure material benefits will be coming your way, as sure as the Devil lives in Texas."

The 'vision'

THE Economist which follows these events more soberly explains: "Under its "Vision for Post-Conflict Iraq", America plans to spend more than $1.7 billion immediately to demonstrate a rapid improvement in the quality of life in Iraq. The plan is split into a number of bite-sized pieces, for which requests for tenders are being sent out in secret – a procedure justified due to 'urgent circumstances.' The biggest single contract is worth $600M. This envisages that within just six months the contractor will reopen half of Iraq's 'economically important roads and bridges' – some 1,500 miles – to high-speed traffic; repair 15% of the high-voltage electricity grid; provide half the population with access to 'basic health services;' renovate several thousand schools and supply them with books and other educational materials; and spruce up 5,000 houses and 3,000 slum dwellings.

"Initially, the Bush administration issued tender invitations to a small number of companies, including Halliburton's Kellogg Brown & Root subsidiary. This led to accusations of cronyism, as Dick Cheney, the vice-president, and one of the chief advocates of the war in Iraq, was chief executive of Halliburton until 2000, when he resigned to join the Republican presidential ticket. Kellogg Brown & Root is part of a consortium headed by Parsons Corp, which is believed to be on a shortlist of two, bidding against Bechtel for the work. Halliburton was also initially awarded, without competition, a separate contract by the Army Corps of Engineers to make emergency repairs to Iraq's oilfields. This was originally valued at up to $7 billion, but a new contract is now being drawn up, estimated to be worth a more conservative $600m because the damage was so light. Fluor and Bechtel are both expected to bid for the contract, though Halliburton, perhaps chastened by the cronyism allegations, has yet to say whether it will rebid. The Army Corps of Engineers is also taking bids for work worth up to $500m for road-and barrack-building projects."

Nation rebuilding in the dark

AS of this morning, the lights are still not on in Baghdad. The head of one power plant there complains that the U.S. military has taken over his office and he can't find transport to bring his staff to work despite all the hummers crowding his parking lot. This situation mirrors other realities including under resourced hospitals and a humanitarian crisis that is building. As we know this is not news the Administration wants to see reported.

Recall last weekend's remarks from Secretary of War Rumsfeld, who dismissed reports he didn't want to hear as off the wall, telling reporters "Chicken Little's crying The Sky is Falling, The Sky is Falling". He echoed the now departed Iraqi Minister of Misinformation: "I picked up a newspaper today and I couldn't believe it," he said. "I read eight headlines that talked about chaos, violence, unrest. And it just was Henny Penny – 'The sky is falling'. I've never seen anything like it! And here is a country that's being liberated, here are people who are going from being repressed and held under the thumb of a vicious dictator, and they're free. And all this newspaper could do, with eight or ten headlines, they showed a man bleeding, a civilian, who they claimed we had shot – one thing after another. It's just unbelievable . . .'

Privatization on the way

ZNET, on the left, carries a report itemizing more manna from the City on the Hill but also notes that the post war plans call for privatizing the Iraqi economy. What socialism there was there apparently has to go. "The $4.8 million management contract for the port in Umm Qasr has already gone to a U.S. company, Stevedoring Services of America, and the airports are on the auction block. The U.S. Agency for International Development has invited U.S. multinationals to bid on everything from rebuilding roads and bridges to printing textbooks. Most of these contracts are for about a year, but some have options that extend up to four. How long before they meld into long-term contracts for privatized water services, transit systems, roads, schools and phones? When does reconstruction turn into privatization in disguise?

"California Republican Congressman Darrel Issa has introduced a bill that would require the Defense Department to build a CDMA cellphone system in postwar Iraq in order to benefit 'U.S. patent holders.' As Farhad Manjoo noted in Salon, CDMA is the system used in the United States, not Europe, and was developed by Qual-

comm, one of Issa's most generous donors.

"And then there's oil. The Bush Administration knows it can't talk openly about selling off Iraq's oil resources to ExxonMobil and Shell. It leaves that to Fadhil Chalabi, a former Iraq petroleum ministry official. 'We need to have a huge amount of money coming into the country,' Chalabi says. 'The only way is to partially privatize the industry.'"

Ah, yes, those weapons

WE look forward to some news outlet running a chart on all this with frequent updates. Interestingly, BBC World led this morning with a reminder that the weapons of mass destruction alleged to be hidden in Iraq have yet to be found. UN weapons instructor Hanz Blix has offered to go back in to finish the job that, shall we say, was put on hold by preemptive war. No thanks, says Washington which is, nonetheless reportedly hiring 1,000 now out of work UN weapons inspectors do the job under Washington's watchful eye. Colin Powell insists the weapons will be found. Having covered the work of the Drug Enforcement Agency in America for years, I have no doubt they will.

Encouraging the chaos

SLOWLY, stories we haven't seen and claims we haven't heard are emerging. They challenge the unrelieved picture of a beneficent liberation. One is from Sweden's leading newspaper Dagens Nyheter, whose impressive offices I have visited. It interviews Khaled Bayomi, who has taught and researched Middle Eastern conflicts for ten years at the University of Lund where he is also working on his doctorate. He says some soldiers encouraged the looting we saw:

"I had gone to see some friends who live near a dilapidated area just past Haifa Avenue on the west bank of the Tigris. It was the 8th of April and the fighting was so intense that I was unable to return to the other side of the river. In the afternoon it became perfectly quiet and four American tanks took places on the edge of the slum area. The soldiers shot two Sudanese guards who stood at their posts outside a local administration building on the other side of Haifa Avenue. Then they blasted apart the doors to the building and from the tanks came eager calls in Arabic encouraging people to come close to them.

"The entire morning, everyone who had tried to cross the road had been shot. But in the strange silence after all the shooting, people gradually became curious. After 45 minutes, the first Baghdad citizens dared to come out. Arab interpreters in the tanks told the people to go and take what they wanted in the building.

"The word spread quickly and the building was ransacked. I was standing only 300 yards from there when the guards were murdered. Afterwards the tank crushed the entrance to the Justice Department, which was in a neighboring building, and the plundering continued there . . .

"I stood in a large crowd and watched this together with them. They did not partake in the plundering but dared not to interfere. Many had tears of shame in their eyes. The next morning the plundering spread to the Modern Museum, which lies a quarter mile farther north. There were also two crowds there, one that plundered and one with watched with disgust.

Are you saying????

"**ARE** you saying that it was U.S. troops who initiated the plundering?"

"Absolutely. The lack of jubilant scenes meant that the American troops needed pictures of Iraqis who in different ways demonstrated hatred for Saddam's regime."

"The people pulled down a large statue of Saddam?"

"Did they? It was an American tank that did that, right beside the hotel where all the journalists stay. Until lunchtime on April 9, I did not see one destroyed Saddam portrait. If people had wanted to pull down statues they could have taken down some of the small ones without any help from American tanks. If it had been a political upheaval, the people would have pulled down statues first and then plundered."

Media post mortems

THE media post mortems have begun with growing doubts being expressed over the effect on war reporting of the embedded journalists program. At the symposium I attended put on by the Edward R, Murrow School at Washington State University, mainstream journalists from AP, the Oregonian and the Wall Street Journal admitted that the whole story has yet to be told, and that the embeds, who most insisted were not censored or suppressed, could only see one part of the story. I keep trying to argue that most Americans get most of their news from TV, and that while many newspapers did offer more detailed reporting, there was more selling of the war than telling on the cable nets. I didn't get much of an argument.

Off with their heads

JOURNALISTS who offered negative commentary were often targeted by pro-war media outlets. The Poynter Institute reports on a story you saw here first: "Michael Wolff received over 3,000 hate e-mails after asking Gen. Vincent Brooks at a Centcom briefing: 'Why are we here? Why should we stay? What's the value of what we're learning at this million-dollar press center?' He was also told by a CENTCOM civilian, 'a thirtyish Republican operative': 'Don't f-- with things you don't understand. This is f--ing war, asshole . . . No more questions for you.'

In Los Angles, one website reports: "The executive producer of a CBS miniseries about Adolf Hitler's rise to power has been fired after giving an interview in which he compared the current mood of Americans to that of the Germans who helped Hitler rise to power. According to The Hollywood Reporter, Gernon was fired Sunday (April 6) from Alliance Atlantis, the production company making 'Hitler: The Rise of Evil' for CBS. He had worked there 11 years and was head of the firm's long-form programming division. Neither Gernon nor Alliance Atlantis is commenting on the matter . . ."

Get Michael Moore

THE New York Post claims that a website "Revoketheoscar.com has been set up try to strip filmmaker Michael Moore of his prize for best documentary. The San Francisco Bay Guardian's Steven T. Jones reports, "Instead of being back at work writing his technology column for the San Francisco Chronicle last week, Henry Norr was at home nursing a deep bruise on his leg, the result of being shot with a wooden dowel by Oakland police during an antiwar demonstration.

"His two-week suspension from the paper for calling in sick and being intentionally arrested on the first full day of the war should have ended April 3, but he has been neither formally fired nor invited to return. And he probably won't be welcomed back on terms he can accept, given a policy change unilaterally implemented by editor Phil Bronstein. On April 2, Bronstein issued what he labeled a 'clarification' to the Chron's conflict-of-interest policy, stating in a memo to staff, 'Our responsibility as journalists can only be met by a strict prohibition against any newsroom staffer participating in any public political activity related to the war.'" •

APRIL 22: WAR IS OVER, NOW IT'S TIME TO MOVE ON

SAY Goodbye to The War on Iraq, as brought to you daily by all your news channels, and welcome back television as usual. With the war "won" and victory to be officially proclaimed by General Franks as early as today, the story is over. Right?

Wrong.

But no matter. Chad was back in action as the weatherman this morning on CNN and search as I did, I could find no more forecasts on TV for Basra. Imagine more sandstorms predicted and we will know nothing of them!

"It never happened"

GET ready to yawn when you hear about the war

again; it's the old story of overexposure and simplification driving out more nuanced coverage and follow-up. Leave it to the Guardian in England to spot the trend in America, reporting today:

"One month after the beginning of the Iraqi conflict, America is returning to its normal diet of reality TV – including a presenting debut for one Monica Lewinsky.

"Suddenly, it's as if the war had never happened. Stefano Hatfield, a contributor to an advertising magazine explains: 'War is God's way of teaching Americans geography,' said the writer Ambrose Bierce. Well, the war is apparently over because those lustrous locations, Brooklyn and Queens, have elbowed Baghdad and Umm Qasr out of the news.

"The hour-long rightwing rant known as Fox News contained not a single Iraqi name check. Is it over then? As I look north out of my apartment window, I can just about make out the red, white and blue lighting on the Empire State Building through the clouds. It's a giant Zoom ice lolly that will remain patriotically lit until 'we' had 'won.' Or so we were told. It's an eloquent symbol of the confusion reigning over how to define victory.

"All around us, life has returned to what passes for normal. Scott Peterson, the platinum-blond husband who allegedly murdered and decapitated his pregnant wife, is the top story. The Central Park Jogger has a book out, Madonna a "controversial" new CD.

While New York City has a budget crisis, the Yankees are laying waste to all around them. Michael Jordan has retired (again) and OJ Simpson is set to be an 'expert' commentator on Robert Blake's murder trial.

Besting the West

IT is not just Al-Jazeera by the way that has emerged with new respect in this war. Islam Online is carrying a report today from Cairo arguing "Western Media No Longer the Best." It reads in part: "When the First Gulf War erupted in 1991, Egyptian TV was almost entirely dependent on CNN coverage of the war. The logo of the American news channel appeared on almost every feed about the war.

"For many years Western media had represented the best option for Arab viewers. First, it possessed the necessary resources for high quality news coverage, resources that Arab media lacked. Secondly, it was generally viewed as being free and unconstrained by political considerations. It had gained a reputation of being motivated solely by professional incentives, in which the first and most important objective is to seek and present the truth as it is. This was in contrast to Arab media, which had gained a reputation of being a mere propaganda tool.

"Now, with the outbreak of the Third Gulf War, things might be changing, and there is evidence to suggest that Western media might be losing its edge in the Arab world. "Several Arab satellite channels, notably Al Jazeera, Abu Dhabi TV, El Manar TV and possibly the new member of the MBC group, Arabiyya, have proven to have a high degree of technical and professional ability."

Was BBC biased?

AND what about the western media? How well has it done? The Guardian today looks into the controversy about BBC coverage. Media researcher David Miller of Stirling Research writes: "The BBC was attacked by both sides over the Iraq war. It was the only news organization apart from the Sun that was targeted by anti-war demonstrators, and senior managers apologized for the use of biased terms such as "liberate" in their coverage. Meanwhile, ministers publicly criticized the BBC's alleged bias towards Baghdad. The BBC argued that criticism from all sides showed it must be getting something right. The empirical evidence, however, suggests a pro-war orientation.

"The BBC, as the national broadcaster, has always found it difficult to resist government pressure. During the Falklands war, for example, it was attacked as traitorous for airing doubts about the war, but its senior management was clear that the bulk of its output had either not reported Argentinean claims or had 'nailed' them as 'propagandist lies.'

"The level of public opposition to the war in Iraq was difficult for the BBC to navigate. The war exposed a serious disconnection between the political elite and the public, so the usual method of ensuring 'balance' – interviewing politicians – was never going to be enough. Other channels, including even ITV's lightweight Tonight program, tried new ways of accessing opposition, while the BBC cautioned its senior management, in a confidential memo dated February 6, to 'be careful' about broadcasting dissent.

Imagine that: ABC had more anti-war coverage than the BBC

YOU may be surprised to learn that our associates at Media Tenor in Germany which studied coverage in six countries found that the BBC featured the lowest level of coverage of dissent of all. Its 2% total was even lower than the 7% found on ABC in the U.S.

Fisk: "It's going wrong"

MEANWHILE, new stories are emerging that seem to challenge the perceptions that the government with the help of many media outlets are fostering. Robert Fisk of the Independent may be hard line but, if so, so many of his American colleagues are softer than soft. His latest just rips the veil off an emerging era of "good feelings:"

"It's going wrong, faster than anyone could have imagined. The army of 'liberation' has already turned into the army of occupation. The Shias are threatening to fight the Americans, to create their own war of 'liberation.'

"At night on every one of the Shia Muslim barricades in Sadr City, there are 14 men with automatic rifles. Even the U.S. Marines in Baghdad are talking of the insults being flung at them. 'Go away! Get out of my face!' an American soldier screamed at an Iraqi trying to push towards the wire surrounding an infantry unit in the capital yesterday. I watched the man's face suffuse with rage.

"'God is Great! God is Great!'" the Iraqi retorted.

"'Fuck you!'"

"The Americans have now issued a 'Message to the Citizens of Baghdad,' a document as colonial in spirit as it is insensitive in tone. 'Please avoid leaving your homes during the night hours after evening prayers and before the call to morning prayers,' it tells the people of the city. 'During this time, terrorist forces associated with

213

the former regime of Saddam Hussein, as well as various criminal elements, are known to move through the area . . . please do not leave your homes during this time. During all hours, please approach Coalition military positions with extreme caution . . . '

"So now – with neither electricity nor running water – the millions of Iraqis here are ordered to stay in their homes from dusk to dawn. Lockdown. It's a form of imprisonment. In their own country. Written by the command of the 1st U.S. Marine Division, it's a curfew in all but name."●

APRIL 23: NOW THE RESISTANCE AND POLITICAL TURMOIL

YOU can't help thinking that someone of self-importance and consequence in some safe room in the bowels of Washington power was watching Nic Robertson's CNN report this morning "LIVE FROM KARBALA" and having a twinge of second thoughts about what liberation has wrought. As thousands of the Shia faithful flagellated themselves for Allah while denouncing the United States occupation of their country, some in the Bush brigade must be waxing just a bit nostalgic for the bad old days of Saddam Hussein, the demon we loved to demonize. "He," you can hear them mutter, "at least kept the Sharia crowd in check; he was a strong man we could do business with. He opted for a civil state, not a religious one. He was such a useful bad guy to rail against."

But, for better or worse, they no longer have Saddam to kick around. As the good poet once said, when the center doesn't hold, things fall

apart. And it will take more than the hapless General Jay Garner to put Humpty Dumpty back together again. The New York Times is leading with this tale of woes today as well with several stories such as, "As Baghdad Awaits Aid, Feeling Grows Against U.S. Islamic passions suppressed under Saddam Hussein escalated in Karbala. In Baghdad, Iraqis awaited material help from the U.S." And then there is: "Iranian-trained agents have crossed into Iraq and are working to advance Iranian interests, according to U.S. officials."

Reporting on the WMDs

CYNTHIA COTTS notes how some media outlets have handled the WMD issue in this week's Village Voice. She writes: "Since the war began, the military and its media have trumpeted one WMD discovery after another that turned out to be a dud. Searches of 'sensitive sites' have turned up gas masks, protective suits, antidotes, manuals, white powder, barrels of chemicals, and a cache of mystery shells but no smoking gun. The military types who could not wait another week for UN inspectors to do their job are now saying their own WMD search will take weeks, maybe months.

"This is all so peculiar it calls for a heightened level of skepticism. But after weeks of false alarms, some major media outlets have fallen into the habit of reporting the absence of news. Last week, CNN began a WMD report with the words 'No smoking gun yet,' and the headline on a recent New York Times story read, 'U.S. Inspectors Find No Forbidden Weapons at Iraqi Arms Plant.' On Monday, the Times reported that an unnamed scientist who claims to have worked for Iraq now says WMD evidence was destroyed just days before the war began.

"Sure, unambiguous proof of the hidden stockpiles may turn up any day now. But the threat of Iraq's WMD may also turn out to be the biggest media hoax since Y2K."

Not Comical Ali

WE still have had no attempt at accounting for the number of civilian casualties in Iraq. But, as if to salve our conscience, media attention has predictably enough been focused on one child, a poster boy for children in need. His name is Ali Ismail Abbas. He is 12. He lost his father, his mother (who was pregnant at the time) and his brother to "coalition bombing." He lost part of his body, too. Poor Ali has aroused the conscience of the west. You have probably seen him on TV. Mary Riddel wrote about him in the Observer:

"Today, he is recovering in Kuwait, where his publicity shots show a sweet face above the blankets masking his scorched torso and stumps. He has eaten a kebab and obliged visiting journalists from British newspapers with quotes. 'When will my arms grow back?' he asked.

"Ali, the iconic image of war, is the centerpiece of half-a-dozen charity appeals, which have raised several hundred thousand pounds, as against the $20 billion cost of the conflict, or the $1.3bn needed by the World Food Program. Of that, only $296 million has been offered. Though comparatively small, the Ali appeals prove that the dry plea of bureaucrats cannot compete as a can-rattler for humanity.

"The formula is not difficult to read. Hope, the magical ingredient of childhood, sells. Despair

does not. No one can predict whether Ali will ultimately be glad of the officious mercy accorded him, but few would argue it was wrong for him to have his chance. Nor is it reprehensible to make him the face of good causes. His exploitation lies, instead, in the propaganda implicit in his story . . . Ali is the human emblem of the case for war, not for the arguments against. A wonder of modern surgery, masterminded by the U.S. and Britain and performed in the Middle East, is an exact metaphor for the outcome the coalition wants for Iraq. Nor is Ali a sting to Western consciences. Instead, he is their balm. Despite the correct insistence of Unicef that he should be the figurehead for all Iraqi children, the spotlight on a single child distracts from the countless number who die this Easter because the miracle workers of the West cannot switch on their electricity or offer clean water or bring oxygen and aid into flyblown wards where the mattresses stiffen with other people's blood."

Ignored warnings

REMEMBER Peter Arnett? Recall that he was working in part for National Geographic. I always wondered about what their interest was in Iraq. As it turns out they were fully aware of the country's cultural treasures and warned of looting WELL BEFORE IT OCCURRED.

Here is a report just sent to me. It is dated March 21 – It was given scant coverage at the time: "Iraq War Threatens Ancient Treasures. Brian Handwerk for National Geographic News (Updated March 21, 2003).

"The looming war in Iraq is likely to take a heavy toll in terms of lives and property. But in a country regarded as the 'Cradle of Civilization,' there may also be substantial harm to irreplaceable cultural heritage in the form of damage to ancient structures, archaeological sites, and artifacts.

"The first immediate danger to Iraq's cultural sites is bombing or combat damage. In the first Gulf War, damage of this kind appears to have been fairly limited. "There are millions of sites in Iraq," said Selma Radhi, an independent scholar and consultant archaeologist who has excavated and restored ancient monuments all over the Middle East. "How could one choose two that should not be bombed?"

The greater worry

WHILE such damage is a concern, it's likely not the greatest worry. "We're not so worried about errant bombing," explained McGuire Gibson, an Iraq specialist at the University of Chicago's Oriental Institute. "It could happen, but it's that period of uncertainty that would come with the war that would be a problem."

"Gibson and many other prominent archaeologists are most concerned about looting. It's been an ongoing problem in Iraq since the first Gulf War, when Iraq's formerly robust Department of Antiquities began to decline. In the event of combat and/or unrest, looting could become much worse."

Debating BBC coverage

YESTERDAY, I also carried excerpts from a Guardian article lambasting the BBC for its war coverage. I queried BBC News chief Richard Sambrook for his response. He wrote back – one of the few news executives willing to respond to critics – saying, "There is a real critique to be done of our coverage of course, but that wasn't it." He then included a response which later appears in part in today's Media Guardian:

"David Miller's attack on the BBC's journalism (Taking Sides 22.4.03) is a lazy cobbling together of disparate evidence taken out of context in an attempt to reach a pre-ordained conclusion. He is also factually wrong in a number of instances.

"The BBC has not argued that because we are criticized by all sides we must be right – we have suggested it shows the case from either side is not straightforward.

"Mr. Miller suggests we virtually ignored opposition to the war. Yet in many programs, across radio and TV, opponents to war were regularly given the opportunity to express their views, anti-war demonstrations were reported and opinion polls showing the balance of public opinion fully analyzed. (DISSECTOR: On this point, and for what it is worth, I would interject that I was interviewed several times on BBC Radio, and only once on CNN. A BBC world service reporter came along to a demonstration in New York that I was covering.)

"Mr. Miller selectively quotes research carried out for the Frankfurter Allgemeine Zeitung. He doesn't, strangely, mention that the same survey showed the BBC, uniquely out of the broadcasters analyzed, was even-handed in its reporting of the U.S. military action and in reporting of coalition and civilian casualties. Presumably it didn't fit his argument."

I have not watched as much BBC coverage as I would have liked. Many of our readers preferred it to the U.S. cable nets. But there are many in England, especially around the website MediaLens which have compiled more detailed critiques. Without passing judgments, I would only say that at least in the UK, there are debates about these issues in many newspapers. They are taken seriously. This is less true in the USA.   ●

APRIL 24: WAR COVERAGE UNDER FIRE FROM BBC CHIEF

JUST I was wallowing in the thrill of victory as more wanted Iraqis experience the agony of defeat, just as I thought it was safe to eat French food again – as I did last night with fava beans on the side. Shades of Silence of the Lambs – word comes that secretary of State Powell intends to "punish" France. Sorry Colin, the food has already been recycled. And then there was this morning's shocker coming from the land of coalition cronies and Blair Baathists: Our TV System is under attack.

BBC: Shock, no awe

A NEW front in the media war erupted across the Atlantic when the "topper" (to use a Variety-ism) of the BBC opened up on American television. Embroiled in some criticism in the home counties for less than objective war coverage, Greg Dyke is shifting attention across the seas. And in this case, hitting his mark in a gutsy manner that we have yet to hear from most of his U.S. counterparts. The Guardian reports:

"BBC director general Greg Dyke has delivered a stinging rebuke to the U.S. media over its unquestioning coverage of the war in Iraq and warned the government against allowing the UK media to become Americanized.

"Mr. Dyke said he was shocked to hear that the U.S. radio giant Clear Channel had organized pro-war rallies in the U.S., and urged the government to ensure new media laws did not allow U.S. media companies to undermine the impartiality of the British media.

"We are genuinely shocked when we discover that the largest radio group in the United States was using its airwaves to organize pro-war rallies. We are even more shocked to discover that the same group wants to become a big player in radio in the UK when it is deregulated later this year," Mr. Dyke said.

"Mr. Dyke singled out Fox for particular criticism over its pro-Bush stance, which helped the Rupert Murdoch-owned broadcaster to oust CNN in the U.S. to become the most popular news network.

"Commercial pressures may tempt others to follow the Fox News formula of gung-ho patriotism, but for the BBC this would be a terrible mistake. If, over time, we lost the trust of our audiences, there is no point in the BBC," he said in a speech delivered at Goldsmiths College in London today."

Targeting the Middle East

EVEN as the BBC blasts U.S. broadcasting, a U.S. government TV venture is good to go in the Middle East. It's run by a man who comes out of Infinity Broadcasting, the radio monopoly owned by Viacom and known for the wit and wisdom of Howard Stern. Again, it is a British newspaper we must turn to for a report on an American Media venture:

"Washington's battle to win public support in

the Arab world has begun in earnest with the first broadcasts of what officials say will become a 24-hour satellite television network aimed at changing minds throughout the region by American-style morning chat-shows, sports, news and children's programs.

"Iraq and the World, the prototype channel being beamed into the country from a U.S. air force plane, began showing American evening news bulletins this week. A full-service version should be broadcasting 24 hours a day to 22 countries in the Middle East by the end of the year, Mr. [Norman] Pattiz, chairman of Westwood One, said. Faces familiar to U.S. audiences, including Dan Rather of CBS and Tom Brokaw of ABC, are appearing with their words translated into Arabic.

"We don't do propaganda," he insisted.

Give me the pictures, I will give you the war

At the start of the Spanish American War, newspaper magnate William Randolph Hearst reportedly said to a staff illustrator: "Give me the pictures, I'll give you the war." That comment was thought to have ushered in the era of the "yellow" (i.e. sensationalized) press. Clearly, for the media at least, war is good business. That suggests at the same time that conflicts and tensions will be pumped up through press coverage.

Already, new media layoffs are in the offing, with temporary employees brought in to assist with war "coverage" being dispatched to the unemployment lines. Ponder the implications of this report from the LA Times: "Cable news viewing continued to decline last week, with the combined audience for Fox News, CNN and MSNBC slipping over 30% from the previous week."

If wars take time to organize, watch for more sensational stories to boost ratings.

As for time to organize, Ted Koppel let loose a factoid last night of interest. He noted that the U.S. Army started its war plans for Iraq last June. That came up in a discussion with Andrew Natsios who runs the Agency for International Development, the government arm tasked with helping the poorer countries of the world. He is now in charge of the $1.7 BILLION dollar reconstruction effort in Iraq.

This is the agency that gave the biggest contract to Bechtel. Ted was asking why there had been no competitive bidding and why the cost plus contract. The AID Administrator explained how it takes time to draw up the documents outlining the scope of work. He revealed that work started last September, while Washington wonks were still publicly saying no decision had been made. While the public was being fed a line of lies, the agencies were planning the future destruction and reconstruction of another country.

Media man implicated in looting

IF this is not a form of looting, what is? Yet it is not being covered as such. Instead reports are dribbling in that U.S. soldiers and even media employees had sticky fingers in Iraqi treasures. AP reports:

"WASHINGTON – Members of the news media and U.S. soldiers are being investigated for taking art, artifacts, weapons and cash from Iraq, with criminal charges already brought in one case, federal officials said Wednesday.

"At least 15 paintings, gold-plated firearms, ornamental knives, Iraqi government bonds and other items have been seized at airports in Washington, Boston and London in the last week, according to the bureaus of Customs and Border Protection and of Immigration and Customs Enforcement. So far, only Benjamin James Johnson, who worked as an engineer for Fox News Channel, has been charged. But officials said more charges could be brought and more seizures of stolen items are expected in what is being dubbed "Operation Iraqi Heritage.""

Warnings of the TIMES

READING The New York Times today, one is confronted with two warning stories, from right to left, side by side. The first is a warning to Iran not to interfere in Iraq because apparently only Washington has that right.

Says one more unknown and unidentified "Senior" Administration official, "It's clear we have to step in a little more forcefully." To the right of this article is another reporting on warnings to Iraqi politicians against stepping into the power vacuum.

He warned that no one challenging American authority (note no use of the term coalition here) would be subject in the press. Also on page one is a story about the fate of Afghan detainees still sweltering in the prison camp in Cuba. CNN's Aaron Brown quipped last night that this is not a story we have been hearing about. (No shit, Sherlock!) There was no mention on page one of the children in the camp. The Australian Broadcasting company featured this Reuters story more prominently.

CNN on the media

PR SPIN reports: "The media watchdog FAIR/Extra! has studied the guest list of CNN's Reliable Sources to see how many critical voices were heard on the program that claims to "turn a critical lens on the media." Covering one year of weekly programs, the FAIR study found that Reliable Sources strongly favored mainstream media insiders and right-leaning pundits. In addition, female critics were significantly underrepresented, and ethnic minority voices were almost non-existent." ●

APRIL 25: THUG LIFE, BAGHDAD STYLE

IT is April 25th. On this day, in another war for democracy, The New York Times reminds us that the United States and Soviet forces linked up on the Elbe River, in central Europe, a meeting that dramatized the collapse of Nazi Germany. What happened next, as we know were hopes for peace dashed by distrust and power games among the allies, and a cold war replacing that hot war. All the allies, not just the United States, later tried Nazi war criminals.

I raise this after watching Nightline's John Donovan compare the now surrendered (by his son) Iraqi Minister Tariq Aziz to a Nazi war criminal and denounce the thugs who ran Iraq. That same word, "thugs," was used again by frequent "expert," neo-con Daniel Pipes this morning on Fox who called for the U.S. soldiers to step into the background and find a "strongman" to place in power.

A call for a strong man

FUNNY, how much we like "strong men" preferring authoritarianism to democracy, which in Iraq anyway, could easily lead to the selection of anti-American politicians. If only because weeks after the never-doubted successful invasion, the U.S. occupiers have still not managed to get the lights and water back on in the desert town of Baghdad. As we know the eve of destruction is always easier than the morning of construction.

It was odd to hear about "thugs." a word that may even understate human rights crimes in New York. What about Guantanamo? CNN was reporting on that, offering more dirty details about the incarceration of suspects detained in a high security hole in Cuba's Guantanamo Bay. I learned we still don't know how many there are, who they are, what they are being charged with, and why there are children among them. This latter disclosure raises still more questions about U.S. violations of international treaties governing the treatment of prisoners. But no – this is not "thuggish" behavior. The New York Times reported yesterday that the detainees are provided with new Korans and lots of fattening food twice a day. They reportedly have gained ten pounds apiece. I am waiting for the Newsweek cover on OBESITY in our prisons: is it humane punishment?

Was The New York Times used?

PROFESSOR Gary Leup writes in Counter Punch about Judith Miller's recent article in The New York Times, "Illicit Arms Kept Till Eve of War, an Iraqi Scientist Is Said to Assert" (New York Times, April 21). According to a report on Media news, it raised eyebrows in The Times newsroom where its veracity was questioned by some. Leup believes the Administration used The Times:

"You allow a New York Times reporter, who was not permitted to interview the scientist, nor visit his home, nor permitted to write about this momentous discovery for three days, whose copy was submitted for a check by military officials, to reveal this information to the world. You announce that this is the best evidence 'to date' (as though one or more other shreds of evidence had been unearthed recently), adding, 'it may be the discovery,' so others might not be necessary.

Quite brilliant. You have to admire such audacity. But I think of the opening passage of the samurai epic, Heike Monogatari, that chronicles the inevitable downfall of a ruling circle less obnoxious than the one now wreaking havoc on Iraq. "The proud do not endure, they are like a dream on a spring night; the mighty fall at last, they are as dust before the wind."

In the meantime, let us not let them throw dust in our eyes.

War games lead to . . . war games

IF you missed the Iraq War, you can play the game. Maureen Clare Murphy of Electronic Iraq: "The war on Iraq has not caused any severe disruptions to the generally comfortable American lifestyle. Even Americans' favorite prime-time sitcoms have been spared from pre-emption. What many disconnected Americans conceive, as the war is what they see on CNN: green video of explosions over Baghdad narrated by a correspondent in a flak jacket.

"However, many young men in America have decided to 'participate' in the war by purchasing or downloading video games that are set in Iraq. In 'Conflict: Desert Storm,' by Gotham Games, the gamer's mission is to find and capture (or kill) Saddam Hussein. In 'Gulf War: Operation Desert Hammer,' by 3DO, players head a technologically sophisticated tank, and seek out the 'Desert Beast,' a dictator that can easily be inferred as Saddam Hussein."

Although these games were developed before the U.S. bombing campaign began, their timely releases certainly seem opportunistic. "Conflict: Desert Storm" has sold out at video game stores, and "Gulf War: Operation Desert Hammer" has significantly surpassed its previous sales estimates.

How long can you watch?

IN this country, the cable news nets have driven the coverage. Tim Goodman in the San Francisco Chronicle (the newspaper that just fired a reporter who took a day off to protest) had some provocative things to say. Mark Gould of New College sent it along.

"CNN, Fox News, and MSNBC have gorged on Iraq and come up for air bloated, slow and confused. Anyone watching these broadcasts sees the same explosions repeated endlessly. Stories that could be told in 30 seconds or a minute suddenly drag on for five minutes, with long pauses between anchors and field reporters. Not much is either explained or answered in these live interviews, and yet the same verbal dance takes place again 15 minutes later. This cycle has diminished the ability to watch cable news.

"Where the first week – even 10 days if you wanted to be overly indulgent – offered the hardcore news junkie ample time to marvel at the wonders of the modern, live war played endlessly on cable television, that fascination has now faded. It has also rubbed off the patina of competent journalism. What emerges now, for those still putting in the hours, is the inevitable impression that without editors, without reflection or even a modicum of critical doubt, is coverage more seemingly defined by the military.

"With no one stopping for a breath, anchors repeat essentially what's told to them by the government, with phrases and lingo largely intact. Coalition forces are "pounding" or "hammering" the opposition, viewers hear, and while this is true in the bigger context, it ceases to be relevant when it's repeated ceaselessly." ●

APRIL 28: TRUTH CRUSHED TO EARTH WILL RISE AGAIN

I AM sure someone among the perception managers in the information operations division of the ministry of "newsspeak" considered adding an extra 6. Saddam Hussein (spelled interestingly Saddam Husayn Al-Tikriuti on the ace of spades playing card) is 66 today. 666 would have been perfect don'tcha think? He is also very much alive according to Tariq Aziz, not always known as a truth teller, having reportedly survived two decapitation strikes.

Carol Morello of the Washington Post was on MSNBC today talking about the disappointment many Iraqis expressed to her about not being able to celebrate the big B-Day as they have in years past. (Notice how many newspaper reporters are now being milked for stories by the cost-cutting cable nets. Are they getting paid?)

She said that most of the folks in the streets of Baghdad she talked with believe he is alive. Many are apparently pissed at him NOT because of all of the dreadful things about his regime that bombard us daily but because he did not, as promised, defend the capital and them.

More 'revelations' debunked

SECRETARY of Defense Rumsfeld, who was not "inclined" to tell reporters at a briefing last week where he was going, has showed up to thank his military forces for a job well done. The President will offer a more subdued victory statement later in the week. Meanwhile four more U.S. soldiers were wounded in another sniping incident as General Jay Garner begins his democracy building-reconstruction exercise. There has been more debunking of false stories in the media. The Mail and Guardian reports: "Western intelligence officials are playing down the significance of documents appearing to show that Saddam Hussein's regime met an al-Qaeda envoy in Baghdad in 1998 and sought to arrange a meeting with Osama bin Laden."

Also, a bunch of barrels widely reported as having chemical weapons now apparently, on closer inspection, did not. One thousand more "experts" are on the way to join the elusive weapons hunt. (My suggestion: send in the DEA, they always find the illicit substances–one way or another.)

Weapons search a mess

THE Times is reporting that the search for weapons, the nominal purpose of the war, is righteously screwed up. "Disorganization, delays and faulty intelligence have hampered the Pentagon-led search for Saddam Hussein's suspected weapons of mass destruction, causing growing concern about one of the most sensitive and secretive operations in postwar Iraq, according to U.S. officials and outside experts familiar with the effort.

"The slow start has created so many interagency squabbles that a National Security Council military staffer at the White House has been assigned to mediate among the Defense Intelligence Agency, the Defense Threat Reduction Agency, the CIA, the Energy Department, and other government agencies involved in the hunt.

"And some weapons experts warn that the lapses have even raised the threat of arms proliferation from Iraq."

"Selective use of intellligence, exaggeration"

THE Independent on Sunday yesterday said that intelligence agencies in the U.S. and Britain are now saying (where were they before the war?) that their findings were misrepresented. Raymond Whitaker reported: "The case for invading Iraq to remove its weapons of mass destruction was based on selective use of intelligence, exaggeration, use of sources known to be discredited and outright fabrication.

"A high-level UK source said last night that intelligence agencies on both sides of the Atlantic were furious that briefings they gave political leaders were distorted in the rush to war with Iraq. 'They ignored intelligence assessments which said Iraq was not a threat,' the source said. Quoting an editorial in a Middle East newspaper which said, 'Washington has to prove its case. If it does not, the world will forever believe that it paved the road to war with lies,' he added: 'You can draw your own conclusions.'"

ABC News is reporting on another aspect of what was suspected but now confirmed as intentional deception: "To build its case for war with Iraq, the Bush administration argued that Saddam Hussein had weapons of mass destruction, but some officials now privately acknowledge the White House had another reason for war – a global show of American power and democracy."

"Not lying"

OFFICIALS inside government and advisers outside told ABC NEWS the administration emphasized the danger of Saddam's weapons to gain the legal justification for war from the United Nations and to stress the danger at home to Americans. "We were not lying," said one official. "But it was just a matter of emphasis."

The crimes of war

IN addition to the widely reported human rights crimes, possible war crimes are surfacing. AP reports: "Military officials are investigating a Marine who says he shot an Iraqi soldier twice in the back of the head following a grenade attack on his comrades.

"The Marine Forces Reserve announced the preliminary inquiry of Gunnery Sgt. Gus Covarrubias on Friday, the day the Las Vegas Review-Journal published an interview in which he described the killing.

"Covarrubias, 38, of Las Vegas, said that during an intense battle in Baghdad on April 8, he pursued a member of the Iraqi Republican Guard who fired a rocket-propelled grenade at his unit.

"I went behind him and shot him in the back of the head. Twice," Covarrubias told the Review-Journal. He said he also shot the man's partner, who tried to escape. He showed what he said were the men's ID cards."

"Whitewashing the facts"

HUMAN Rights Watch is disputing Pentagon claims on the use of cluster bombs. The story in The Times: "U.S. Misleading on Cluster Munitions." The U.S. Army has used ground-based Multiple Launch Rocket System (MLRS) and other artillery-launched cluster munitions in populated areas of Baghdad and other Iraqi cities, Human Rights Watch said.

U.S. Chairman of the Joint Chiefs Staff Gen. Richard B. Myers told a press conference in Washington that coalition forces dropped "nearly 1,500 cluster bombs of varying types" during the war in Iraq, and that only 26 of those fell within 1,500 feet of civilian neighborhoods, causing only "one recorded case of collateral damage."

"But Myers did not mention surface-launched cluster munitions, which are believed to have caused many more civilian casualties. 'To imply that cluster munitions caused virtually no harm to Iraqi civilians is highly disingenuous,' said Kenneth Roth, executive director of Human Rights Watch. 'Instead of whitewashing the facts, the Pentagon needs to come clean about the Army's use of cluster munitions, which has been much more fatal to civilians.'"

The moral universe
of Thomas Friedman

"AMERICA did the right thing here," argued Thomas L. Friedman, minister of conventional wisdom, on The NY Times Op-ed page yesterday. "It toppled one of the most evil regimes on earth." And so a new rationale of the war is emerging post-hoc, picturing the Bush Administration as human rights avengers, "globo-cops" out to right wrongs. Friedman uses a skull of one of Saddam's many victims as a symbol of why the war was worth it. I read that with a certain degree of mirth because as every serious student of U.S. human rights policy knows Washington's stance on human rights is selective, guided by perceived U.S. interests, not morality.

Isn't it interesting how Saddam's crimes are being splashed across our TV screens now, but so many others in so many countries, over so many years were ignored, or criticized without commitment to action. Today, while the Bush Administration points to human rights abuses in Iraq, it will not support an International Criminal Court to try offenders. Talk of human rights abuses in the U.S. is verboten.

Thomas Friedman waffled for weeks about the justification for going to war with Iraq. Now that war has been "won" he is out front supporting it as a humanitarian intervention. Come on. Last week Philip Weiss skewered Friedman's pretensions in The NY Observer. This week, some letter writers speak about this self-described liberal with a clarity that bears repeating.

Cathryn Carrol of Annapolis writes, "If people wrote about blacks, the way he writes about Arabs, he metaphorically (and justifiably) would be drawn and quartered." She also lambastes Friedman's certainty, his sanctimonious insight, and his pseudo-depth.

Jim Furlong of Connecticut takes on his core ideas: "democracy and love of capitalism flow from the barrel of a gun: that seems to be our new idea. It is a variant of the idea that the ends justify means." Henry Bright of Florida charges that Friedman "has become an intellectual captive of the people he admires: the titans of industry and globalization."

Remember Cambodia

FRIEDMAN holds up the skulls of Saddam's victims as reason enough for the intervention. I wonder if he remembers the Vietnamese invasion of Cambodia to topple the genocidal Khmer Rouge who piled up many more skulls that Saddam ever did. That invasion was condemned by all the policy wonks in the U.S.. Washington later supported the killers, not those liberators. But then again, there was no huge supply of oil in Cambodia.

I was talking the other day with a Falun Gong practitioner who reminded me that 50,000 of her fellow non-violent colleagues are in jail, many tortured or dead, thrown out of buildings and trains. Have we heard a peep about that? We do business with China and so can pragmatically overlook their treatment of Tibetans or pro-democracy activists.

You need a comment from Saddam

I WAS reminded also of a personal experience. Along with my colleagues here at Globalvision, we produced a special on human rights, which included a segment on Saddam's gassing of the

Kurds. At that time, in the Bush years, the neocons were demanding more "balance" at PBS. Local programmers took a mechanistic approach to that problem. We were shocked when we found our human rights program rejected because we didn't have a personal response from Saddam to the charges leveled against him. Have you ever seen a documentary on the holocaust rejected because the Nazis didn't have the right to respond?

Later, our series Rights and Wrongs, was rejected by PBS not because the journalism was inadequate but because the subject was considered superfluous. "Human rights, we were told, "is an insufficient organizing principle for a television series." Unlike gardening or home repair! We finally did get our series on many local PBS stations where it ran for four years. But once our funders experienced "fatigue," the run ended. No network has since aired regularly scheduled programming about human rights.

60 Minutes on Iraq

DID any of you see 60 Minutes last night? It opened with a strong piece about juicy no-bid contracts to politically-connected corporations for the reconstruction of Iraq. It represented compelling investigative journalism showing how Dick Cheney used his connections to build the Halliburton company, which is now being rewarded with a contract paying $50,000 a day for a five-man fire fighting team. The third segment of show featured Mike Wallace in Syria where he interviews the foreign minister. He asks him why he thinks the U.S. invaded Iraq. The guy suggests that it has a lot to do with those post-war contracts, which were given out

before the war began. Mike looks askance. Clearly, he had not seen the first segment of his own show. The Syrian may have been conspiratorial but so was 60 Minutes. Where there's smoke . . .

White House correspondents cheer Bush

AS for media coverage of the war, it was distressing to see so many at the White House correspondents dinner cheer President Bush's defense of the war. His presence there is supposedly a sign of respect for the office, not compliance with his policies. The New York Times described the dinner as a tepid affair. There was nary a word of dissent. The outgoing president of the Correspondents Association said some members had suggested the Dixie Chicks or Harry Belafonte as the entertainers. "Can you believe that?" he asked his colleagues. "You can't make this stuff up." After watching the dinner, I couldn't make that up either. Disgraceful, except for the award to Dana Milbank of the Washington Post for challenging presidential claims on a regular basis while the rest of the crowd sleeps on.

The Observer yesterday reported on how the owners of virulent pro-war media outlets are gloating over the outcome of the war. Yet, their sales are going down. Peter Preston writes: "So, who really won the war? Conrad Black doesn't seem to have many doubts. 'We [that's his Daily Telegraph] have obviously surpassed our competition – and even bear favorable comparison with the New York Times ,' he tells his staff.

"But the loudest cock-a-doodle-doos surely belong to Lord Black's most ferocious competitor, Rupert Murdoch.

"His Fox News won the cable-ratings conflict. His New York Post was top of the pops. His Weekly Standard is now the neo-conservative organ of Bushy choice. He finally took DirectTV as the Marines took Baghdad. A forthcoming Federal Communications Commission review looks certain to let him own more papers and TV stations. He's on a roll; a big, big winner.

"It seems almost churlish to spoil the fun, to point out that circulation wars have little in common with shooting wars (except self-deception and mendacity). But let's examine the March ABC wisdom with a leery eye. The Telegraph was down 7.56 per cent, year on year: selling 926,500 a day, including 27,137 sales in foreign parts, 15,775 bulk copies, 307,596 pre-paid subscriptions, and 40,666 one-off cheapies. The Times was down 6.91 per cent, year on year, including 30,167 foreign copies, 32,892 bulks, 101,986 subscriptions and 14,673 cheapies.

"Neither title, in short, has anything much to crow about."

Pilger: Corruption in journalism

ALSO from London, John Pilger skewers his colleagues for the role they played. "Something deeply corrupt is consuming journalism. A war so one-sided it was hardly a war was reported like a Formula One race, as the teams sped to the checkered flag in Baghdad.

"I read in the Observer last Sunday that 'Iraq was worth $20m to Reuters.' This was the profit the company would make from the war. Reuters was described on the business pages as 'a model company, its illustrious brand and reputation second to none. As a newsgathering organiza-

tion, it is lauded for its accuracy and objectivity.' The Observer article lamented that the 'world's hotspots' generated only about 7 per cent of the model company's $3.6 billion revenue last year. The other 93 per cent comes from 'more than 400,000 computer terminals in financial institutions around the world,' churning out 'financial information' for a voracious, profiteering 'market' that has nothing to do with true journalism: indeed, it is the antithesis of true journalism, because it has nothing to do with true humanity.

"There is something deeply corrupt consuming this craft of mine. It is not a recent phenomenon; look back on the 'coverage' of the First World War by journalists who were subsequently knighted for their services to the concealment of the truth of that great slaughter."

The art of propaganda

HERE is a must read. It speaks to how media strategists shape public perception through a skillful use of "message development."

This particular document was prepared for pro-Israel activists by Frank Luntz's research companies, an agency that worked for the Bush presidential campaign, and most recently for MSNBC. As you evaluate it for yourself, think about the similar media plans that were used by the Administration to sell the war to the media and the public.

The Arab Anti-Discrimination Commission (ADC) sent me a copy, calling it a "vital propaganda strategy document for the period following the war in Iraq. The document, entitled "Wexner Analysis: Israeli Communications Priorities 2003," was prepared for the Wexner Foundation, which operates leadership training programs such as the "Birthright Israel" project, which offers free trips for young Jewish Americans to Israel.

Here is a taste of the "analysis" and recommendations:

1. "SADDAM HUSSEIN are the two words that tie Israel to America and are most likely to deliver support in Congress. The day we allow Saddam to take his eventual place in the trash heap of history is the day we lose our strongest weapon in the linguistic defense of Israel.

2. "IRAQ COLORS ALL. Saddam is your best defense, even if he is dead. For a year, a SOLID YEAR, you should be invoking the name of Saddam Hussein and how Israel was always behind American efforts to rid the world of this ruthless dictator and liberate their people."

"3). It DOES NOT HELP when you compliment President Bush. When you want to identify with and align yourself with America, just say it. Don't use George Bush as a synonym for the United States.

"4) SECURITY sells. The settlements are our Achilles heel, and the best response (which is still quite weak) is the need for security that this buffer creates.

"5) A LITTLE HUMILITY GOES A LONG WAY. You need to talk continually about your understanding of 'the plight of the Palestinians' and a commitment to helping them.

"6) OF COURSE RHETORICAL QUESTIONS WORK, don't they?" ●

THE STATUE SPECTACLE

We wanted it to be true but it wasn't

By TED RALL

NEW YORK, APRIL 16, 2003 – The stirring image of Saddam's statue being toppled on April 9th turns out to be fake, the product of a cheesy media op staged by the U.S. military for the benefit of cameramen staying across the street at Baghdad's Palestine Hotel. This shouldn't be a big surprise. Two of the most stirring photographs of World War II – the flag raising at Iwo Jima and General MacArthur's stroll through the Filipino surf – were just as phony.

Anyone who has seen a TV taping knows that tight camera angles exaggerate crowd sizes, but even a cursory examination of last week's statue-toppling propaganda tape reveals that no more than 150 Iraqis gathered in Farbus Square to watch American Marines – not Iraqis – pull down the dictator's statue. Hailing "all the demonstrations in the streets," Defense Secretary Rumsfeld waxed rhapsodically: "Watching them," he told reporters, "one cannot help but think of the fall of the Berlin Wall and the collapse of the Iron Curtain."

Hundreds of thousands of cheering Berliners filled the streets when their divided city was reunited in 1989. Close to a million Yugoslavs crowded Belgrade at the end of Slobodan Milosevic's rule in 2000. While some individual Iraqis have welcomed U.S. troops, there haven't been similar outpourings of approval for our "liberation." Most of the crowds are too busy carrying off Uday's sofas to say thanks, and law-abiding citizens are at home putting out fires or fending off their rapacious neighbors with AK-47s. Yet Americans wanted to see their troops greeted as liberators, so that's what they saw on TV. Perhaps Francis Fukuyama was correct – if it only takes 150 happy looters to make history, maybe history is over.

Actually, they were 150 imported art critics. The statue bashers were militiamen of the Iraqi National Congress, an anti-Saddam outfit led by one Ahmed Chalabi. The INC was flown into Iraq by the Pentagon over CIA and State Department protests. Chalabi is Rumsfeld's choice to become Iraq's next puppet president.

Photos at the indispensable Information Clearing House website place one of Chalabi's aides at the supposedly spontaneous outpouring of pro-American Saddam bashing at Firdus Square.

"When you are moving through this country there is [sic] not a lot of people out there and you are not sure they want us here," Sgt. Lee Buttrill gushed to ABC News. "You finally get here and see people in the street feeling so excited, feeling so happy, tearing down the statue of Saddam. It feels really good." That rah-rah BS is what Americans will remember about the fall of Baghdad – not the probability that Buttrill, part of the armed force that cordoned off the square to protect the Iraqi National Congress' actors, was merely telling war correspondents what they wanted to hear. In his critically acclaimed book "Jarhead," Gulf War vet Anthony Swofford writes that Marines routinely lie to gullible reporters.

ABC further reported: "A Marine at first draped an American flag over the statue's face, despite military orders to avoid symbols that would portray the United States as an occupying - instead of a liberating – force." Yet another lie. As anyone with eyes could plainly see, American tanks are festooned with more red, white and blue than a Fourth of July parade. And that particular flag was flying over the Pentagon at the time of the Sept. 11, 2001 attacks. The Defense Department gave it to the Marines in order to perpetuate Bush's lie that Iraq was involved in the 9-11 attacks.

Patriotic iconography is a funny thing. I've known that the Iwo Jima photo was fake for years, but it nonetheless stirs me every time I see it. Firdus Square's footage will retain its power long after the last American learns the truth.

The phony war ends, the phony liberation begins

IT was a fitting end for a war waged under false pretexts by a fictional coalition led by an ersatz president. Bush never spent much time thinking about liberation, and even his exploitation is being done with as little concern as possible for the dignity of our new colonial subjects.

What a difference a half-century makes! American leaders devoted massive manpower and money to plan for the occupation of the countries they invaded during World War II. What good would it do, they asked, to liberate Europe if criminals and tyrants filled the power vacuum created by the fleeing Nazis?

Thousands of officers from a newly-established Civil Affairs division of the U.S. Army were parachuted into France on the day after D-Day, while bullets were still flying, with orders to stop looting, establish law and order and restore essential services.

GWB is no FDR. Three weeks after the U.S. invaded Iraq, Civil Affairs was still stuck in Kuwait. Rumsfeld's war plan didn't allow for protecting museums and public buildings from looters, or innocent Iraqi women from roving gangs of marauding rapists. At the same time thousands of irreplaceable archeological treasures from the National Museum of Iraq were being sacked by thousands of looters, dozens of American troops were hanging around the Saddam statue videotaping, trying to be quotable. ●

229

CHAPTER NINE

REMEMBERING THE FALLEN

AFTER THE WAR: CALL FOR A MEDIA CRIMES TRIBUNAL

Look at sins of commission, omission and blinkered patriotism

B y late May, no one in Washington wanted to talk about Iraq any more. Iran had become the enemy du jour as all the familiar tools of media demonization were trotted out as if they were in some playbook of well-worked but successful scenarios for orchestrating crises. The same neo-conservative cast of strategists that gave us the Iraq War seemed to be cranking up a new confrontation with Tehran.

Oddly, some of the Terror War advocates here recommend assisting (i.e., arming) opposition movements that the Iranians brand as terrorists. A Pentagon warning that it will seek to "destabilize" the Tehran government has given that country's right-wing mullahs new arguments to label reformists traitors. Another country is on the verge of imploding.

Meanwhile, Iraq is still coming apart at the seams. More U.S. soldiers are dying in incidents that lead the Independent's Middle East correspondent Robert Fisk to say that an armed resistance is emerging as complaints about a lack of services and self rule spread. Politically, demography appears to be destiny. Reports William O. Beeman in the Los Angeles Times: "The war in Iraq has produced an unintended consequence — a formidable Shiite Muslim geographical bloc that will dominate politics in the Middle East for many years. This development is also creating political and spiritual leaders of unparalleled international influence."

British media outlets seem ahead of their American counterparts in following up on stories of civilian casualties and the lack of discoveries of weapons of mass destruction. The Guardian's Jonathan Steele says Iraqis don't make distinctions between those killed defending their country and innocent victims.

He writes: "All over Baghdad on walls of mosques or outside private homes, pieces of black cloth inscribed with yellow lettering bear witness to the thousands of Iraqis killed in the American-led war. Only if they were officers do these notices make clear whether the victims were soldiers or civilians. As far as Iraqis are concerned all the dead are "martyrs," whether they fell defending their country or were struck when missiles or cluster bombs hit their homes."

On the very day that Tony Blair was staging a triumphant visit to see his "boys in Basra," the

British press was revealing that Downing Street had doctored a dossier on Iraq's weapons program to make it "sexier." This is according to a senior British official who claims intelligence services were unhappy with the assertion that Saddam's weapons of mass destruction (WMD) were ready for use within 45 minutes, The Guardian reports.

New information about the war itself is emerging. Pacific News Service reports that the seeming successful invasion of Baghdad may have been staged. It reports on a story "making headlines around the world – but not in U.S. media," and goes on to say: "European newspapers are reporting that a notorious Republican Guard commander mysteriously left off the U.S. card deck of 55 most-wanted Iraqis was bribed by the United States to ensure the quick fall of Baghdad."

Pacific News Service also says: "A San Francisco Chronicle interview with Iraqi soldiers suggests that Saddam himself may have double-crossed his soldiers and made a deal. Saddam refused to follow a military plan established before the war to launch the street war to defend Baghdad, despite the repeated statements of the leadership that the Iraqi army would fight from one house to another to defend the capital."

The London-based, Saudi-owned newspaper Al-Hayat says: "For the first time, Iraqi soldiers have revealed the details of the fall of the Iraqi capital Baghdad, explaining why the American troops entered it without meeting any resistance. One of the main reasons is that Qusay, the youngest son of former Iraqi President Saddam Hussein, issued a number of orders during the last days of the war, which resulted in the death of the Iraqi Republican Guards' elite outside the city. This enraged the military leaders, who decided to return home calmly, and let the city fall at the hands of the invading troops."

Slowly but surely, new information like this is trickling out, calling into question the rationale for the war and the coverage of its most celebrated moments. The International Press Institute says that an estimated 3,000 journalists covered the war, making it one of the most reported events in history. Many of their stories seem to confirm the institute's finding that "propaganda, bias and disinformation were more prevalent than accurate and relevant information."

This propaganda offensive was all too successful in the way it influenced media coverage and permitted the Bush Administration and its perception managers to dominate the media and drive all other voices to the margins. Stories came so fast and furious that there often wasn't time for follow-up, clarifications and diverse interpretation. Breaking News broke up our attention spans, lurching from one new development to another.

In its postmortem, the International Press Institute concludes: "At least 15 journalists died in the conflict. Two are still missing. Journalists and media outlets were targeted and attacked; journalists were beaten, harassed, jailed and censored. The battle over the airwaves and public opinion was seemingly as important to the belligerents as the battles over territory and air superiority."

And yet if you were watching the news on TV, rare were the admissions that the news was managed, manicured, sanitized and spun. It all seemed so authoritative even when it wasn't. It was produced to be believable even when it wasn't.

As Linda McQuaig wrote in the Toronto Star: "Accordingly, a terrified American public was kept under the mistaken illusion that Saddam Hussein had 'weapons of mass destruction,' and would soon strike America if America didn't strike first."

She indicts the administration for its deception – but also the media for marching in lockstep. "This media docility has allowed the Bush Administration to go largely unchallenged as it adopts the mantle of an imperial presidency," she writes.

An environment of patriotic correctness in the media led to more selling than telling on the part of many journalists. When historians began to construct the real story of this war, it is safe to predict that they will indict the media along with the administration.

In the best of all possible worlds, there would be a war crimes investigation into this dreadful war. A media crimes tribunal should accompany it. ●

CPJ RELEASES REPORT ON PALESTINE HOTEL ATTACK

NEW YORK, May 27, 2003 – The Committee to Protect Journalists (CPJ) released an investigative report today about the April 8 shelling of the Palestine Hotel in Baghdad by U.S. forces, which killed two journalists and wounded three others. CPJ's investigation, titled "Permission to Fire," provides new details suggesting that the attack on the journalists, while not deliberate, was avoidable. CPJ has learned that Pentagon officials, as well as commanders on the ground in Baghdad, knew that the Palestine Hotel was full of international journalists and that they were intent on not hitting it. However, these senior officers apparently failed to convey their concern to the tank commander who fired on the hotel.

Written by Joel Campagna, CPJ's senior program coordinator responsible for the Middle East, and research consultant Rhonda Roumani, "Permission to Fire" is based on interviews with a dozen reporters who were at the scene of the attack, including two embedded journalists who monitored radio traffic before and after the shelling occurred, and journalists who witnessed the strike from inside the Palestine Hotel.

During the intense fighting that occurred on the morning of April 8, a U.S. battalion encountered stiff resistance from Iraqi forces. It was determined that an Iraqi forward observer, or spotter, was guiding the attacks against the Americans, and a frantic search for the spotter began. During this search a U.S. tank officer believed he had sighted a person with binoculars in the Palestine Hotel, and received permission to fire on the building a short while later.

Journalists covering the U.S. military command headquarters in Baghdad that morning told CPJ that commanders there were aware that the Palestine Hotel was in the vicinity of the fighting, and that journalists were staying in the hotel. That information, and the location of the hotel, apparently wasn't relayed to the tank battalion until it was too late

Conflicting responses

In the aftermath of the attack, U.S. military officials have given a variety of explanations for the shelling of the Palestine Hotel, mainly alleging

235

that U.S. forces came under "significant enemy fire" from the hotel, that there was an Iraqi bunker next to the hotel, and that Iraqi fire was coming from the hotel's lobby. However, according to the report, "There is simply no evidence to support the official U.S. position that U.S. forces were returning hostile fire from the Palestine Hotel. It conflicts with eyewitness testimonies of numerous journalists in the hotel."

"Based on the information contained in this report, CPJ calls afresh on the Pentagon to conduct a thorough and public investigation into the shelling of the Palestine Hotel. Such a public accounting is necessary not only to determine the cause of this incident, but also to ensure that similar episodes do not occur in the future." ●

ROSTER OF THE DEAD AND MISSING

Terry Lloyd, ITV News, Date unknown, Iman Anas

Paul Moran, free-lancer, March 22, 2003, Gerdigo

Kaveh Golestan, free-lancer, April 2, 2003, Kifri

Michael Kelly, Atlantic Monthly, Washington Post, April 3, 2003, outside of Baghdad

Christian Liebig, Focus, April 7, 2003, outside Baghdad

Julio Anguita Parrado, El Mundo, April 7, 2003, outside Baghdad

Tareq Ayyoub, Al-Jazeera, April 8, 2003, Baghdad

José Couso, Telecinco, April 8, 2003, Baghdad

Taras Protsyuk, Reuters, April 8, 2003, Baghdad

NON-COMBAT-RELATED DEATHS:

Veronica Cabrera, America TV, April 15, about 24 miles from Baghdad

Mario Podestá, free-lance, April 14, about 24 miles from Baghdad

David Bloom, NBC News, April 6, 2003, outside Baghdad

Gaby Rado, Channel 4 News, Date unknown, Suleimaniya

OTHER MEDIA WORKERS KILLED IN ACTION:

Kamaran Abdurazaq Muhamed, translator for BBC, April 6, 2003, northern Iraq

MISSING IN IRAQ:

Fred Nerac, French, 43 years old

Hussein Othman, Lebanese, 28 years old

Source: Committee To Protect Journalists, April 26, 2003

SOME FACTS FROM FAIR (Fairness and Accuracy in Reporting)

AMPLIFYING OFFICIALS, SQUELCHING DISSENT

During the Iraq war, the guest lists of major nightly newscasts were dominated by government and military officials, disproportionately favored pro-war voices and marginalized dissenters, a new study by FAIR has found.

Starting the day after the invasion of Iraq began, the three-week study covered the most intense weeks of the war (March 20 to April 9, 2003). It examined 1,617 on-camera sources in stories about Iraq on six major evening newscasts: ABC World News Tonight, CBS Evening News, NBC Nightly News, CNN's Wolf Blitzer Reports, Fox News Channel's Special Report with Brit Hume and PBS's NewsHour With Jim Lehrer.

Some key findings:

■ **Official voices dominate:** 63 percent of all sources were current or former government employees. U.S. officials alone accounted for more than half (52 percent) of all sources.

■ **Pro-war chorus:** Nearly two thirds of all sources – 64 percent – were pro-war.

■ **Anti-war voices missing:** At a time when 27 percent of the U.S. public opposed the war, only 10 percent of all sources, and just 3 percent of U.S. sources, were anti-war. That means the percentage of Americans opposing the war was nearly 10 times higher in the real world than on the news.

■ **Sound bytes vs. interviews:** When anti-war guests did make the news, they were mostly relegated to man-on-the-street sound bytes. Not a single show did a sit-down interview with a person identified as being against the war.

■ **International perspectives scarce:** Only 6 percent of sources came from countries other than the U.S., Britain or Iraq. Citizens of France, Germany and Russia – countries most opposed to war – constituted just 1 percent of all guests.

The six shows' guest lists had a lot in common, but there were a few differences. Of U.S. sources, NBC Nightly News had the smallest percentage of officials (60 percent) and the largest percentage of anti-war guests (4 percent), while CBS Evening News had the highest percentage of officials (75 percent) and fewest anti-war voices (a single sound byte from Michael Moore's Oscar acceptance speech).

"When independent policy critics and grassroots voices are shortchanged, democracy is shortchanged," said FAIR's Steve Rendall. "Not one show offered proportionate coverage of anti-war sentiment. If media are supposed to foster vigorous, inclusive debate during national crises, it's clear that during the Iraq war, TV news let the public down." ●

CHAPTER 10

WHAT CAN WE DO ABOUT IT?

A CALL FOR MEDIA ACTIVISM

Now's the time to press the press and move the media

I f we want better media coverage, then we have to make it happen! It is time for a campaign to PRESS THE PRESS AND MOVE THE MEDIA. Every activist knows that American media has slanted the coverage of the war, distorted coverage of the anti-war movement by understating its size and marginalizing its message, is prone to distorting the anti-war message and demonizing the messenger. Most of us are outraged by the way the size of demonstrations are downplayed and minimized. As this book makes clear, propaganda was pervasive, and truth was distorted. If you think it is bad now you haven't seen anything yet. The Bush administration perfects its media spin machine while the Republican-dominated FCC gives more power to media moguls. Significantly, one of its arguments for more consolidation in the industry is that only big companies can cover the war the way this one was reported.

Our movements have to take this orchestration and abuse of the media as our challenge. It has to become an issue, not just a complaint. PR-oriented responses are an important, but not a sufficient response. It is no longer enough to just hold press conference, put celebrities on TV or buy ads that often don't air. It is the relentless media spin of the story and the content of the programming that affects what Americans think they know. Mainstream media coverage helped prepare America for this war, and it was promoted through uncritical reporting.

The media was not just a conduit for administration positions. It was a communications collaborator. While they talked endlessly about weapons of mass destruction, they functioned as weapons of mass deception.

That is why we have to make this problem an issue. What can be done about it?

First we have to decide that the fight for media fairness and truth is central to our collective agenda. We need to raise money and mobilize people to fight the media war as we combat other wars. We need to ask ourselves: How can we get people to recognize that changing the media frame is a key to changing policy?

The real problem is ideological, and institutional, a function of concentrated media power, news management, censorship and self-censorship. News bias is not only about what is reported – but what is left out. It involves the way stories are framed and given one-sided pro-government tilts. It has to do with what points of view are heard, and which are excluded while 'consent is manufactured' for war. Today, "patriotic correctness" rules the airwaves.

We need to launch a campaign to press the press for more openness, diversity of news sources, more skepticism towards government claims, balanced treatment for dissenters. One way to change government policy is to get more coverage and airtime for our views.

This will take a campaign and real organizing including protests, critiquing on a daily basis, letter writing, petitions, selective pressure on advertisers, law suits, and a counter media propaganda campaign to delegitimize phony news.

It will require insider lobbying, educational forums, mobilizations of well-known journalists and activism within the profession.

We need to create some positive goals and fight for our values and visions, not simply against theirs. I think we should develop a Media and Democracy Act, an omnibus bill that could be a way of showing how all of these issues are connected. This is not unlike the Contract for America in that it will create one easy to market and explain package of proposals that can forge a coalition with many stakeholders and constituencies. We are far stronger together than pushing separately. We have to simplify and project a united message.

At the same time, we need to support alternative independent media and promote it to our organizations and e-lists. It is not enough to get an occasional progressive sound-bite on the air. We need to find a way to work together in a sustained effort, perhaps even create a united media appeal to try to create a serious fund for this type of long term multi-track media work. It will take a big push. It can be done.

We at Globalvision launched Mediachannel.org as global network for media change. We started with 20 groups. We now have well over a thousand. We also started the Globalvision News Network (GVnews.net) to offer syndicated coverage from 350 news partners to offer a different kind of news from around the world. We want anti-war activists to know about these offerings. We want to help syndicate and distribute media content. We have worked with and would like to do more with World Link TV, Free Speech TV, and Indy media projects to cross-promote and cross market.

As a media person with a 30-year track record (CNN, ABC, WBCN etc), I know that media companies are responsive to pressure when it is sustained, sophisticated and well executed. If we don't like the news, then we have to do something about it – with a well thought out strategy to press the press and move the media. Let's discuss it – and do it.

Your ideas are welcome . . . share them with me by writing: dissector@mediachannel.org. ●

NEW YORK, JULY 1, 2003

AFTER THE WAR: THE SUMMER OF SUMMING UP

Soldiers die, questions go unanswered

The war is over but the Iraq debate goes on as summer erupts in the West and heat rises to insufferable degrees in the deserts of Arabia. By early July 2003, the Iraq story had become an unending catalogue of deadly incidents claiming the lives of British and U.S. soldiers. There were also daily reports of seething unrest and festering anger by a visibly unpurified and often enraged Iraqi population. It seems clear that if "we" won the war, we may have already lost the peace, if there ever was any. Alongside, the reality of the post-war war has been a non-stop parade of allegations, debates and political recriminations over the status of the still unsuccessful hunt for weapons of mass destruction.

The term "deception" that critics use to challenge the coverage is now being liberally applied to characterize the political leaders who started the war. Clare Short, a former member of the British Cabinet admitted to Parliament that there had been willful inconsistencies, mistruths, and embellishments in the pro-war speeches and dossiers offered by Prime Minister Tony Blair. She called it "honorable deception."

And so, at last, the "d-word," the idea of deliberate deception enters mainstream discourse. This leads to another question, of course. If officials – including heads of state – whether 'honorably' or not, were deceptive, why didn't the media catch them in the act, or even try to verify or debunk their claims. Why were all the half-truths and the self-serving spin that they came wrapped in reported with little scrutiny?

The truth is that most media organizations refused even to make the effort. After the war, Michael Getler, the Washington Post ombudsman asked some questions that should have been shouted before the conflict got underway: "The question for news organizations is whether these claims should have been reportorially tested and challenged sufficiently. Were news organizations inhibited for fear of seeming unpatriotic after September 11th?"

THE PATRIOTISM POLICE

THERE is no question that there was pressure on the media to stay in line. Eric Sorenson who ran the coverage at MSNBC told The New York Times, "Any misstep . . . and you can have the

Patriotism Police hunt you down." Fear of being so hunted led broadcasters to do some hunting of their own, perhaps to keep any potential critics at bay. In the unbrave world of broadcasting, Sorenson fired Peter Arnett for the crime of saying on Iraqi TV what he had been saying on MSNBC.

When MSNBC correspondent Ashley Banfield publicly criticized some of the war coverage as "sanitized," she was "taken to the wood shed" and chastised publicly by her bosses. This intolerance towards dissent in the ranks sent an unmistakable message to any others who might raise similar questions. (It is still not clear if her contract will be renewed.)

Was it just fear and intimidation that led so many in the media to become willing boosters of the "coalition of the willing?" Why was the prospect of war constantly projected as inevitable, and then widely accepted, even eagerly anticipated, as "the next big thing?" It seems clear that large sectors of the media were not duped but rather complicit, even enthusiastic flag-waving partners with the military

THE SEDUCTIONS OF EMBEDDING

THE embedding program helped breach the wall between the media and the military, between subject and reporter. Few investigated the origins and financing of this program. Thanks to Milwaukee Magazine, we now know why:

"Who paid for this media training, transportation and equipment? Unwittingly, American taxpayers picked up the tab for these and many other expenses in the military's embedded media program.

"That's one way of looking at it," concedes Maj.

Tim Blair, Pentagon officer in charge of the program. Another way of looking at it is the embedded media, by accepting military handouts at taxpayer expense, betrayed the public's trust and venerable journalism policies against freebies."

WHAT IT SOUNDED LIKE

CARTOONIST Aaron McGruder captured the frequent flavor of the exchange between studio and journalist in one of his Boondocks strips. His principal character, Huey Freeman, is watching the tube:

"I'm Aaron Brown, this is CNN. We're talking to one of our brave correspondents in Iraq. Hello?

"Hey, Aaron" is the response.

"You are so brave to be out there.

"Thanks Aaron, I am brave but our troops are braver.

"Yes our troops are brave. But you are very brave as well.

"Yes Aaron, there is a lot of bravery here."

"There sure is a lot of Bravery – IN YOU, my friend.

" . . . And that's it. From Iraq, back to you Aaron."

This invented exchange captures a psychic subtext of self-promotion and mission identification. For many covering the war, the task clearly had a personal dimension, the sense journalists crave of doing something important, and being part of history. In years past, this type of satisfaction came from crusading, muckraking, 'speaking truth to power.' Today, it seems to come from serving power and its many servants.

A MILITARY VIEW

EVEN experienced military people were turned off by all the media pandering. Writing in Army Times, Gulf War 1 veteran Ralf W. Zimmerman wrote:

"Often contradictory news coverage of our war on terror has made me a bit suspicious of the control the Pentagon and other government agencies are exercising over what can and can't be reported. Without access to the Internet (despite all its flaws) and other reliable western media sources, I'm afraid I'd have a rather incomplete picture of what is really shaping up in the world around us.

"American war reporting seems to be governed by extremes, especially on television. We get either a sketchy tabloid report or the Pentagon's edited party line. Both are readily available and mainly strive to entertain the public or to whip up superficial patriotism."

Many media organizations became an adjunct, to the selling of the war for political and economic reasons as well.

Why?

There were three principal reasons:

1. Institutional changes in our media system.
2. A shift in our media culture.
3. A new sophistication by the military and government in the art of news management.

MEDIA SYSTEM CHANGE

THE American media system today is totally corporate dominated, market driven and hence, at its core, conservative in the sense that it rarely rocks the boat or challenges the status quo. It is more consolidated and, more paradoxically, frag-

mented than ever. Diverse in appearance, it tends towards uniformity in content and conformity in method. Most news outlets act more alike even as they seem more different through positioning and "branding."

All fight for market share and "mind share." All target the same demographics, covet the same advertisers, and offer similarly formatted and formularized programming. Infotainment has been dominant for 20 years on television. As entertainment companies took over news organizations, showbiz techniques were fused into newsbiz presentation style.

This institutional dimension to the problem has been overlooked by most critics.

The rise of Fox News has not changed this dynamic, even if it has added more polarization and patriotic correctness to the television spectrum. Studies have shown that whenever a broadcaster seems to be winning the constant race for ratings and revenues, others clone their look and adapt their attitude. Fox built its format on the experience of right-wing talk radio, adding personality, harder edge politics, and aggressive posturing to a news business known for centrism and blandness. As the new kid on the block, it played the patriotic card by hitching its wagon to a popular president who understood how to play to fear and insecurity while wrapping himself in the red, white and blue to boost approval ratings.

By positioning itself as an alternative and antidote to a non-existent liberal media, it appealed to a hard core audience and those estranged by mainstream middle-of-the-road news. It served as the media shock troops for the Bush war offensive often framing news in a pro-administration direction while insisting on its fairness and balance.

Media outlets which long ago abandoned any sense of serving as the nation's conscience or social mission were blindsided by Fox's bullying approach and rushed to emulate it. It was easy for Fox, who claimed to believe in something to score points against outlets which believed in nothing, save their bottom line.

That fact that most had abandoned any real commitment to investigative reporting or interpretive journalism, not to mention in-depth anything, made it far easier for the Administration to get its views over. By substituted simplistic slogans for substantive policies, the Bush media team was bold and convinced of the righteousness of their cause. Mainstream outlets, which tend to mirror and reflect dominant ideas, as well as reinforce them, was well-suited as a transmission belt. When major opinion leaders line up behind a policy, the media falls in line.

MEDIA CULTURE SHIFT

IN a desperate bid for younger viewers, most of the networks had already pushed out their gray-haired eminences. The older, more experienced, journalists with commitments to journalistic traditions were disposable. Inside news organizations, the "thinkers" were out; the marketers were in. Images became information. Perception trumped reality.

Soon newscasts became faster – "more news in less time" – to quote a claim of a station in New York. World news was cut way back as symbolized by a Fox feature called "The world in a Minute." CNN followed shamelessly with the "Global Minute." The proliferation of digital channels enabled CNN to offer one "brand" of news-lite in the US and another more substantial and more international newscast for foreign viewers.

Inside the networks, the media culture had shifted. The premium now was on younger hipper anchors, happy talk and dumbing down by design. As economic hard times rocked the media business, insecurity spread. Soon there were more lowest common denominator shows – anything to bring viewers into the tent.

Staffers understood that you got along by going along and not standing out for the wrong reasons. During World War II, it was said that loose lips sunk ships. Today, the right botoxed lips raise media ships. Dissenting documentaries and hard-nosed investigators became a thing of the past in the age of "you news" and constant entertainment updates.

In what some scholars call a "post journalism era," media institutions had become experts at engineering news as a spectacle with one story dominating all others, with more money spent on promos and graphics than programs. Sensationalism was in along with tabloid formats. Soon, there was the year of O.J. Simpson trials followed by two years of Monica news and the Clinton scandal. That gave way to the missing intern story and a summer of shark attacks.

Until the day that changed everything.

AND ALONG CAME 9/11

AFTER September ll, media companies saw their role as reassuring an anxious public and playing to the sense of patriotism that always surfaces at a time of national crisis. They gave the administration a pass when it came to serious criticism. A president who one day was being dismissed as a global village idiot was transformed into a statesman overnight.

9/11 provided the opening for rolling out a pre-packaged and orchestrated strategy of deception and demagoguery, which would be amplified on the airwaves, endlessly recycled and repeated.

When the decision to go to war was made, in early September 2002, the media offensive began. The country was prepared for the "inevitable" in a rollout that resembled a product launch. Speech after speech hit the same themes positioning a strategy of aggression into a posture of defense and victimization. The alarmist note was enunciated by the President in Cincinatti on Oct. 7, 2002, "The Iraqi dictator must not be permitted to threaten America and the world with horrible poisons and diseases and gases and atomic weapons."

Was America and the world at large ever so threatened? Were there horrible poisons, and diseases and gases and atomic weapons just waiting to be deployed? Were there other weapons of mass destruction being hidden for later use? Was there a link between Saddam Hussein's secular regime and the 9/11 Islamic jihad junkies presumably following orders from Osama bin Laden?

GOVERNMENT MEDIA MANAGEMENT

AS preparations for a war with Iraq moved up on the Administration's agenda, plans were made to sell the story. Journalists were easy prey for media savvy ideologues in Washington who had perfected a strategy of perception management, and knew how to play the media as an orchestra conductor directs different instruments.

The Administration understood how to get its message out and did so relentlessly. Corporate PR techniques were implanted early on with the Iraq war "rolled out' like a product with a multi-tiered campaign to sell the policy to the public through the media. Sheldon Rampton and John Staunber of PR Watch tell this story in detail in a new book on "the uses of propaganda in Bush's War on Iraq." Like this one, it is about weapons of mass deception; only their emphasis is on the PR campaign and media management techniques used by the Administration and the Pentagon through a network of PR firms, think tanks, lobbying groups, disinformation specialists military operators and international marketing efforts. Among their findings:

" • Top Bush officials advocated the invasion of Iraq even before he took office, but waited until September 2002 to inform the public, through what the White House termed a "product launch."

" • White House officials used repetition and misinformation – the "big lie" tactic – to create the false impression that Iraq was behind the September 11th terrorist attacks . . .

" • Forged documents were used to "prove" that Iraq possessed huge stockpiles of banned weapons.

" • A secretive PR firm working for the Pentagon helped create the Iraqi National Congress (INC), which became one of the driving forces behind the decision to go to war."

From a war fighting perspective, media is now viewed as a target for IO – Information Operations – a key component of what military people call Psy-ops. "Information is the currency of victory," says one military manual. Winning the media war is as important as winning on the battlefield.

And, hence, the deployment of a well-trained

network of advocates, lobbyists, experts, retired military and intelligence officers, and covert operators to work the media on the inside and out. The news army had to be managed lest it go "off message". Media messages were framed on the basis of polling and research. They were field tested with focus groups. Presidential speeches and other administration utterances were calibrated and coordinated for maximum effect.

A variety of pundits were placed on TV programs to reiterate and repeat the same message, that Saddam is a threat, a menace, and an evildoer. His weapons of mass destruction became their boogie man. Mere assertions were accepted as evidence. In the absence of an equally visible coherent counter-narrative, this government-promoted line became the dominant media line. Every tactic was used – selective leaks, authoritative assertion, references to intelligence documents that could be shown and in some instances were faked, infiltration, cultivation, co-optation, embedding and denigration.

And oddly enough, this strategy of deception was justified in terms of the need to challenge deception by the other side. Pentagon media chief Torie Clarke told a panel after the war: "I knew with great certainty if we went to war, the Iraqi regime would be doing some terrible things and would be incredibly masterful with the lies and the deception. And I could stand up there at that podium and Secretary Rumsfeld could stand up there and say very truthfully the Iraqi regime is putting its soldiers in civilian clothing so they can ambush our soldiers. Some people would believe us and some people wouldn't. But we had hundreds and hundreds of credible, independent journalists saying the Iraqi regime is putting their soldiers in civilian clothing."

"YOU DID WELL"

WHEN the President said, you are either with us or against us, he had the media in mind as well. He ignored the protesters and rolled over the doubters. And his administration appreciated the outcome. Dick Cheney, never a media fave, told the annual dinner of the American Radio and Television Correspondents Association "You did well -- you have my thanks."

Is it any wonder that so many journalists in this country look to non-Americans like they have sold out and sold in? Journalists in other countries are increasingly putting down their American counterparts. In a recent article, Justin Webb, who covers Washington for the BBC, lorded it over his U.S.-based colleagues, asking: "Are American journalists simply spineless? Do they toe the line because they love the President? Or because their employers do?"

There is no denying that there is the stench of obedience and deference among far too many media people. Legends in business are noticing it as well.

Here's Newsday's Jimmy Breslin, an icon among newspaper columnists, who now says, "news reporters go about the government like gardeners, bent over, smiling and nodding when one of the owners shows up. You only have to look at a White House news conference to see how they aggressively pursue your right to know.

"The newspeople stand when the president comes into the room. They really do. They don't sit until he tells them to. You tell them a lie and they say, 'Sir.' . . . Newspeople like to be called 'journalists' and write of 'the need to protect sources.' They don't have any. . . . The newspeople are comfortable with being known as the "media." That is a dangerous word; all evil rises around those afflicted with it."

Please, Jimmy, don't just blame the reporters. They don't assign themselves stories. They don't edit their work or decide how much time or space to allocate for it. They work in an industry. They are paid to do a job, and disciplined when they stray from the appointed path. Being a team player is rewarded; being a troublemaker is not.

THE MASTER NARRATIVE

IT is fair to ask which major media companies had the gumption or the guts to deviate from the official story and "master narrative" adopted with such ease on so many seemingly competitive outlets. It is hard to name many reporters who challenged the hourly and daily onslaught of rah-rah newspeak built around constant briefings, endless "breaking news" bulletins and utter contempt for critics?

Could there be another explanation for this culture of compliance? Could the economic interests of the media cartels have had something to do with it? Especially at a time when economically challenged media companies had lucrative business pending before the FCC, a government body headed by the son of the Secretary of State, a high profile salesmen for the war policy.

Earlier in this book, I argue that there was a connection between war coverage and FCC deliberations. For a long time, I felt very alone in suggesting such a link, since few other media writers explored the relationship. But now, New York Magazine's Michael Wolff, who covered the CENTCOM briefings in Doha, is making me feel like I am not crazy of conspiratorial to think this way.

"It's important to understand how much this FCC ruling means to these companies," he writes. "News (especially old-fashioned headline news) is a sick business, if not a dying game. For newspaper companies, the goal is to get out of the newspaper business and into the television business (under the old rules, it's a no-no to own newspapers and television stations in the same market). For networks with big news operations, the goal is to buy more stations, which is where the real cash flows from. The whole point here is to move away from news, to downgrade it, to amortize it, to minimize it . . .

"All right then. The media knows what it wants, and the media knows what the Bush people want. So is it a conspiracy? Is that what I'm saying? That the media – acting in concert – took a dive on the war for the sake of getting an improved position with regard to the ownership rules? Certainly, every big media company was a cheerleader, as gullible and as empty-headed-or as accommodating-on the subject of WMDs as, well, Saddam himself. But conspiracy wouldn't quite be the right word.

"Negotiation, however, would be the right one. . . . The interesting thing is that in most newsrooms, you would find lots of agreement as to this view of how businessmen and politicians get the things they want. A general acceptance of the realities of ass-kissing, if not a higher level of corruption"

The sad truth is that the truths that are now truckling out were known before the war began. There was no secret about the Administration was up to. On September 11, 2001, Bill Kristol, editor of Rupert Murdoch's Weekly Standard, and the founder of the Project for a New American Century, the lobby group that mapped a the plan for unilateral preemptive intervention that the

Bush Administration has followed since, appeared in the News Hour with Jim Lehrer on PBS. He revealed that the Administration was planning to link Saddam Hussein to Osama Bin Laden.

The cat was out of the bag. Others reported Dick Cheney's call for war on Iraq on that day. It was not classified. None of it was. None of our media wanted to say that the emperor had no clothes, if just possibly, just plausibly, and parenthetically, he did.

Taking on this naked 'Emperor' also meant being willing to incur the wrath of what the head of MSNBC called the "patriotism police," aided and abetted by an ascendant Fox News Channel which smartly exploited the political environment that the Bush Administration cultivated.

THE MEDIA FAILURE

AN examination of the sordid story of media coverage of this war reveals a media failure as blatant and troubling as the record of failures by the Administration in Iraq and the war on terror.

Less than a year after Bush's exaggerated and alarmist proclamation in Ohio, and just a few months after the war in Iraq was said to end, fresh doubts about the reasons for the war are being raised by pundits, members of Congress and the "we-told-you-so" activists of the largest anti-war movement in history.

No one is still clear on the real agenda for the war. Was it oil, power, or global imperial ambition? Was it regime change or region change? Was it to satisfy the macho needs of unhappy white males who found new role models in Bush's new action army, as writer Norman Mailer opines. Or was there a higher power involved, some divine purpose as suggested by

the President himself, who said in June, 2003 while visiting the Holy Land that "God instructed me to strike at Saddam."

"You can't put it plainer than that" Chris Floyd commented in The Moscow Times, "The whole chaotic rigmarole of Security Council votes and UN inspections and congressional approval and Colin Powell's whizbang Powerpoint displays of "proof" and Bush's own tearful prayers for "peace" – it was all a sham, a meaningless exercise. "No votes, no inspections, no proof or lack of proof – in fact, no earthly reason whatsoever – could have stopped Bush's aggressive war on Iraq. It was God's unalterable will: the Lord of Hosts gave a direct order for George W. Bush to "strike at Saddam."

A TIME FOR REASSESSMENT

COLORFUL polemic aside, these issues will be debated for years to come. Already the journalism reviews and op-ed columnists are debating the role the media played-or refused to play. This is a time for reassessment.

One thing is certain: that the war coverage of the US invasion of Iraq is unlikely to win the kind of praise that Supreme Court Justice Hugo Black heaped on major media outlets in the aftermath of the Pentagon Papers case. "In my view, far from deserving condemnation for their courageous reporting, The New York Times, the Washington Post, and other newspapers should be commended for serving the purpose that the Founding Fathers saw so clearly, " he wrote.

"In revealing the workings of government that led to the Vietnam War, the newspapers nobly did precisely that which the Founders hoped and trusted they would do." ●

NEW YORK, AUGUST 2, 2003

MANHUNTS AND MEDIA MYOPIA

Media debates as body count mounts

t is now early August. The war in Iraq has a new face and a continuing stream of casualties. The quagmire talked about during the war was evidently premature then. It seems undeniable now. The death toll of U.S. soldiers killed in the post-war grows daily with fresh sniping incidents that have finally been acknowledged officially as a form of guerilla war. By mid-summer, media critics were complaining that the Pentagon was underreporting its dead and wounded as well as the skyrocketing costs of a volatile and insecure occupation.

The U.S. military response was to try to cajole other countries to dispatch troops so that U.S. soldiers can eventually be withdrawn. India is being promised aid concessions and other goodies for sending its boys to take the heat. A debate in Japan's Parliament erupted into fisticuffs when that member of the "coalition" was pressured to do its duty by sending a few contingents, for humanitarian duty of course. To the degree possible, Washington is "privatizing" the war by contracting out to specialized companies to provide support services and even security.

Propaganda expert Paul de Rooij predicted, after analyzing discrepancies in the body counts and the downplaying of casualties, "All told, expect the war in Iraq to become like the wars in Orwell's 1984; these were only used to stoke jingoism and rile the crowd and would occasionally yield a glimpse of a captured enemy in a cage on display. Every other facet of those wars was not reported on. In Iraq, soon, too, reporting on the daily carnage will be a thing of the past – wars will be something occurring far away, and the plight of the mercenaries fighting them will not be something the home crowd will have to know anything about."

THE GREAT SADDAM HUNT

THE big news now seems to have been inspired by Cowboy and Indian movies and tales of the old West when posses saddled up to catch the bad guys. Saddam Hussein is the prey this month just as Osama bin Laden had been in an earlier unresolved war in Afghanistan not that long ago. His sons were captured and slaughtered in what sounded like a reprise of Hollywood's "Shootout at the OK Corral."

A U.S. government which chastised news outlets for running pictures it didn't like, and had condemned Al Jazeera for transmitting them and some U.S. outlets for carrying them, was soon hawking the most grotesque images of their kill. (Left out of the picture was the body of the 14 year old boy slain with them as well as a bodyguard.)

To most of the world, this PR maneuver backfired, as PR columnist Mark Borkowski noted in the Guardian on August 1st, "Since this is war, this is PR and the Uday and Qusay photograph incident, planned as a surgical media strike, has turned mucky (both in media and military terms) because no one had the sense to think through the PR implications properly. It's been a total PR disaster."

Meanwhile a non-stop manhunt for Saddam began to feel like the earlier tracking of Osama bin Laden. Like the elusive caliph of Al Qaeda, the on-the-run Iraqi leader began releasing messages to rally his supporters and taunt his pursuers. In the Arab world, SH, was, like OBL, becoming an icon of resistance. News anchors followed the "action" closely with video of soldiers breaking into Iraqi homes in hot pursuit. They began reassuring viewers that it was only a matter of hours, and then of days.

It all began to take on a soap opera-ish quality. Sometimes it felt like reality TV shows such as COPS with endless chase sequences. But bear in mind, in the TV industry at least, much of the reality programming is fabricated. Years ago a TV syndicator rejected a TV series I was co-producing on real world human rights issues because "we only do reality TV."

By the time you read this, Saddam have left the material realm and entered into the mythic pantheon of martyrs. Long time anti-war activist Tom Hayden saw the end coming in time for the next commercial break, writing, "To judge from the excited build-up, Saddam Hussein will be killed very soon. Once his location is identified, the spectacle of his death can soon be orchestrated. To have the greatest impact, perhaps it will be televised in all time zones on a weekday,

avoiding the competition of weekend sports. There must be burnt offerings and a triumphal revelation of the corpse. For an insecure America, this killing will be a "ritual of blood," a "compact of fellowship" – terms used by West Indian sociologist Orlando Patterson in the context of ritual lynchings in the Old South."

A BAD MEMORY,
NOT A RIGHTEOUS MISSION

AS the dog days of August grew nearer, the Iraq war was on its way to becoming thought of as a bad memory, not a righteous mission. What media focus there was shifted to battlegrounds closer to home, to the lies and distortions in the alarmist claims that were used to stoke the war.

In Britain, Tony Blair was holding off mounting skepticism in a scandal that included the dramatic death of a high level weapons expert who had been fingered as the source of BBC reports that the government had "sexed up" its dossier warning that the Iraqis could hurl Weapons of Mass Destruction at its enemies within 45 minutes.

Not only was the claim later debunked as preposterous but also the weapons themselves had not been found. Soon the government was shifting attention away from its actions to challenging the BBC. A government deception had triggered a media controversy.

In the U.S., it was 16 words in a presidential speech attributed to British intelligence claiming that the African country of Niger had sent uranium to Iraq for its nuclear weapons program. Even though the claim had been thoroughly investigated and found to be based on forgeries prior to the President citing this "evidence" in a

State of the Union address, it was used anyway. A media storm ensued only to be doused when the president "accepted responsibility" and promptly went on vacation. Throughout this controversy, his supporters in the press and the Congress were arguing that the weapons issue was never all that important. Thomas Friedman in The New York Times was now scolding the Administration for raising the weapons issue in the first place since Iraq, in his view, was always a "war of choice," not necessity. The rationales began to shift like sand in the Arabian Desert.

THE FCC BACKGROUND BECOMES THE FOREGROUND

DURING the war, media companies were lobbying the FCC for regulatory concessions while at the same time downplaying and barely covering the FCC issue. Yet, thanks to brilliant grass roots organizing, the issue mushroomed in importance. More than a million people wrote the FCC or their legislators opposing pro-industry rule changes voted June 2. This is unprecedented. Conservative and liberal groups made common cause. The result: Congress voted 400-21 against the Bush Administration policy, prompting a threat of a veto.

Washington Post media writer Howard Kurtz was startled by the response. "Nobody much likes Big Media these days," he wrote. "But who woulda thunk that it would become a hot political issue? Not me ... this issue has struck some kind of nerve."

New York Magazine's Michael Wolff went further in suggesting that there is a wave of revulsion building against the media itself, as well as the FCC. He told me in an interview: "We're all media consumers. It stinks and nobody's happy. Nobody can find what they want. Nobody is pleased ... there are so many people who work in the media business and those people are also saying this stinks. These companies that we work for don't work anymore. They're dysfunctional because they're too large and now you want to make them bigger?"

The public has yet to turn against the media for its propagandistic coverage but a wave of scrutiny had finally begun. At last, the coverage of the wars seemed to be striking a nerve, too, within parts of the media world.

In England, the BBC coverage of the Blair government's dossier justifying the war became embroiled in controversy with top government officials and members of Parliament denouncing its reporting. When the BBC's principal source of information, weapons expert David Kelly committed suicide under intense pressure from the government, the story dominated the headlines.

In retaliation, there were calls by Tony Blair's supporters for regulatory supervision of the BBC by a new FCC-type commission called OFCOM. While the Beeb defended its impartiality, a Cardiff University study on its war coverage was released documenting not an anti-war bias but a pro-government tilt in much of its coverage.

JOURNALISTS DEBATE

JOURNALISTS on both sides of the Atlantic began debating the coverage and speaking out. I covered two conferences dealing with the issues raised in this book. One in England was sponsored by Reporting The World. Another, in New York, was co-sponsored by The Guardian and New York Magazine.

Reporting the World's roundtable was hosted by journalist Anabel McGoldrick who posed important issues about the role of the media in covering the conflict:

"ENABLING DEBATE – Did we do a good job of equipping readers and audiences to form their own views on the merits – or otherwise – of attacking Iraq?

"MISSING PERSPECTIVES – What about the alternatives to war – non-violent ways of bringing about regime change? What other evidence was there about Iraq's weapons programmes?

"WHY – Why did we go to war? Was it over weapons of mass destruction? Removing Saddam? Oil? To help establish a 'New American Century' by force of arms?

"CONTEXT – How effective were the embeds? Did we risk losing sight of the bigger picture? Did they distract us from real fighting and real casualties, such as the bombardment of the Republican Guard positions around Baghdad?

"MISINFORMATION – Were facts 'created' in order to be reported? What really happened to Private Jessica Lynch; how many times did we hear that Umm Qasr had fallen or that there was an uprising in Basra? And was there anything staged about the fall of the Saddam statue in Baghdad?

"SECURITY – Is the world now a safer or more dangerous place? Is Iraq now becoming a quagmire? Was Iraq liberated or did the war leave it as a chaotic, seething hotbed of resentment? How is it affecting the war on terrorism?"

I was asked to have a say in the very heady company of newspaper editors and the head of news for the BBC. Happily, there is a transcript of my intervention to draw on so I can get it right:

"The war that you saw in Europe, the war that people saw in the Middle East and the war that we saw in America were the different wars with different focus and a different emphasis. And I believe that CNN's decision to offer two distinct newsgathering services, and I speak as a former CNN producer by the way, I believe that was because Chris Cramer and Rita Golden and their people knew that the rest of the world would not accept the jingoistic news coverage that was being fed to people in the United States and they were right to take pride in what they did.

"But I challenge this notion that was very common in the top media executives, that we can't get ahead of our audience, the audience was gung-ho for the war, therefore we have to give the audience what it wants and I think in doing so there was an abdication of journalistic responsibility."

TWO NATIONS, TWO WORLDVIEWS

THE New York conference showcased the differences between British media discourse and our own. It was clear that the journalists from London were far more outspoken and adversarial than their American counterparts.

Gary Younge of The Guardian noted that the U.K. media had covered Northern Ireland and French media had covered Algeria in much the same way that the U.S. media covered Iraq. But he was also blistering in his assessment of U.S. media telling me: "… Just a half an hour of any kind of news TV show or reading the papers, you're wondering, you think you've lost half of the paper. Where's the bit where you criticize, where you analyze, where you go into some depth and rip this thing apart?"

New York Magazine's Michael Wolff challenged the journalists present to think about the degree that the war coverage was self-referential, media framed with journalists at its center. Was it, he wondered, "all about us?" He also asked if the U.S. media had sold out? Many of the positions in the debate were predictable, but at least the issue was raised. The U.S. media coverage was being challenged before a media audience.

"When the President comes into the room, American journalists stand erect with their backs rigid, British journalists stay slouched in their chairs," the New Statesman's John Kampfner said. "American journalists regard the people in authority as good men who should have the benefit of the doubt. In Britain, we work on the assumption that they need to prove to us that we should believe them."

The New York Observer's Phillip Weiss praised the British journalists for speaking out: "However spineless or greasy he has seemed to be, this is Tony Blair's gift to America: The English have provided us with a left wing, a conscience wing that must be taken into account. This conscience wing is now leading the United States on the Middle East peace plans, and leading the American press in the furore – soon to become a furor, one hopes – over the manipulation of intelligence preceding the war.

"At the same time, the war has made the American press docile and flaccid. Imagine that Bill Hemmer, the anchor of a leading network, CNN, could go before the New School audience and defend the network's policy of vetting its armchair generals through the Pentagon by saying that the network was only trying to check out their "credentials." "We were trying to make sure they were worth their weight," he said. And

he's proud of that."

EMBEDS SENT "TO COUNTER LEFTIST PROPAGANDA?"

EMBEDDED journalists insisted for the most part that their work was not censored although several acknowledged that they did not show us the whole war. John Danvan of ABC's Nightline admitted that Iraqi voices were rarely heard and that the picture overall was sanitized. He told me: "I've covered enough wars to be able to say this that I, believe me, have never shown the viewer what it's really like; how horrible war is. And partly you can't show it, because you never can capture it, and partly because the camera does catch it but we can't show it. There's certain close ups, blood spatters and dead children that we don't show because it violates certain long term practices, 'Don't put gore on television'. And it's a very tough issue. I only say to friends who see that pictures, 'it was just a lot worse than that'. I'm not sure they could take it. I don't know."

While the Embeds defended their coverage while admitting its limits, war supporters on the right saw the embedded journalists in a more political light. Tom Kilgannon of the right-wing Freedom Alliance contended that there was a reason the Pentagon permitted embeds in the first place, and it was not to provide impartial coverage. "The Pentagon sent hundreds of imbedded (sic) reporters to Iraq," he said, "to show America the heroic nature of the men and women in uniform, and counter decades of leftist propaganda about the U.S. military." Even though reporters would hate to be characterized as counter propagandist, that is how many of the war's most fervid backers saw them.

SOUND BITES OVER TOKYO

AND so, at long last, months after the war was prematurely deemed over, the media role was being reconsidered. Many top editors and some TV correspondents turned up. But there was only one TV news executive present and, even more disturbing, no U.S. TV outlets there.

This debate has still not been exposed to the public at large.

I was covering the conference for a documentary Globalvision is trying to make about the issues raised in this book. As of now, we have no funding and no certainty that we can finish the film or get it in the air in the television environment that manufactured the coverage I have been dissecting.As those of you who have read this whole shameful story know, as Susan L. Car-

ruthers of the University of Wales put it in her book length study, The Media At War (2000).

She writes: "Following the lead of the state, mass media are frequently more willing accomplices in war time propaganda than they care to admit, and may even play a significant role in instigating conflict."

Is there air time in our vast universe of so many TV channel to tell this "Weapons of Mass Deception" story,? And if there is, can we find the funding to make the film and get it seen? Stay tuned

I reported earlier that no TV teams came to document the conference raising these issue of the media and the Iraq War, I was wrong. There was one. From the other side of the world. Japan's NHK had a camera and producer present. I know because at least they interviewed me.

If nothing else, I may get my fifteen seconds of fame in Tokyo.   ●

A LETTER TO EDWARD R. MURROW

Dear Ed:

I got the idea of writing to you after visiting the Edward Murrow School of Communication out in the wheatfields of Washington State. I had come to debate the coverage of the Iraq war with a group of mainstream journalists, who surprised me by how they were willing to be candid outside their institutional settings.

While I was out there I tried to commune with your spirit. You have never died for me because it was your work that got me into the media racket in the first place. It was as a kid that I was awed by your TV programs, See It Now, Harvest Of Shame and even Person To Person. (Yes, I know, you did celebrity interviews, too, and even changed your name from the awkward Egburt Roscoe Murrow to the more impressive Edward R. Murrow.)

In elementary school, I even memorized one of your "I Can Hear It Now" 78-rpm records that crisply recapped recent history with all the sounds that made it special. Your work shaped my idea of what a journalist should be. Your guts in taking on Joe McCarthy later showed me that a reporter could stand up for truth.

You used to talk about "illuminating" issues, not just reporting them.

Anyway, here we are in 2003. You have been long gone, and I am trying to honor your memory by pounding away at what's happened to media institutions that "back in the day" showed such great promise. I don't want to overdo the "golden age" of TV bit, but clearly this profession has gone downhill, as news became an industry. Despite all the channels and choices, there are few voices today as commanding as yours. The only illumination these days in TV studios comes from the light bulbs.

When I was at your old school library, I dipped into the archives and discovered a set of letters you wrote in lavish penmanship to a girl named Hermine Duthie who you were enticing but not committing to. You seemed to love her physical attentiveness but were keeping her at a distance with exaggerated tales of perpetual busyness. That gave me the sense that even a media icon could be a real and flawed person like the rest of us.

I would have loved to get your reaction to the way the Iraq war was covered. Many remember you, Ed, as the best dressed daddy of all war correspondents covering what was then the mother of all bombings, the blitz in London. You were the quintessential war reporter we all looked up to, standing there in well-tailored suits, cool under fire, microphone in hand, painting visual pictures with sound.

"This is London," was your signature. Memorable language reportedly dictated to a secretary, but rarely written down, was your method. You learned how to speak conversationally in

257

speech class. Your first concern was the human story, the suffering people, and the traumatized city. According to Gerald Nachman's "Raised on Radio," Murrow "picked up his basic speech patterns from his Quaker mother, who often spoke in inverted phrases like 'This I believe.'" Many don't recall that you were dispatched to London as CBS's "director of talks," not of news.

I can hear it now.

"Tonight, as on every other night, the rooftop watchers are peering out across the fantastic forest of London's chimney pots. The anti-aircraft gunners stand ready.

"I have been walking tonight – there is a full moon, and the dirty-gray buildings appear white. The stars, the empty windows, are hidden. It's a beautiful and lonesome city where men and women and children are trying to snatch a few hours of sleep underground."

It was only years later that I learned most of those memorable talks/reports were not delivered live but instead carefully crafted and, then, only broadcast three days after the incidents they reported on. Some had been censored; others were self-censored, clearly reflecting the war "message" and propaganda of those times.

There were, for example, no reports I know of in the early years about the then unfolding holocaust that many news organizations including the BBC knew about but did not broadcast for fear of confusing war goals. Some British leaders believed that the English people (perhaps like themselves) were anti-Semitic and would not fight if the war were pictured as a battle to save the Jews. So they muzzled the biggest crime of the century by decree. The truth came out much later, sadly, after the fact, after the destruction of a people.

Fortunately, Ed, your moving reports from the death camp at Buchenwald helped drive the horror home with its reference to "bodies stacked up like cordwood."

Your broadcasts are still listened to in journalism classes, still revered. How much of the media coverage of the Iraq War will ever be regarded that way? Alas, so much of what we produce today is forgettable, disposable, even embarrassing. Sometimes it is thought of as "product" to be recycled into retrospectives or used as archival material as today's breaking news becomes grist for tomorrow's History Channel specials.

The pressures journalists felt in covering this war were not new. Ed, you experienced them yourself. A profile I found on the Internet explained the internal tensions that existed within your own beloved CBS between you, the journalist, and your bosses.

Quote: " . . . though he and William Paley, head of CBS, were soulmates during the war, fighting a common enemy, that closeness was becoming strained. Paley felt he had to compromise with the government, the sponsors. Murrow felt, at first, that broadcast news could not suffer, should not be compromised. It would eventually take its toll on Murrow as he tried to straddle both worlds."

What you had then is what so many of today's self-styled experts and oh, so authoritative newscasters lack today – a sense of humility that admits that none of us are know-it-alls. It is a stance that concedes that today's news is just a first and often flawed draft of a history still to be written. You knew that Ed, and you said it plain: "Just because the microphone in front of you amplifies your voice around the world is no reason to think we have any more wisdom than we

258

had when our voices could reach only from one end of the bar to the other."

A final relevant recollection comes from one of your producers, Joe Wershba, who wrote a book about your work and times. He tells of a moment when many at CBS had second thoughts about going after McCarthy's Red Hunt. They wanted to kill the broadcast. You observed, as you listened but did not bow to the fears of your colleagues: "The terror is right here in this room."

And so it was – and so it is today when journalists hesitate to challenge the dominant storyline for fear of appearing unpatriotic. Dan Rather, of today's CBS, voiced his concerns about stirring a backlash and being bullied in an interview with the BBC on May 22, 2002. He worried he would be "necklaced" in the way some South Africans had been, with burning tires put around their necks if he stepped out of line. For him, that was a metaphor – but what a metaphor, what a nightmare to have embedded itself in his brain. Talk about intimidation. Talk about "the terror" in the room.

Some things don't change. Media institutions remain citadels of conformity, conservatism and compromise. Courage is in short supply in our unbrave world of news because it is rarely encouraged or rewarded, especially if and when you deviate from the script. Ask Peter Arnett. There is little space, airtime or support for those individuals in the media who stand alone, who do it their way, who at times dissent to challenge the paradigm or who suspect that today's emperor has no clothes.

Ed, today's news business hands out awards in your name by the bushel. They revere your legend and embellish its impact. But few are willing to battle the way you did or take the stands you

did because when you come right down to it they stand for so little.

Today, the challenge news people face involves how to get along by going along, how to keep their heads down to survive cutbacks in a volatile cut-throat news world. A young woman told me of her work at MSNBC during the war. She was part of a team of eight whose job was to monitor all the news on the other channels around the clock, "We didn't want Fox doing stories or features we didn't do," she explained. There was constant pressure to do what the others did and not fall behind. Competition became, in effect, cloning. When the war "ended," so did her job.

Is the war over? Not on the evidence. Occupation breeds resistance in Iraq as it does on the West Bank. American soldiers are dying and so is the dream of the Administration to go in, get it over with, proclaim democracy and steal the oil. They knew how to pummel a far weaker fighting force. They prepared for that with unequalled force and a war plan that used psy-ops, bribery, and deception as much as not such awesome or shocking bombing raids. They won, or have they?

Seven weeks after the President landed in triumph on the deck of an aircraft carrier to strut in uniform and proclaim victory (even if that was not the term he used), the storyline has changed. Ten weeks after the "fall" of Baghdad, new questions are being raised that sound an awful lot in tone like those raised during Watergate. What did the President know and when did he forget he knew it? Is he lying or did he merely "exaggerate."

On June 22, 2003, The New York Times prominently displayed a lead Week in Review analysis headlined: "Bush may have exaggerated but did he lie?" The report leaned to a toned-down "all presidents use selective interpretation". A week earlier, in contrast, the Economist in London put a picture of Tony Blair on its cover with less equivocation and beating around the bush. It blared about Blair: "LIAR." In testimony before a Parliamentary Committee, Clare Short, one of Blair's Minister who resigned in protest, catalogued deliberate distortion in her former Government's position. She called it – echoing the title of this book – "Honorable Deception."

In the United States, the focus has been on intelligence failings and how the Administration abused its spy agencies and concocted a threat that was not there to stage a war that may not have been needed. This focus has been misplaced – and even so – not fully pursued. As Maureen Dowd put it in late June: "They're scrutinizing who gathered the intelligence rather than those who pushed to distort it." For more detail on this whole sordid tale, see the New Republic's take out, Deception and Democracy in its June 30th, 2003, issue. The magazine focuses on government deception.

This book looks at how media outlets bought this whole distorted story, and then brought it to the rest of us.

This book was rushed out almost like a Samizdat publication in the old Soviet Union; clearly, it lacks the more considered perspective of the many that will follow. There is more to dig up and some of it may lead believers in a free press to throw up,

That does not mean that many American journalists are willing to concede they had been used and had their trust abused. Few see a connection between the June 2nd, 2003, FCC rule changes that sailed through a body headed by the son of the Secretary of State as a reward to media companies for a job well done.

Many media people remain defensive, far more willing to point their fingers at government deception than their own. "I really want to read a book by someone who wasn't there," was the dismissive response I received when I offered to send this book to a military correspondent on a newspaper in Atlanta.

That may sound like fair point. But, the fact is that many of those who were there had no idea of the picture that most of were getting, or how it was hyped, exaggerated and shorn of context. The value of news has to be evaluated by its consumers, not its originators.

Writes Chris Hedges who has covered many wars for the New York Times:

"I doubt that the journalists filing the hollow reports from Iraq, in which there are images but rarely any content, are aware of how they are being manipulated. They, like everyone else, believe. But when they look back, they will find that war is always about betrayal."

He believes that journalists are used to disseminate myths, justify war and boost the morale of soldiers and civilians. "The lie in war time is always the lie of omission," he wrote in The Nation.

Perhaps it's too soon for many in the media to recognize these truths. At the same time, I am sure that much of what I have to say, and perhaps even how I say it, is far too "unobjective" for many in the media trenches to "get." Most distrust personality-inflected commentary from independent journalists who deviate or dissent from the straight and narrow, or even from the more predictable left-right divide.

In the words of Lord Tennyson, "Theirs is not

to reason why." Sometimes, not to reason at all.

So Ed, I just wanted you to you to know that war reporting today has become just as controversial as some of your programs on the red scare were way back when.

I am writing to you just days before my 61st Birthday. I am thinking of how in the early 1960s, you left broadcasting to lead the Voice of America. (A few years later your partner Fred Friendly who went on to head CBS News would quit when the network refused to broadcast an important hearing on the Vietnam War and instead ran reruns of I Love Lucy).

War coverage built your career, Ed. A war ended your partner's network presidency.

And, it is war and its coverage that still defines the media in these times.

My hunch is that the analysis offered in these pages may have seemed too far out to some in the war's immediate aftermath, but will, in its essentials, be accepted down the line.

As you put it once, "the obscure we see eventually. The completely apparent takes a little longer."

Danny Schechter
June 27, 2003

THE NETWORKS AND NEWS MANAGEMENT

The Takingsides.blogspot.com site published some internal memos in and documents in April 2003 that strike me as believable, given my own experience as a producer inside two TV networks. They speak to the amount of micro-management that takes place within news divisions at a time of national crisis. The site describes these documents this way:

"Recently, a mid-level executive of one of the three major American television networks sent on over 1,500 pages of memos from the corporate offices of his network in New York to the head of their television news division.

"These memos contain a multitude of instructions concerning the presentation of national and international news for the network's viewers. It would be impossible to show all of these revealing documents but selections are certainly possible. What is not possible, obviously, is to reveal either the name of the conscience-stricken media executive nor the company that employs him."

Excerpts:

"February 10. It is not permitted at this point to use or refer to any film clips, stills or articles emanating from any French source whatsoever.

"February 26. It is expected that coverage of the forthcoming Iraqi campaign will be identical with the coverage used during Desert Storm. Shots of

GIs must show a mixed racial combination. Any interviews must reflect the youthful and idealistic, not the cynical point of view. The liberation of happy, enthusiastic Iraqis can be best shown by filming crowds of cheering citizens waving American flags. Also indicated would be pictures of photogenic GIs fraternizing with Iraqi children and handing them food or other non-controversial presents. Of course, pictures of dead U.S. military personnel are not to be shown and pictures of dead Iraqi soldiers should not show examples of violent death. Also indicated would be brief interviews with English-speaking Iraqi citizens praising American liberation efforts. All such interviews must be vetted by either the White House or Pentagon before public airing.

"March 26. U.S. alliances with the Turkish/Iraqi Kurdish tribes should be played down. This is considered a very sensitive issue with the Turks and American arming and support of the Kurds could create a severe backlash in Ankara. Kurds should be depicted as 'Iraqi Freedom Fighters" and not identified as Kurds.

"March 2. Further references to the religious views of the President are to be deleted.

"March 15. Photo opportunities of the President and members of his cabinet, especially Secretary Rumsfeld, with enthusiastic GIs.

"March 25. No mention of either Wolfowitz or Pearle should be made at the present time.

"March 10. Pro-Government rallies are to be given the fullest coverage. If anti-Government demonstrations are shown, it is desired to stress either a very small number of "eccentrics" or shots of social misfits; i.e., with beards, tattoos, physical deformities, etc. Pro-Government supporters should be seen as clean cut with as many well-groomed subjects as possible. Subjects should stress complete support for the President's programs and especially support for American military units en route to combat. Also interviews with photogenic family members of participating GIs stressing loyalty and affection. American flags are always a good prop in the background." ●

CHAPTER ELEVEN

INTERNATIONAL PERSPECTIVES

THE WAR AGAINST IRAQ ON TELEVISION: A SPLIT REALITY

By Raimund Mock and Markus Rettich

The war in Iraq is and remains foremost a political affair. The question about its necessity has divided whole societies before, during and after the beginning of the military actions and continues to do so. But the evaluation of causes and consequences of armed conflicts depends greatly on political, moral or economical beliefs and interests - this goes for politicians as well as for journalists (and, for that matter, media researchers).

Media Tenor, the independent and non-partisan media analysis institute with offices in Bonn, New York, Dover, Ostrava and Pretoria conducted a detailed analysis of the main evening news broadcasts of three U.S., one British, three German, two Czech and two South African TV networks between March 20 and April 16 to determine how news of the war was presented to their respective audiences.

The analysis, examined on behalf Frankfurter Algemeine Zeitung's cultural desk, was conducted on the level of individual verbal and visual statements. In order to determine the tone of the coverage, both explicit and implicit positive and negative statements were recorded.

But we are not going to attempt to answer the question whether the war was right or wrong, as we don't have a clear overview of all relevant information necessary to decide this question. For the same reason, the science of media analysis cannot decide what type of coverage of the war was right and which was wrong.

However, media content analysis can show how the war was presented to TV audiences: which issues did journalists choose to report on, how did they evaluate them? The subject of this analysis is not reality, but the mediated depiction of reality.

Several questions must be raised in the context of media coverage of the war: To what degree are American patriotism and European anti-Americanism a by-product of news coverage of the war?

What were the actual benefits of embedding journalists with the troops? Perhaps most importantly, but also most difficult to discuss: To which degree were journalists in the U.S. and abroad serving the interests of their governments, intentionally or not? Was the media merely part of a larger war strategy?

Visualization pushes old journalistic principles to the background

WAR is unpopular: Not only does it cost lives, but also money, and its benefits are hard to see initially. It has thus always been an integral part of strategic war planning to win over public opinion at home, since, at the end of the day, it is the public and their elected representatives who must provide the money and supply the soldiers.

The information ministry is not an invention of Saddam Hussein. Television's visual dominance increasingly dictates the tactics in the fight for public opinion. According to US political legend, the Vietnam War's days were numbered when popular TV news anchor Walter Cronkite publicly expressed his opposition to it. The mass medium of television has turned every question of this conflict into a subject of public debate. This has led to a situation where the war has to be justified on moral rather than on political grounds.

In the 1991 Gulf war this was accomplished with the help of dubious reports on Iraqi atrocities in Kuwait. A similar dynamic was at work before the war in Kosovo, when news coverage focused on atrocities committed by the Serbs. It would seem as if the public will only support a war if it is directed against mass murderers, baby killers or rapists.

The war of weapons is anticipated by the war over public opinion. However, most journalists say they do not want to be used as instruments in this game. At the beginning of the war, many correspondents broke an unwritten rule of journalistic conduct and made their own working conditions and status a focus of their reports. It is questionable to which extent this coverage was

really necessary.

If some journalists became the story, the sourcing of their stories quickly became an issue. As has been known for decades , journalists are dependent on information, butinformants usually act out of self-interest. This is why each source must be treated with utmost scrutiny. News should not be driven by images alone; reports must be topical and relevant. And yet, the images often come first.

This is the dilemma of television at the heart of its appeal and its limit: It needs images. Visualization pushes old journalistic principles to the background, because they often conflict with the constant challenge to break news. At the beginning of the war, for example, German news channel N-Tv boasted of having been the first station to report news in Germany in the middle of the night. In fact, they had managed only to switch over to CNN one minute ahead of their competition. But is it really an indicator of journalistic achievement when one technician presses a switch more swiftly than another?

Some media outlets solved the dilemma of needing to be both quick and believable by reporting on its limitations, thereby shifting the responsibility to the audience: Journalists reflected on their working conditions continuously throughout the war, in terms of their physical well-being and practical conditions as well as the access they were given to information.

On the news programs outside of the U.S that Media Tenor analyzed, there was an overwhelmingly negative tone about the coverage of journalists' working conditions. This specifically relates to the ability of journalists to get access or operate in a secure setting. As much as a third of the coverage on this subject - 34% on Germany's public broadcaster ARD - was explicitly or contextually negative. Even on BBC news, generally moderate and unemotional in other aspects of its coverage, journalists had almost nothing positive to say about their working conditions, but negative statements of the latter stood at over 25%.

U.S. journalists apparently did not experience, or at least did not feel the need to emphasize, the same degree of difficulty as their European colleagues. On NBC and especially on CBS, journalists reported more positively on their working conditions by a wide margin. Only ABC journalists offered a slightly more negative tone on their experiences. Of course, compared to most of their foreign colleagues, American journalists, by virtue of being embedded with troops, did gather more first hand information, However, there was little reflection on the potential shortcomings of their relatively narrow view of events on the battlefield. After all being embedded did not necessarily guarantee the factual accuracy of the information, a question on which American journalists had little to say, or assure reports with perspective and scope. German journalists in particular appeared to complain the most without offering solutions, thereby shifting the blame at least partly to their viewers.

This can be very tricky with no clear cut solution. The traditional idea of giving access to "both sides" can lead to the dissemination of lies and propaganda. Identifying a source as as liar is also problematic and naïve An army at war will never be entirely truthful, unless it makes sure beforehand that its opponent does not have access to television for its claims. When a journalist is faced with two potential liars, is it satisfactory to give both of them a chance to speak.

Clearly, more contextualization and background is needed.

Radically different representations of war

OBJECTIVELY observed, the situation in Iraq had to look the same for all reporters. But in fact, they all reported very differently, particularly if one compares the media coverage internationally. American broadcast news coverage of the war assumed a tone that was as positive as that of European coverage was negative. The overall pattern on the three U.S. networks was similar: After initial restraint, the tone of the coverage approached something like euphoria. This was in line with opinion polls conducted at the same time. They frame as our analysis.

An ABC News/Washington Post poll of 504 adults nationwide shows that approval of U.S. military actions spiked on April 9, with 80% of the respondents supporting U.S. war efforts.

The similar development of media approval and public support do not seem coincidental. When it came to coverage of American military actions - by far the most widely covered topic in the context of the war in all analyzed news media - the margin of difference between positive and negative coverage was notably greater on CBS Evening News than on NBC Nightly News and ABC World News Tonight, where the tone of coverage concerning U.S. war actions did not become overwhelmingly positive until the third week of fighting, although the tone remained more positive than negative throughout the time frame of the analysis on all three networks' evening news.

Differences were greater among U.S. news

programs in the tone in which the President was covered. ABC World News Tonight was very polarized in its portrayal of Mr Bush as the Commander-in-Chief, with an equal 19.4% positive and negative average implicit and explicit statements with the President as the subject – a number of negative statements on par with those of most European news programs.

On NBC, the tone of the coverage was clearly more positive, while the difference between positive and negative statements was most glaring on NBC, where it was explicitly or implicitly positive 41.9% of the time the President was its subject, compared to 7% negative statements.

While U.S. news programs portrayed the President and the war in a more positive light overall, they nevertheless did so from different angles and at different degrees of enthusiasm, leaving us to wonder to which extent ideological differences may account for variations in the news coverage. These differences become more apparent when we look at the frequency with which voices of dissent were featured on the news.

German TV presented a different reality: its bias become obvious in the newscasters' evaluation of U.S. military actions. In the beginning of the war one out of five verbal or visual portrayals by RTL journalists was negative, only six percent of all statements on the Americans were positive. The coverage was particularly critical by the end of March, as U.S. advances, according to the journalists, were beginning to slow down and the end of the war was not yet in sight,. Instead, there was talk of the threats of house-to-house fighting or the deployment of biological and chemical weapons. The BBC, on the other hand, assessed the American war effort in an overall balanced manner, despite American 'friendly fire' incidents leading to the deaths of British troops.

In the Czech Republic, a member of the war alliance, the assessment of U.S. military actions was slightly negative, while in South Africa a more differentiated picture emerges: Whereas the public broadcaster, English-language SABC NEWS portrayed the American military more positively than negatively, the private television station E-TV criticized them harshly. This program, which targets South Africans of Indian origin ended their newscasts day after day with the same remark. So far, E-TV would say, the Americans have not found any weapons of mass destruction. Of all analyzed media, only the BBC maintained an equilibrium of sorts of positive and negative coverage, mostly remaining ambivalent in tone, with far fewer explicitly positive or negative statements than its German or U.S. counterparts.

International differences became even clearer when it came to the choice of protagonists of the news coverage. In the U.S., more than half of the protagonists of news stories on the war were either U.S. politicians or military personnel (ABC: 53%; NBC: 54%; NBC: 58.1%), more than twice as many as on the average foreign news program.

More tellingly, while TV news outside of the U.S. made frequent reference to British and other coalition troops, British troops figured little in U.S. coverage of the war and coalition troops from other countries played almost no role at all. U.S. TV news coverage was thus arguably as unilateral as the actions of the Bush administration, a point further illustrated by comparing the amount of coverage on military actions to that of international politics.

By far the majority of the coverage on evening news programs in the U.S. focused only on U.S. military actions. On BBC news, in comparison, U.S. politicians and military personnel made up 25.1% of the featured protagonists, while British politicians and military personnel comprised 12.8%. German and British news programs also referred much more often to the allies as an entity than U.S. news programs (ARD: 8.9%, ZDF: 9.5%, RTL: 9.5%, BBC: 9.9%).

When U.S. politicians and military personnel were the subject of the coverage, it was most frequently in the context of military actions, compared to which the consequences and political ramifications of the war received only scant attention. In the context of U.S. society, as mentioned before, only NBC showed concern for politics to a significant extent, with 86 statements (ABC: 5, NBC: 4). On German news programs, reports on military actions figured less prominently in the coverage of public broadcasters ARD and ZDF than on RTL, the private network (ARD: 44.7%, ZDF: 47.3%, RTL: 55%). The BBC spent 58.3% on its news coverage reporting on military actions, slightly more than the Americans (ABC: 52.3%, NBC: 55.8%, NBC: 56.3%).

In comparison, international politics played a far greater role on ARD and ZDF, with 20.9% and 17% of the coverage, respectively, than on any other network in the three countries. BBC news programs devoted 9.1% of their coverage to international politics; among U.S. network news the share of the topic exceeded 10% only on NBC (ABC: 9.7%, NBC: 12.7%, NBC: 9.8%).

One could argue this merely goes to show that there is no room for politics on the battlefield, but it also raises the question about whether the overwhelming focus on military actions, both in the overall coverage and in regard to politicians and military personnel, may not have served to obscure and detract from the political issues underlying the conflict. Coverage of international politics suffered the most from the latter.

The rule of thumb here seems to be, the greater the share of coverage of military actions on any network, the lower the share of coverage of international politics – a phenomenon not limited to TV news in coalition countries.

We should also note that there is no clear correlation between the share of coverage of military actions on any of the analyzed programs and the share of reports filed by journalists embedded with troops for each. Several of the non-U.S. news programs, including the BBC, managed to report just as much on military actions as their U.S. counterparts without relying on embedded journalists, instead supplementing their reports with footage bought from U.S. or Arabic networks or reporting from Baghdad or the studio.

The narrow focus on the battlefield was thus largely endemic, although reports from embedded journalists certainly shortened the supply lines for the newsrooms of all analyzed programs. As a consequence, the coverage of the war was largely de-politicized and journalists were running the danger of merely providing infotainment instead of contributing to public debate by focusing more on the political issues surrounding the war, both domestically and internationally.

TV news programs outside of the U.S. tended to focus more on Iraqi civilians, though not by as much as one might have expected. On German news programs, around 15% of protagonists featured on all three programs were Iraqi civilians, on BBC they comprised 17.1%. NBC Nightly News was the only news program in our analysis on which Iraqi civilians made up less than 10% of the featured protagonists, while the numbers were slightly higher on the other networks (ABC: 13.7%, NBC: 9.6%, NBC: 12.1%).

The American way of reporting I: unseen U.S. casualties

ANOTHER category in which American news programs fell markedly behind in their coverage was the depiction of American casualties. After Al-Jazeera was sharply rebuked by U.S. officials for broadcasting images of dead and captured POWs, the depiction of U.S. casualties in particular seemed to become taboo on U.S. news programs.

Short of saying that news producers and journalists were cowed into withholding information, Media Tenor's data clearly shows a much greater reluctance on the part of U.S. news programs to show images of American dead and wounded than on foreign news programs, even though they had no problems depicting dead or wounded Iraqis – on NBC, the share of visual depictions on dead or wounded Iraqis even exceeded the share of verbal statements.

Of all statements on dead, wounded or missing American soldiers on both ABC and NBC, 80.6% were delivered verbally, while only 19.4% were delivered in the form of visual depictions. On NBC, the share of visually depicted dead, missing or wounded was significantly higher, with 42.4% of all statements on the subject.

The coverage of Iraqi casualties offers one of the most obvious differences between coverage in the U.S. and abroad, particularly if one considers that the number of American casualties was lower than in the Persian Gulf war, while the number of Iraqi casualties, both military and civilian, numbers in the thousands. In the U.S., allied casualties comprised up to two thirds of all casualties reported on in evening news (ABC: 58.9%, NBC: 60.5%, NBC: 67%). On BBC news programs, allied casualties made up 44.2% of casualties reported on; 50.6% were Iraqis. In Germany, the picture was almost the exact opposite from the U.S. On the low extreme, only 26.5% of casualties on ARD were allies, while 69.9% were Iraqis (ZDF: 35.9%/ 58.8%, RTL: 42.3%/ 55.1%).

The American way of reporting II: CBS silences dissent

IN their reports on U.S. society during the war, we found significant differences among U.S. news programs in the amount of coverage given to protests against the war. ABC World News Tonight reported most frequently on protests (101 statements), followed by NBC Nightly News (68 statements). With only 6 statements on protests in the U.S. in the time frame of our analysis, CBS Evening News hardly ever exposed its viewers to news of dissent among Americans. Only NBC featured a notable amount of coverage on both protests and political affairs in reference to societal protagonists in the U.S.

With a geographical focus on non-allied countries, all three networks featured a comparable amount of coverage on these political aspects, but, once again, the disparity between the networks in their coverage of protests was glaring, with ABC taking the lead and NBC barely acknowledging protests abroad.

But, surprisingly, protests did not play a particularly great role on European news either.

In the overall comparison of coverage of protests, Germany's ARD, with 5.2% of its coverage, is alone at exceeding the share of coverage ABC granted to protests. On the BBC, protests were the main focus of only 1.3% of the coverage. There were also no great variations internationally concerning the frequency with which the legitimacy of the war was the central aspect of the coverage – around 4% of the coverage in Germany, Britain and the U.S. dealt with this topic.

Another similarity between news programs in the three countries is the extent to which they reported on the justifications for war provided by the allies. The combined topics peace, human rights and weapons of mass destruction comprised a mere 1.2% of the coverage on ARD news programs and even less on all others. In the news coverage as on the ground in Iraq, WMDs were mostly absent. The combined topics will of the people, democracy and dictatorship, on the other hand, received significantly more coverage. In the U.S., all three networks dedicated more than 3% of the coverage to topics associated with the liberation of the Iraqi people, with NBC in the lead (ABC: 3.1%, NBC: 3.1%, NBC: 3.6%).

The U.N. dropped out of the coverage almost entirely with the beginning of the war. On the rare occasions in which it was the subject of reports, it was mostly in terms of politics, followed by discussions of Iraq after the end of the war. Of the three evening news programs in the U.S., only NBC was reporting on the international organization in the context of military actions or their consequences, but even here, mentions of the U.N. were so scarce as to be almost negligible.

In Germany, the public broadcasters ARD and ZDF in particular reported much more frequently on the U.N., while the BBC's reports on the U.N. were almost on par with NBC's in terms of their frequency (ARD: 2.3% of all reports, BBC: 0.9%, NBC: 1%).

Compared to the other two networks, ABC stood out in giving space to voices of dissent and relied less on embedded journalists. It showed a greater capacity for self-criticism and offered a more balanced – though highly polarized – depiction of the American President. ABC also featured a higher share of footage originating with Arabic networks, showed a greater interest in the rebuilding of Iraq and the consequences of war and gave slightly more room to Iraqi casualties than the other two news programs. NBC's coverage was less balanced in most of these categories, but did comparatively well in the depiction of American dead and wounded. Of all three, Dan Rather's NBC EVENING NEWS went to the most extremes, firmly toeing the government line in terms of its tone of coverage of the war and in the issues it chose to disregard. NBC was also among the highest in using emotionally charged coverage (5.2% of all verbal and visual statements).

The German way of reporting – a good example?

THE war is over but the problems still remain in post-war Iraq. In German TV news, the military actions had been depicted largely as a U.S. war against Iraqi civilians. The Americans were the subject of criticism on all three analysed news programs, particularly on private Broadcaster

RTL. The German network also made less of a switch toward more positively-toned coverage, as the military success of the American operation became apparent. In the discussion on whether or not the war was justified, ARD and ZDF ignored the fact that Anglo-Saxon experts on international law did not agree with their German colleagues. ARD in particular focused its coverage heavily on anti-war protests. ZDF led in reporting on the issue of the allies ignoring popular will worldwide.

On the other hand, the topic 'Dictatorship in Iraq' only played a noticeable role in the Heute Journal. The question whether the intervention would result in liberating Iraq was practically left out of the coverage in the first two weeks of war.

With the benefit of hindsight: did German TV journalists do a better job than their American colleagues? Editors and executives of German TV stations think so: "Better than during the first gulf war in 1991," this is how representatives of ARD, ZDF and RTL assessed their coverage of the war in Iraq in the German financial paper Handelsblatt on April 11th.

'Better' does not necessarily mean good, however; nor even good enough. The analysis of German TV news coverage on the war in Iraq reveals the basic journalistic decisions that were taken: Which issues were important to them in international comparisons, and how they chose to describe the situation.

For the German media, the war was a mega-event that was given more coverage that the catastrophic Elbe flood of the past summer, a major story in Germany. Almost two thirds of the news coverage broadcast during the first week of the war dealt with Iraq, and this does not even take into account a large number of special news specials. By the end of March the exceeded that on the Kosovo war in 1999.

In comparison, in the last week before the 2002 German parliamentary elections, the latter received only half as much attention as the war in its first week. The leader in the ranking was private broadcaster RTL Aktuell, which had practically eliminated all non-war reporting – a marked difference from how it covered the Kosovo conflict. The dominance of this issue cannot be explained solely in terms of its relevance.

First: The war did not come as a surprise: Failing diplomacy in Washington, Paris and Berlin as well as the poker game played in Baghdad made it seem inevitable for months. The German federal government's loudly announced goal to prevent the war at the eleventh hour was at best an indication of the unrealistic assessment of its negotiating power.

Second: German soldiers were not involved, they did not fight or die in Iraq. It is true that German interests were at stake in regard to global security and oil. But those key topics were missing from discussion.

Third: Facts from the news front were in short supply, for reasons mentioned above.

Fourth: 'Solidarity with the suffering Iraqis' as a reason for the strong media interest would be little more than hypocrisy, at least when taking Chechnya into account; and also, in retrospect, from the Iraqi perspective, whose suffering under the dictatorship was always of marginal importance to the German news media.

Fifth: Outlawing war might have been a noble goal in and of itself. But that was rarely analyzed along with what the intervention might mean for future wars and threats. US arguments pointing in that direction, however, were simply portrayed as propaganda, put forward to mask power and business related interests.

This leaves us with one explanation for the strong focus on the war: the fascination of horror, the entertainment value of war. The sad truth: We are used to the fact that TV stations have torn down almost all moral barriers, as if to say that privacy is theft., Years ago Tucholsky said. "Satire is free to do anything." Today this quote could read: Television is free to do anything. Reality in itself is no longer enough to attract viewers; it is Joe Millionaire, not Joe Schmo, who heralds the mainstreaming of hyper-reality, while the war is pictured as an ultimate showdown between good and evil.

In order to boost the ratings, the boundaries of taboo are under attack. They are pushed further each time, only to be transgressed anew.

It is well known that CNN rose to being a respected international news source with Peter Arnett's reporting on the roof of a Baghdad hotel in 1991. The development of transmission technology continues to permit new feats in breaking news coverage.

German stations have also focussed on these "gee whiz" aspects. Even compared with international coverage it is striking how RTL rejoiced in the fact that one of their reporters, Ulrich Klose, accompanied the allied troops. Public broadcaster ZDF, on the other hand, in the newscast Heute Journal, primarily relied on its correspondent in Baghdad, Ulrich Tilgner. The men on both sides of the front suggest proximity to the events. But are they also able to keep their journalistic distance?

On April 8th, after three international journalists had died under American fire in Baghdad, correspondent Stephan Kloss appeared on the newscast TAGESSCHAU, wearing a bullet-proof vest. On the subsequent special edition BRENNPUNKT, his colleague Christoph-Maria Fröhder conjectured (without a bullet-proof vest) that the Americans, bothered by the coverage they received, were no longer showing consideration for journalists. One has to wonder, though, what war correspondents had expected before heading out on their dangerous, but also highly prestigious assignments. (ZDF's Tilgner, as well as his colleague Antonia Rados, reporting from Baghdad for RTL, are due to receive the German Hanns-Joachim-Friedrichs Award for Journalism this year.)

The scenario we have been sketching underscore the limitations of war coverage. Correspondents cannot report freely, even if they did not have conditions to meet, watchdogs and censors to deal with or pre-selected perspectives to portray. It is not surprising that Ulrich Tilgner, who was so intensively questioned by ZDF anchors, comes in second in the "don't know"-ranking, a statisical measure of the number of statements which clearly expressed an assumption or the admission of being unable to answer a question from the studio in Germany. However, he had good company in the guessing game.

Even highly praised colleagues like Anne Will, Steffen Seibert and Peter Kloeppel presented their audience with assumptions and feature prominently in the rankings. In retrospect, it is striking how many of the infinite number of prognoses turned out to be speculations without any foundation or evidence to substantiate the claims. At first the Iraqis were reputed to be too weak and unmotivated to fight back. Then, all of a sudden, we were told they would engage in tough house-to-house fighting and a long war.

At first, the Americans were chararacterized as e hated by the Iraqi people. Then they were projected as liberators. Conjectures as to the extent of casualties did not coincide with numbers. The question is whether the ambition to be first justifies everything. The first lesson a journalism trainee learns is that unconfirmed news is not news. It is unlikely that any audience would really chose quick and unchecked information over thoroughly researched news if they had the choice,

RTL not only relied on its military correspondent Ulrich Klose, but also on its reporter Antonia Rados in the Iraqi capital. As cited earlier, ARD and RTL correspondents in Baghdad put the main emphasis on the suffering of civilians, rather than on warfare, whenever Iraqi protagonists were in the picture. The newscast RTL Aktuell even devoted a slight majority of coverage to this topic. German television reporting on victims clearly focused on the Iraqi side. Since Rados and Tilgner will receive a journalism award for this type of coverage, it must mean that it is considered to be proper and even politically correct

German journalists had ventured into the coverage of the war with real concerns. They felt they did not want to be taken for a ride by the Americans (again). This they did manage. But there was also a sense of self satisfaction among German TV executives that appeared out of place.

The question arises, did the news coverage went to another extreme: After assuming a position of sharp criticism of the American military actions, which was abandoned only with the increasing success of the operation, and after fixating on the Iraqis as suffering victims, they created a representation of the war for the German television-viewing public which was neatly in line with the position of the German government. Critical questions, concerning, e.g., the extent to which the unrelenting German position contributed to the escalation of the conflict, were thus widely kept from public scrutiny.

An alternative approach?

MOST worrisome, across the board, was the overt reliance on coverage of military actions, compared to which political discussion took a back seat. This was true both in Europe and in the U.S. Journalists appeared as reluctant to allow for arguments of the other side as their respective governments, leaving us to wonder whether the goal of journalistic objectivity was missing or misappropriated in the name of infotainment, while political and moral arguments were presented in an almost indistinguishable fashion.

News programs in the U.S. and abroad were drawing a very sharp line between talk and action. But, what about all the repetition. Anyone who subjected themselves to a few evenings of war coverage on TV will to attest to the level of redundancy which rose steadily with each hour of viewing. Action, we learned, can be cheap, too, especially when it is dotted with flags and interspersed with dramatic musical interludes aimed at consolidating the national spirit.

To escape the patriotic sheen, viewers had to turn to other media outlets, foremost the BBC. An April 28 article in Business week described how "'the Beeb' is gaining viewers from around the globe with its sober, authoritative coverage of the war," citing Nielsen Media Research data of a 28% increase in viewers of BBC World in the U.S. since the beginning of the war. The networks might want to take note.

These concerns were raised, but then quickly sidelined by discussions of national complacency and/or naiveté about the world. How the US intelligence apparatus could have missed this was taken only as evidence that it needs more money, not a different policy to serve. No mention was made of course of the cutback in international news coverage that keeps Americans so out of touch with global events.　　　●

For more of Media Tenor's reports, visit: www.mediatenor.com

LAST WORDS

DECEPTION AS POLICY

As investigative reporter Seymour Hersh discovered, a small group of neo-conservative ideologues, calling themselves the Cabal and stationed at the Pentagon's Office of Special Plans, reworked U.S. intelligence on Iraq's weapons of mass destruction to help justify a U.S. invasion. Hersh also quoted a former Bush Administration intelligence official as saying he quit because, "They were so crazed and so far out and so difficult to reason with – to the point of being bizarre. Dogmatic, as if they were on a mission from God."

Hersh found, too, that Wolfowitz and other key neo-conservatives at the Pentagon were disciples of the late political philosopher Leo Strauss, who believed that some deception of the population is necessary in statecraft. "The whole story is complicated by Strauss's idea – actually Plato's – that philosophers need to tell noble lies not only to the people at large but also to powerful politicians," said Stephen Holmes, a law professor at New York University. [See The New Yorker, May 12, 2003] – Robert Parry, Consortium News.

CREDITS

DANNY SCHECHTER
Dissector/Writer/Director/Producer

anny Schechter is a television producer and independent filmmaker who also writes and speaks about media issues. He is the author of "Media Wars: News At A Time of Terror (2003); "The More You Watch, The Less You Know" (Seven Stories Press) and "News Dissector: Passions, Pieces and Polemics" (Akashic Books and Electron Press). He is the executive editor of Mediachannel.org, the world's largest online media issues network, and recipient of the Society of Professional Journalists' 2001 Award for Excellence in Documentary Journalism.

He has produced and directed many TV specials and documentary films, including "Counting on Democracy" about the electoral fiasco in Florida narrated by Ossie Davis and Ruby Dee; "We Are Family" (2002), "Nkosi: A Voice of Africa's AIDS Orphans" (2001) narrated by Danny Glover; "A Hero for All: Nelson Mandela's Farewell" (1999); "Beyond Life: Timothy Leary Lives" (1997); "Sowing Seeds/Reaping Peace: The World of Seeds of Peace" (1996); "Prisoners of Hope: Reunion on Robben Island" (1995, co-directed by Barbara Kopple); "Countdown to Freedom: Ten Days that Changed South Africa" (1994), narrated by James Earl Jones and Alfre Woodard; "Sarajevo Ground Zero" (1993); "The Living Canvas" (1992), narrated by Billy Dee Williams; "Beyond JFK: The Question of Conspiracy" (1992, co-directed by Marc Levin and Bar-

bara Kopple); "Give Peace a Chance" (1991); "Mandela in America" (1990); "The Making of Sun City" (1987); and "Student Power" (1968).

Schechter is co-founder and executive producer of Globalvision, a New York-based television and film production company now in its 16th year. He has specialized in investigative reporting and producing programming about the interface between popular music and society. His career began as the "News Dissector" at Boston's leading rock station, WBCN.

Later, Schechter was a producer for ABC NEWS 20/20. He produced profiles of such stars as Bruce Springsteen, Bob Dylan, Tina Turner and pioneering segments on hip-hop and heavy metal. Working with Springsteen guitarist Little Steven Van Zandt, he produced SUN CITY, the hit record and video featuring 54 top artists speaking out against apartheid. In 1991, he worked with Lenny Kravitz and Yoko Lennon on a video remake of John Lennon's classic "Give Peace a Chance" with 39 stars. He was a producer on the Nelson Mandela concert at Wembley Stadium in London in 1990.

A Cornell University graduate, he received his Master's degree from the London School of Economics, and an honorary doctorate from Fitchburg College. He was a Neiman Fellow in Journalism at Harvard, where he also taught in 1969.

After college, he was a full time civil rights worker and then communications director of the

Northern Student Movement, and worked as a community organizer in a Saul Alinsky-style War on Poverty program. Then, moving from the streets to the suites, Schechter served as an assistant to the Mayor of Detroit in 1966 on a Ford Foundation grant.

Schechter joined the start-up staff at CNN as a producer based in Atlanta. He then moved to ABC as a producer for 20/20, where during his eight years he won two National News Emmys. Schechter has reported from 49 countries and lectured at many schools and universities. He was an adjunct professor at the Graduate School of Journalism at Columbia University.

Schechter's writing has appeared in leading newspapers and magazines including the The Nation, Newsday, Boston Globe, Columbia Journalism Review, Media Studies Journal, Detroit Free Press, Village Voice, Tikkun, Z, and many others. ●

Danny Schechter can be reached at dissector@Mediachannel.org

COLDTYPE.NET

ColdType (http://coldtype.net) is a Canadian web site devoted to *Writing Worth Reading From Around The World*. The site contains books, magazines, newspapers, essays and photo-essays, all produced in pdf format for downloading. Everything on the site is free.

Contributors include international correspondents such as top British commentators Robert Fisk, John Pilger and George Monbiot, U.S. media critics Norman Solomon, Michael I. Niman and Danny Schechter, Antonia Zerbisias from Canada, and noted South African writers Denis Beckett and Rian Malan.

ColdType is edited by Tony Sutton as an adjunct to running the international newspaper design consultancy, News Design Associates Inc., which provides services to clients in Europe, Africa, North America and Australasia from its base in rural Ontario, Canada.

Before becoming a consultant, Sutton – an award-winning editor and designer – worked for daily and Sunday newspapers in his native Britain, and was executive editor of Drum magazine in South Africa (where he was also a consultant to the apartheid-era alternative press). He moved to North America in 1990 to become design director of Toronto's Globe and Mail, later joining Thomson Newspapers as head of design for its North American operation before becoming a newspaper consultant.

Sutton also spent five years as editor of Design magazine, the quarterly publication of the U.S.-based international Society for News Design.

He is the author of Creative Newspaper Design and Creative Magazine Design. ●

Tony Sutton may be contacted at editor@coldtype.net